In Harmony Framed

Habent sua fata libelli

Volume XXI
of
SIXTEENTH CENTURY ESSAYS & STUDIES
Charles G. Nauert, Jr., General Editor

Composed by NMSU typographer Gwen Blotevogel, Kirksville, Missouri
Cover Design by Teresa Wheeler, NMSU Designer
Printed by Edwards Brothers, Ann Arbor, Michigan
Text is set in Bembo II 10/12

In Harmony Framed

Musical Humanism, Thomas Campion,
and the Two Daniels

by Erik S. Ryding

Volume XXI
Sixteenth Century Essays & Studies

This book has been brought to publication
with the generous support of
Northeast Missouri State University

Library of Congress Cataloging-in-Publication Data

Ryding, Erik S., 1953-
  In harmony framed : musical humanism, Thomas Campion, and the two
Daniels / by Erik S. Ryding.
      p.   cm. – (Sixteenth century essays & studies ; v. 21)
  Includes bibliographical references and index.
  ISBN 0-940474-22-0
  1. English poetry – Early modern, 1500-1700 – History and criticism. 2.
Music – England – 16th century – History and criticism. 3. Campion, Thomas,
1567-1620 – Criticism and interpretation. 4. Daniel, Samuel, 1562-1619 –
Criticism and interpretation. 5. Danyel, John, 1564-ca. 1626 – Criticism and
interpretation. 6. English poetry – Classical influences. 7. Courtly love in
literature. 8. Music and literature. 9. Humanists – England. 10. Humanism –
England.
  I. Title. II. Series.
  PR535.M85R9   1993
  821'.309 – dc20   92-21689
                                                                          CIP

Ad Patrem

Contents

Examples

Preface

I began work on this study in 1981, when my goal was to write a doctoral dissertation. Shortly after the defense in 1986, I began revising with the end of producing a book. While my strategy and my central thesis remain what they were in the dissertation, I have made numerous changes throughout the new work. Much has been cut, much added. Many errors have been corrected. Having discovered, after a reexamination of the material, that I no longer agree with all my original assessments, I have accordingly altered some of my opinions.

The reader I have in mind is one interested in poetry and song but better acquainted with literature than with music, though a musicologist might well find the discussions of humanist literary theory and practice enlightening. I undertook the survey in the first three chapters partly because it seemed a useful context for viewing the Campion-Daniel debate and partly because I thought no one had attempted such a survey before. I was therefore surprised to discover, in a collection of the late Edward Lowinsky's essays, *Music in the Culture of the Renaissance* (Chicago: University of Chicago Press, 1989), that Lowinsky had also offered a survey of musical humanism in Germany, France, and Italy, and that mine and his overlapped in several areas. (Lowinsky's essay, "Humanism in the Music of the Renaissance," appeared originally in *Medieval and Renaissance Studies* 9, ed. Frank Tirro [Durham, N.C.: Duke University Press, 1982], 87-220.) Despite the inevitable overlaps, the surveys are different in method and purpose. Lowinsky does not examine parallel literary sources, as I do, and he does not extend his discussion of musical humanism to include England, which is one of my chief goals. For the remaining chapters, my emphasis is on Campion and the brothers John and Samuel Daniel. I have tried to present discussions of the music that will be intelligible to nonmusicologists with some knowledge of music and that will not prove wholly unprofitable reading for those interested principally in music history.

When I began this study, the term "musical humanism" had a fairly limited meaning. A modern term, apparently invented by Paul-Marie Masson in 1906, it was first used mainly to describe German and French settings of quantitative verse that were rhythmically governed by the long and short syllables of the texts. D. P. Walker broadened the meaning of the term in the 1940s, and in the 1980s, Claude Palisca and Don Harrán found reflections of humanism in many different facets of Renaissance music. I have retained the phrase for convenience' sake, though I have used it in its older sense and would now perhaps avoid it altogether since it suggests a unified musico-philosophical movement that never existed. Still, many sixteenth-century classicists expressed similar opinions on music, often derived from ancient sources, and some term to describe these opinions seems necessary.

Another term, *fin'amors*, was in fact used frequently in the Middle Ages, though medieval authors seem to have had several meanings for it. I have tried not to be too specific about the meaning of *fin'amors*, lest it should become – like "courtly love" – first overdefined, then nearly useless. In using the Provençal term, I do not mean to suggest that either Thomas Campion or Samuel Daniel would have been familiar with the phrase. It does, however, describe a kind of love encountered frequently in the Middle Ages, and I believe that Renaissance writers recognized its characteristics and saw them as distinct from the amatory conventions of, say, the ancient Augustan poets.

I have incurred many debts while writing this book. I consider myself fortunate indeed to have worked closely with James Mirollo, Joel Newman, and Anne Lake Prescott – scholars whose erudition and encouragement proved a source of constant pleasure to me. Kathy Eden and Richard Katz, who also read the original version of this study in its entirety, offered useful suggestions for improvement. Barbara Russano Hanning, Mary McLaughlin, Sandra Pinegar, and Brian Spence kindly read through portions of this study and caught a number of slips and infelicities. I am also grateful to the following scholars – better skilled than I at interpreting ablatives – for discussing various Latin passages with me: Nathalie Hanlett, Eugene Rice, Jr., James Runsdorf, and Ernest Sanders. Though busy and soon to give birth to twins, Letizia Alvisi-Seirup consented to check the passages in Italian and their accompanying translations. (I alone, of course, am responsible for any inaccuracies in the translations; those not attributed to others are mine.) With admirable patience and goodness of spirit, Cornelia Praetorius and Elizabeth Randell between them sang through all the lute-songs of John Daniel and Thomas Campion for me. Rebecca Pechefsky and Sandra Pinegar enthusiastically played through the musical examples, calling my attention to dubious accidentals, wrong notes, missing flags, and so on. Two anonymous readers for this series spotted superfluous material and offered much constructive criticism. Special thanks go to Rachel Aubrey, whose wise and humane counseling helped me to overcome several personal problems threatening my professional and emotional well-being. Barnard College and the Charles A. Dana Foundation allowed me the luxury of having two student interns: Mary Firmani, who meticulously proofread numerous passages, and Stephanie Promish, who carefully checked references. Librarians at the Beinecke Rare Book and Manuscript Library at Yale, The Pierpont Morgan Library, and the New York Public Library generously let me examine their rare books, while Kathleen Haefliger and Kevin Piccini, former librarians at the Columbia University Music Library, called my attention to recent books on my subject and helped me to find out-of-the-way sources. My greatest debt is to a scholar I have mentioned briefly in one footnote, though his influence, as he may recognize, runs throughout this study; my oldest and closest friend, he is also, through a stroke of good fortune, my father.

Note:
Passages cited follow the spelling of the edition used, though I have silently expanded abbreviations and followed modern practice regarding *i/j, u/v,* and so forth. Except when quoting, I have consistently used the spellings "Daniel" (rather than "Danyel") and "Campion" (rather than "Campian"). Passages from Campion's poetry generally follow the texts in Walter Davis' edition of *The Works of Thomas Campion,* though I have sometimes altered his text when it differs from that in the Scholar Press facsimile editions of Campion's ayres. All poetic passages from John Daniel's songs are based on the texts in the Scholar Press facsimile edition, though the longer passages follow the full texts presented under or beside the songs while the shorter passages, cited in connection with the music, follow the texts presented in the songs. G- and f-clefs have been used throughout in place of c-clefs. References to Shakespeare's works, unless otherwise noted, are to *The Riverside Shakespeare,* ed. G. Blakemore Evans (Boston: Houghton Mifflin, 1974). The following abbreviations have been used in citations:

AIM   American Institute of Musicology

CMM   Corpus Mensurabilis Musicae

CNRS   Centre National de la Recherche Scientifique

DTÖ   Denkmäler der Tonkunst in Österreich

New Grove   Stanley Sadie, ed., *The New Grove Dictionary of Music and Musicians*

NUC Pre-1956   *National Union Catalog Pre-1956 Imprints*

OED   *Oxford English Dictionary*

Strunk *SR*   Oliver Strunk, ed., *Source Readings in Music History*

VfMW   *Vierteljahrsschrift für Musikwissenschaft*

Warburg   *Journal of the Warburg and Courtauld Institutes*

Preamble

The wisdom of the ancients inundated sixteenth-century Europe. Painters, poets, musicians, dramatists – all those involved with the arts found their opinions on aesthetics confirmed or contradicted by the *auctores* whose texts spread through the continent and eventually crossed the English Channel. Though many ancient treatises had been available to scholars throughout the Middle Ages, a great number of long-neglected texts came to light in the Renaissance and – thanks largely to printing, translation, and popularization – quickly reached a pan-European audience. Faced with this sudden increase in knowledge, poets and musicians found themselves wrestling with difficult questions. Should they follow the moderns or the ancients? Should they continue to write rhyming poetry and polyphonic music (exposed as inventions of a "barbarous" age), or should they attempt to imitate what the ancient Greeks and Romans had given the world?

Of course, not everyone in the sixteenth century suffered from neoclassical anxiety. But a good many poets and musicians felt compelled to justify their particular way of writing – witness the large number of polemical tracts devoted to poetry and to music. The authors of these tracts generally tried either to reconcile current practice with ancient theory or to alter current practice in accordance with ancient theory. No matter what the approach, one often discovers many a discrepancy when comparing the authors' practice with their theory.

Such is the case in the quarrel between Thomas Campion and Samuel Daniel over the relative merits of rhymed and quantitative verse in English.[1] In his *Observations in the Art of English Poesie* (1602), Campion argues in favor of unrhymed quantitative verse, derogating rhyme as a medieval barbarism; yet nearly all his English poetry is rhymed. Is Campion's treatise, then, an unimportant academic exercise – a futile one at that? Daniel, in his *Defence of Ryme* (1603), would have us believe so. But we should not dismiss this debate as mere pedantic quibbling; for the issues discussed by Campion and Daniel are in large part the central issues of the entire Renaissance, a period

---

[1]Quantitative verse, the norm in ancient Greek and Latin poetry, is determined by temporal length rather than accentual stress; a long syllable should theoretically take twice as long to pronounce as a short syllable and may not always coincide with the stress accent of a word. The average line of English poetry during the Renaissance, in contrast, is composed of accented and unaccented syllables. The first chapter of Derek Attridge's *Well-Weighed Syllables* (Cambridge: Cambridge University Press, 1974) offers a good introduction to classical meters in the Renaissance; see also O. B. Hardison, Jr., *Prosody and Purpose in the English Renaissance* (Baltimore: Johns Hopkins University Press, 1989), chap. 1.

1

whose art is constantly marked by the juxtaposition of medieval and classical elements. Similar debates took place, for example, in the field of music throughout the sixteenth century; indeed, when examining the antecedents to Campion's *Observations* and Daniel's *Defence*, we often find music and poetry discussed as two halves of an aesthetic whole.

Every educated poet in the Renaissance knew that lyric poetry, in theory if not always in practice, was verse apt for singing to the accompaniment of a lyre – or of any instrument like the lyre, such as the lute. As classical scholars discovered more and more about the performance and composition of ancient Greek and Roman poetry, many authors and composers felt challenged to emulate antique song using modern languages and modern music. Twentieth-century scholars use the term "musical humanism" when referring to the efforts of those Renaissance poets and musicians who tried to revivify in their own time the lyric poetry of antiquity.[2] Though by no means a homogeneous group, almost all musical humanists had the goal of making sung texts intelligible to an audience, and they found two principal means of achieving this. One approach was to write what the French called *musique mesurée* – music, usually for several voices, in which the singers declaim the text homorhythmically in two note-values, corresponding to the long and short syllables of the classical or neoclassical text; this brings out the meter of the poem. Monody, the other method, places emphasis on a single voice, most often accompanied by a lute or keyboard instrument. Though they paid careful attention to word rhythm, the monodists generally set modern rhyming verse and concerned themselves with bringing out the dramatic (rather than the prosodic) side of their texts.

Just as poets advocating vernacular quantitative verse disparaged rhyme as a medieval barbarism, so musicians seeking to imitate Greek and Roman song attacked elaborate polyphony as a corruption of ancient musical ideals. Genres that we now regard as the high point of Renaissance music – the highly contrapuntal madrigals, motets, and masses – were sharply censured by the musical humanists, for such pieces obscured their texts. Since Campion was not only a poet but a musician as well, we might expect his lute-songs to reflect the concerns of the musical humanists. And they do. Samuel Daniel's brother, John, also wrote lute-songs; almost predictably, they con-

---

[2]Paul-Marie Masson coined the term "musical humanism" in his pioneering articles "L'humanisme musical en Allemagne au XVIe siècle," *Mercure musical* 2 (Dec. 1906): 394-403, and "L'humanisme musical en France au XVIe siècle" *Mercure musical* 3 (April and July 1907): 333-66, 677-718. Two recent works have considerably widened the meaning of "musical humanism": Claude V. Palisca's *Humanism in Italian Renaissance Musical Thought* (New Haven: Yale University Press, 1985), and Don Harrán's *Word-Tone Relations in Musical Thought: From Antiquity to the Seventeenth Century* (Neuhausen-Stuttgart: AIM, 1986). Palisca shows how deeply ancient theory influenced musical theorists of the Renaissance, and Harrán finds musical-humanist issues in the basic question of text-underlay.

tain nearly every "fault" attacked by the musical humanists. Held in high esteem in their day, Campion and the brothers Daniel have enjoyed a steadily increasing posthumous fame in our own century.[3] By extending the arguments in the *Observations* and the *Defence* to the area of music and by examining what the musical humanists had to say about musico-poetic relations, we gain insight into these two English treatises and achieve a deeper understanding of the Renaissance lyric itself. To appreciate the goals of the musical humanists, however, we must have some idea of what these poets and musicians were responding to and often reacting against – and of why they were doing so. A brief look at some important related issues will help bring our chief topics into sharper focus.

Musical Mathematics and the Problem with Polyphony

University students in the Middle Ages studied music as part of the quadrivium, along with geometry, astronomy, and arithmetic.[4] A music course in the fourteenth century, however, would concentrate largely on speculative music, that branch of music dealing with proportions and closely allied to mathematics. Boethius' *De institutione musicae*, which remained popular throughout the Renaissance, was the standard textbook on the subject in the Middle Ages.[5] It presents the reader with hundreds of pages of mathematical formulas but with little of what one would today associate with music proper. Indeed, it was written "more for the student who aspired to philosophy than for the practicing musician, even though it was the practicing musician's most authoritative theory text for almost a thousand years."[6] Music as *sound* comes into the discussion mainly to illustrate mathematical principles. A student reading Boethius' book should have a monochord – a resonating box with one string and a movable bridge. This instrument provides a musical equivalent, so to speak, of the proportional formulas under discussion. If, for example, the student places the bridge in the middle of a twelve-inch string, the pitch produced will be an octave higher than that produced by the entire

[3]Several books and dissertations have been written on Samuel Daniel and Thomas Campion; see chap. 5, n. 11, and chap. 7, n. 8. John Daniel has received little critical attention in recent times, though long ago Peter Warlock, in *The English Ayre* (London: Oxford University Press, 1926), praised Daniel's music (see chap. 3 of his book), as did Percy Judd, in "The Songs of John Danyel," *Music and Letters* 17 (1936): 118-23.

[4]See Nan C. Carpenter, *Music in the Medieval and Renaissance Universities* (1958; New York: Da Capo, 1972), 115.

[5] Ibid., 117-20. A fourteenth-century condensation of Boethius' work "superseded Boethius in the original as the textbook to be used in many of the medieval universities" (118).

[6]Calvin Bower, "Boethius' *The Principles of Music*, an Introduction, Translation, and Commentary" (Ph.D. dissertation, George Peabody College for Teachers, 1967), 17. Bower has recently published a new translation of Boethius' work, *Fundamentals of Music* (New Haven: Yale University Press, 1989).

length of the string. The octave is a consonant interval – as one might expect, since the ratio 12:6 is inherently consonant (six going into twelve exactly twice). So far, the method is easy enough to grasp. But when Boethius discusses more complicated intervals, the formulas begin to look more forbidding. Proportional exercises abound in *De institutione musicae*. When we read Boethius, we are in the world of Plato's *Timaeus*, in which "the soul of the universe [is] joined together according to musical concord,"[7] and in which that musical concord is the result of mathematical perfection.

Practical music, to be sure, also had some importance in university studies during the Middle Ages.[8] But mere performers – those who could play or sing but had no understanding of the underlying mathematical principles, the eternal truths, of music – were usually condemned by speculative theorists. Even in the late English Renaissance, this condescending attitude, though perhaps moribund, is by no means dead.[9] In John Dowland's translation (1609) of Ornithoparchus' *Micrologus* (1517), for instance, one reads the following:

> Therefore he is truely to be called a *Musitian*, who hath the faculty of speculation and reason, not he that hath only a practick fashion of singing: for so saith *Boêtius lib.* I *cap.* 35. He is called a Musitian, which taketh upon him the knowledge of Singing by weighing it with reason, not with the servile exercise of practise, but the commanding power of speculation, and wanteth neither speculation nor practise.[10]

Augustine's *De musica*, another text well known in the Middle Ages and Renaissance, also treats the mere performer with disdain because, like a bird, such a musician imitates sounds without using reason.[11] Music, for Augustine, includes poetry; in fact, the better part of his unfinished treatise is devoted to subtle discussions of Latin prosody. Like Boethius, Augustine believes that good composition depends on a proportional balance and that this balance pleases because it reflects, in microcosm, the perfection of the universe.[12]

[7]Boethius, *Fundamentals*, 2.

[8]See Carpenter, 120-27, in which the practical side of music is discussed.

[9]See John Hollander, *The Untuning of the Sky* (1961; New York: Norton, 1970), for an account of the decline of speculative music as seen in English poetry from 1500 to 1700.

[10]Ornithoparchus, *Musicae activae micrologus* (1516), trans. John Dowland (1606); both included in Ornithoparchus/Dowland, *A Compendium of Musical Practice*, intro. Gustave Reese and Stephen Ledbetter (New York: Dover, 1973), 124.

[11]St. Augustine, *On Music, Books 1-6*, trans. R. Catesby Taliaferro (Annapolis: The St. John's Bookstore, 1939), 7-9.

[12]See Boethius (*Fundamentals*, 2) and Augustine (bk. 1). The influence of Plato's *Timaeus* which describes the universe in musico-mathematical terms (see esp. 35-36), is strong in these two works. See Palisca, *Humanism in Italian Renaissance Thought*, 37, and, for a broad discussion

But practical musicians, though slighted by theorists like Boethius and Augustine, provided people with the music they listened to and enjoyed. By the late Middle Ages, composers had raised the art of combining independent melodies to a level of great complexity. Of course, simple pieces were also written throughout the medieval period, but masters of counterpoint were hardly reluctant to show off their skill, and their pieces ravish the ear with intricate polyphony. The very intricacy of the music, however, could be regarded as a drawback; since the parts are rhythmically independent of one another, the singers do not declaim the text at the same time, so the words become unclear. Many composers, moreover, assigned different texts to the various voices, which made it nearly impossible for the listener to follow the words. The lack of concern for the comprehensibility of the text that one often encounters in medieval polyphonic music is best illustrated by the polytextual motet, which in its extremest form presents not only different texts but different languages simultaneously.[13]

Like the medieval contrapuntists, most of the great composers of the fifteenth and sixteenth centuries did not try first and foremost to make clear all the words they set. Generally, however, they did respond to their texts: the mood of a piece was often inspired by the words, and key phrases were underscored by the use of homorhythmic declamation. The motet "Rogamus te," by Heinrich Isaac (c. 1450-1517), illustrates these tendencies well. At the core of Isaac's piece is an eight-note *cantus firmus*, appearing several times in the tenor part, each new time in faster note-values. The motive also appears in the other voices, which weave a complex web of polyphony around the *cantus firmus* (Ex. a).[14] Near the end of the piece, the voices declaim in chordal blocks (Ex. b). The shift to a homorhythmic texture strikingly highlights the direct address to Mary; Isaac has clearly kept the text in mind when setting it to music. Certain words – like *te* in the alto line (m. 1) – receive a subtle stress by appearing at the peak of a phrase or in an accentually emphatic position. Still, most of the words in the motet are incomprehensible.

---

of the concept, Leo Spitzer, "Classical and Christian Ideas of World Harmony: Prolegomena to an Interpretation of the Word 'Stimmung,'" *Traditio* 2 (1944): 409-64; 3 (1945): 307-64.

[13]See Richard Hoppin, *Medieval Music* (New York: Norton, 1978), 328-30, for a discussion of the polytextual motet; also John Stevens, *Music and Poetry in the Early Tudor Court* (1961; Cambridge: Cambridge University Press, 1979), 34-35. James A. Winn, in *Unsuspected Eloquence: A History of the Relations between Poetry and Music* (New Haven: Yale University Press, 1981), points out some of the advantages to having simultaneous declamation of different texts; his persuasive argument that composers using this technique can, for example, "express and surpass literary oxymoron" (148) serves as a healthy corrective to the humanists' frequent condemnations of vocal counterpoint.

[14]I thank Richard Taruskin for allowing me to consult his unpublished transcription of "Rogamus te," on which my reduction is based. The original was published by Petrucci in *Motetti C* (Venice, 1504).

Ex. a, Isaac, "Rogamus te" (note-values quartered)

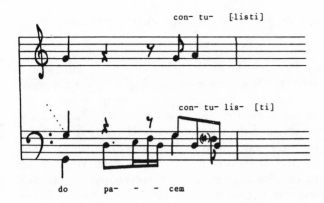

Ex. a, continued

Ex. b, Isaac, "O Domina"

Throughout the first half of the piece, the *cantus firmus* moves so slowly that the listener hears little more than the vowel sounds *o, a, i, a.* Furthermore, the text of the tenor part differs from that of the other parts. Some syllables – like the first of *pacem* in the alto line (m. 6) – are lengthened by the use of melismas, which distort the words. But what most hinders us from understanding the text is the simultaneous singing of different words; at almost any point in the piece, two, three, even four words (or parts of words) are sung at once.

And one is not surprised to find a sixteenth-century version of the piece without any text and with the title "La mi la sol" (these words being the solmization syllables that correspond to the notes of the *cantus firmus*).[15] For the music alone, unattached to a text and based on what seems a purely musical motive, has a life of its own. Even the homorhythmic section has a

---

[15]The instrumental piece can be found in DTÖ 28:87-89.

function other than to make the words suddenly clear: it provides textural variety in the instrumental setting.

Isaac was a well known and highly regarded composer in his day, and his music circulated widely. He worked with the humanist Politian and counted among his patrons Lorenzo the Magnificent and Maximilian I. Yet the music for which Isaac was famous – elaborate polyphonic compositions – was precisely the kind that many musical humanists inveighed against. They argued that such music obscured the texts and violated the rhythm of the words. But unlike literary classicists, who regarded the barbarian invasions as the beginning of the end of great poetry, the musical humanists more commonly blamed "modern" composers for the polyphony that drained music of its power. Of course, the word *modernus* itself could be used in the sixteenth century to mean "medieval" or "Gothic"; for some, the word chiefly implied postclassical aesthetic "pollution," and I suspect that many critics of polyphonic music used the term this way.[16] They certainly knew that music had changed – for the worse, in their opinion – since the days of Horace, and they hoped to restore it to its "untainted," classical state.

Orpheus

Since Orpheus will appear with some frequency throughout this essay, it will be helpful to trace certain important stages in his fortunes from the Middle Ages to the Renaissance. Orpheus earned the respect of medieval writers chiefly because of his connection with Christ (who also entered the underworld with a wooden instrument – the cross – in order to save souls)[17] and because of his great skill. He was the musical craftsman *par excellence.* Chaucer, for example, has Orpheus head a list of famous harpers in the *House of Fame* (lines 1201-8);[18] what distinguishes Orpheus there is that he plays the harp "ful craftely." Similarly, the eponymous harper in the anonymous *Sir Orfeo* (c. 1300) strikes us more as a noble virtuoso than as a demigod (his parents are descendants of King Pluto and "King" Juno). Only once is his playing described in a way that suggests it had supernatural powers:

> & when the weder was clere & bright
> He toke his harp to him wel right
> & harped at his owhen wille.
> In-to alle the wode the soun gan schille,
> That alle the wilde bestes that ther beth

[16]See Erwin Panofsky, *Renaissance and Renascences in Western Art* (1969; New York: Harper and Row, 1972), 33-34.

[17]John B. Friedman, in the third chapter of his *Orpheus in the Middle Ages* (Cambridge: Harvard University Press, 1970), discusses the medieval conflation of Christ and Orpheus.

[18]*The Complete Poetry and Prose of Geoffrey Chaucer,* ed. John Fisher (New York: Holt, Rinehart and Winston, 1977), 601.

For joie abouten him thai teth,
& alle the foules that ther were
Come & sete on ich a brere,
To here his harping a-fine
– So miche melody was ther-in. . . .[19]

But this passage differs little from a fourteenth-century description of Francesco Landini's organ playing, which was said first to have struck birds dumb and then to have set them chattering wildly.[20] Both passages smack of hyperbole, but neither paints a picture of an utterly incredible situation. Animals do, after all, react to sound: and music is sound.

The medieval Orpheus, though a dazzling performer, does not hold the divine secrets of the universe, as his Renaissance counterpart was often thought to do. Some musical humanists had implicit faith in Orpheus' extraordinary musical abilities. Those skeptical about the story of his taming wild beasts could allegorize as Horace had done:

Silvestris homines sacer interpresque deorum
caedibus et victu foedo deterruit Orpheus,
dictus ob hoc lenire tigris rabidosque leones.

While men still roamed the woods, Orpheus, the holy prophet of the gods, made them shrink from bloodshed and brutal living; hence the fable that he tamed tigers and ravening lions. . . .[21]

Even thus allegorized, the story gives Orpheus no little credit for having the ability to soften the mores of wild men.

By Ficino's time, Orpheus had become an amalgam of several discrete personages: the legendary singer – celebrated in Ovid's *Metamorphoses* (bk. 10) and Virgil's *Georgics* (bk. 4) – whose divine singing quieted brutes and arrested activity in Hades; the author of several perhaps pre-Platonic fragments; the composer of some hymns written probably in early Christian times; and a central character in a fourth-century *Argonautica*.[22] Moreover,

---

[19]*Sir Orfeo*, ed. A. J. Bliss (London: Oxford University Press, 1954), 24-25. My text is based on that of the Auchinleck MS.; I have silently modernized the thorn and yogh to "th" and "gh" and have not marked the expanded contractions. Bliss glosses *schille* as "to resound shrilly" and *teth* as "approach."

[20]The story of Landini's playing is in Giovanni da Prato's romance *Il Paradiso degli Alberti* (1389) and is summarized in Gustave Reese, *Music in the Middle Ages* (New York: Norton, 1940), 372.

[21]*Ars poetica* 391-93. In *Satires, Epistles, and Ars Poetica*, trans. H. R. Fairclough, Loeb Classical Library (Cambridge: Harvard University Press, 1929), 482-83.

[22]See D. P. Walker, "Orpheus the Theologian and Renaissance Platonists" *Warburg* 16 (1953): 103, where the last three points are made.

tradition had linked him with Christ and David,[23] and Iamblicus credited Orpheus with being the first to argue that the universe is explicable through numerical formulas – a theory made especially popular by Plato's *Timaeus*.[24] Orpheus could thus become an important link between the Boethian concept of music as a set of proportions echoing the harmony of the universe and the humanist concept of music as a force capable of producing extraordinary emotional and morally edifying effects in the listener – a concept not absent in Boethius, but dealt with rather hastily as a prelude to the loftier matter of *musica speculativa*.

As the author of the various fragments and hymns listed above, Orpheus was a key figure in the history of ideas and of religion; and although many Renaissance thinkers doubted the authenticity of the Orphic fragments, many also "assumed that the Orphica, even if not all literally by Orpheus, were the genuine sacred writings of a very ancient religious tradition."[25]Because he was the oldest Greek of the *prisci theologi* – a group of ancient and sometimes divine writers that included Zoroaster, Hermes Trismegistus, Moses, and Plato (among others) – Orpheus was regarded as the ultimate teacher of Pythagoras and Plato.[26] Indeed, some syncretists believed that Orpheus (who according to the *Argonautica* had traveled to Egypt) had read Moses' works, recognized them as divinely inspired, and in effect retold them in an oblique way. (The obliqueness was necessary because of the divine nature of the text, to be concealed from the uninitiated "lest it should be profaned and despised by the vulgar.")[27]

Orpheus is a fellow harper throughout most of the Middle Ages. True, several medieval treatises list the many amazing deeds that Orpheus, Arion, David, and the rest have accomplished through music; but one feels that the theorists present such catalogues perfunctorily: the ancient lore is the sugar-coating to make readers take their dose of speculative music the more willingly.[28] In the fifteenth and sixteenth centuries, however, classicists looked more critically into these effects. Ficino tried to give a rational explanation of the effects of music, and others, especially those connected with Baïf's *Académie de Poésie et de Musique*, made a concerted effort to restore the ancient effects of music.

---

[23]Friedman, 147-49.

[24]Walker, "Orpheus," 100.

[25]Ibid., 104.

[26]D. P. Walker, "Le chant orphique de Marsile Ficin," in Jean Jacquot, ed., *Musique et poésie au XVIe siècle* (Paris: CNRS, 1954), 22, and Walker, *Orpheus,* 103-7.

[27]Walker, "Orpheus," 106.

[28]See Nino Pirrotta, "Music and Cultural Tendencies in 15th-Century Italy," *Journal of the American Musicological Society* 19 (1966): 136-37.

Ficino and Music

A serious interest in classical literature existed, to an extent, throughout the Middle Ages. Yet it would be wrong to say that in fifteenth-century Italy, nothing new happened in the history of Western thought. Manuscripts that had for centuries lain neglected were newly studied – many written in Greek, a language accessible neither to the general public nor to many scholars. These works required translation. Moreover, a new group of readers, recently made wealthy by trade, wished to acquire knowledge and its attendant prestige. The most famous family of this kind was, of course, the Medici. Cosimo de' Medici wanted to free some of the wisdom locked in the ancient manuscripts, and he chose Marsilio Ficino (1433-99) for this task. According to Ficino, in the preface to his translation of Plotinus (1492), Cosimo wanted to encourage the study of Platonic and neo-Platonic texts after hearing the eloquent Byzantine philosopher Gemistus Pletho (James Hankins questions this account, written well after the fact). In the 1460s, Cosimo supplied Ficino with Greek manuscripts to translate and, in 1463, a house in Careggi in which to work.[29]

Although the most influential works to come out of Ficino's endeavors were his translations of (and commentaries on) Plato and various neo-Platonists, early in his career (1462), Ficino translated the Orphic hymns, which he sang to his own accompaniment on the "lyre" (probably the *lyra da braccio*, a bowed string instrument akin to the modern viola).[30]

In his *De vita* (1489), a study of health and medicine, Ficino discusses, among other things, the salutary influence of the stars and planets, and the effects of music on humankind. Stressing the occult to a surprising degree, Ficino encountered opposition from religious conservatives for the ideas presented in *De vita*.[31] Most important to our study, of course, are his views on music, presented in the third book, chapters 21 and 22.

Numerous ancient authorities – Origen, Synesius, Al-Kindi, Zoroaster, Iamblichus, and others – have agreed (Ficino tells us) that words, especially chanted words, have great power. This belief was also held by the Pythagoreans, "who used to perform wonders by words, songs, and sounds in the Phoebean and Orphic manner" (". . . *Pythagorici verbis et cantibus atque sonis mirabilia quaedam Phoebi et Orphei more facere consueti*").[32] But how

---

[29]See James Hankins, "Cosimo de' Medici and the 'Platonic Academy,'" *Warburg* 53 (1990): 144-62.

[30]D. P. Walker, "Orpheus," Warburg, 102-03; "Le chant orphique," 19; James Haar, "Marsilio Ficino," *New Grove*.

[31]See the Introduction to Marsilio Ficino, *Three Books on Life*, ed. and trans. Carol V. Kaske and John R. Clark (Binghamton, NY: Medieval and Renaissance Texts and Studies, 1989), 55-57.

[32]Ibid., 354-55.

does this affect moderns? The power, Ficino argues, can still be harnessed. One should try, by playing the right music, to draw the beneficial influence from the heavens. After observing how certain kinds of music are played by certain kinds of people, one can determine what kind of music draws what celestial effects.

Like many of his contemporaries, Ficino was interested in sympathetic vibration, a phenomenon best illustrated when one of two strings tuned to the same pitch is struck and, through its vibrations, makes the other string sound. Since, from the time of Boethius onward, music had been divided into three categories – "music of the spheres (*musica mundana*), of man's body, spirit and soul (*musica humana*), of voices and intruments (*musica instrumentalis*)"[33] – Ficino could argue that playing and singing in a certain way would cause the heavens, as it were, to vibrate in sympathy and, in turn, make the music of the human *spiritus* re-echo sympathetically. Done frequently, this practice would alter one's personality. Depending on the kind of songs being sung to the heavens, one would become Jovial, Mercurial, or Venereal – and Phoeban in any case, since Phoebus governs music.[34]

Music has the ability not only to please the sense of hearing but also to feed the intellect and is thus a formidable force. It can affect the *spiritus* ("a certain vapour of the blood, pure, subtle, hot and lucid"), which is especially receptive to sound since the *spiritus* and sound "are living, feeling kinds of air," as D. P. Walker has observed; for Ficino, Walker continues, "music has a stronger effect than anything transmitted through the other senses, because its medium, air, is of the same kind as the *spiritus*."[35]

Though few works in the sixteenth century *directly* echo Ficino's *De vita*, the first two books were translated into German (1505) and French (1541), and in 1582 a translation of all three books was published in Paris, *Les trois livres de la vie*.[36] *De vita* was also republished several times in the middle years of the sixteenth century (Paris, 1547; London, 1560 and 1566);[37] the work thus appears to have enjoyed a wide reading public. But more important than Ficino's careful working out of the effects of music on the listener is his earnest attitude toward music as a powerful force capable of molding a person's moral character. Ficino rarely deals with the mathematical side of

[33]D. P. Walker, "Ficino's *Spiritus* and Music," *Annales musicologiques* 1 (1953): 141. See also Boethius, *Fundamentals*, 9-10, and John Hollander, *Untuning of the Sky*, 25.

[34]*Three Books on Life*, 360-61.

[35]Walker, "Ficino's *Spiritus*," 132-35; in parentheses, Walker's translation of a passage from *De vita*, bk. 1, chap. 2: "*vapor quidam sanguinis purus, subtilis, calidus et lucidus*" (*Three Books on Life*, 110).

[36]Notes on translations of *De vita* are provided in the Introduction to *Three Books on Life*, 12.

[37]See *NUC Pre-1956*, 171:434-36. Also listed is an edition from 1595 (no place).

music;[38] he represents the new humanist respect for practical music, as opposed to speculative music, and was perhaps the "earliest Renaissance writer . . . to treat the 'effects' of music seriously and practically, and not merely as a constituent of the rhetorical topic of the *laus musicae*."[39] His influence on later writers is well attested,[40] and even in England, Ficinian concepts – drawn either directly from Ficino or from an intermediate source – often surface in works devoted to philosophy, love, and music.

---

[38]See Pirrotta, "Music and Cultural Tendencies," 137.

[39]Walker, "Ficino's *Spiritus*," 147.

[40]Paul O. Kristeller, *The Philosophy of Marsilio Ficino*, trans. Virginia Conant (Gloucester, Mass.: Peter Smith, 1964), 19.

Part One

Musical Humanism and "Measured" Verses

Chapter 1

Germany and France

German Settings of Latin Quantitative Verse

The fifteenth-century Italian humanists, producing scholarly editions of ancient literature along with erudite commentaries, inspired similar activity throughout the Renaissance. In southern Germany and Vienna, thanks to the influence of Conrad Celtis, a number of short-lived academies blossomed early in the sixteenth century. Celtis (1459-1508) traveled in Italy in the 1480s and became personally acquainted with Ficino, who was then working on *De vita*. Having journeyed extensively, Celtis returned to Germany with the intention of founding an academy in Ingolstadt. His wanderlust eventually took him to Heidelberg, where around 1495 he formed a *Sodalitas litteraria*, an informal gathering of classical scholars, including the great Johann Reuchlin. The group's goals were ambitious: to explore and encourage the study of ancient Greek, Latin, and Hebrew literature. It seems unlikely, however, that most of the members were fluent in ancient languages other than Latin. Always on the move, Celtis traveled in 1497 to Vienna, where he founded the *Sodalitas litteraria Danubiana*. Eventually other Teutonic academies, dedicated to the publication and dissemination of classical literature and humanist studies, sprang into existence.[1]

As a teacher, Celtis discussed classical prosody. Like many other humanists, he believed that the lyrical poems of ancient Rome had been sung.[2] To teach scansion more effectively and, from a humanist standpoint, more correctly, Celtis had musical settings of Horace's odes made, each using only two note-values (breves and whole-notes) to emphasize the metrical scheme of the poem (consisting of long and short syllables). In 1507, Celtis supervised the printing of nineteen four-part settings of Horace's odes composed by Petrus Tritonius (Treybenreif) and by other members of Celtis' learned society.[3] These pieces are unashamedly pedagogical, their chief aim being to

---

[1] Lewis Spitz, *Conrad Celtis: The German Arch-Humanist* (Cambridge: Harvard University Press, 1957), 12, 21, 46, 50, 56, 59, 61.

[2] Ibid., 81.

[3] Rochus von Liliencron, "Die Horazischen Metren in deutschen Kompositionen des 16. Jahrhunderts," *VfMW* 3 (1887): 26-27; Spitz, 81. The earliest German attempt to illustrate quantitative verse with music appears in Hugo Spechtshart von Reutlingen's *Flores musicae*, written in 1332, revised in 1342, and published in 1488. Karl-Werner Gümpel's edition of the

16

provide a mnemonic device for students struggling with the intricacies of, say, the third asclepiade. Nevertheless, in their homorhythmic movement and their use of only two note-values (cadences excepted), the settings anticipate the musico-poetic experiments of the later sixteenth century, notably those of Baïf and his fellow academicians. "Lydia dic" (Ex. 1.1) illustrates Tritonius' approach.[4]

Ex. 1.1, Tritonius, "Lydia dic"

Flores musicae (Wiesbaden: Akademie der Wissenschaften und der Literatur in Mainz, 1958) contains a facsimile of the "measured" verse (123, line 605). On early German settings of quantitative verse, see 163-78 of Édith Weber's *La musique mesurée à l'antique en Allemagne*, 2 vols. ([Paris]: Klincksieck, 1974), the most thorough study of musical humanism in Germany. See also Günther Wille, *Musica Romana: Die Bedeutung der Musik im Leben der Römer* (Amsterdam: P. Schippers, 1967), 222-25, 228-34, 260-82. Edward Lowinsky, in "Humanism in the Music of the Renaissance," *Music in the Culture of the Renaissance*, ed. Bonnie Blackburn, 2 vols. (Chicago: University of Chicago Press, 1989), 1:154-218, discusses several issues that I have brought up here and elsewhere in my survey of musical humanism.

[4]Tritonius' settings, as well as settings of the same poems by Senfl and Hofhaimer, are reproduced in in original note-values and clefs in Liliencron, "Die Horazischen Metren" 49-91; for convenience' sake, I have halved note-values and reduced the original four clefs to the standard treble and bass clefs.

Though simple, the piece – with its constantly shifting accents – has its attractions.[5] Tritonius' settings were widely popular and, whatever their musical value, influential. They, and other strictly homorhythmic ode-settings, continued to be published throughout the sixteenth century,[6] and similar compositions were used in school dramas.[7]

But Tritonius himself, sensing that his compositions were weak, hoped that someone of superior ability would do justice to the poems. With this end in mind, Tritonius' friend Simon Minervius tried to convince Isaac to set Tritonius' tenors.[8] Isaac declined, but his student Ludwig Senfl, who had already written a quantitative-verse setting, granted Minervius his wish.[9] Senfl's settings appeared in 1534, with an introduction by Minervius. That these arrangements of the odes were meant to be inspirational as *music* is suggested by the following passage from the introduction:

> [Senfl] habet, nescio quomodo, illud sibi singulare, quod ceu poeta quidam egregius et verbis gestum et eorum, qui audiunt, animi affectus tonis suis inspiret, dum grandia elate, moderata leniter, iucunda dulciter, tristia moeste inflat ac modulatur totaque arte cum affectibus consentit.[10]

[5]Edward Lowinsky, in a review of D. P. Walker's *Der musikalische Humanismus im 16. und fruehen 17. Jahrhundert* (*Musical Quarterly* 37 [1951]), argues that the homophonic simplicity of these pieces would have had "the charm of an entirely novel sound to the 16th-century listener . . ." (286). Lowinsky develops this idea in "Music in the Culture of the Renaissance," *Journal of the History of Ideas* 15 (1954): 547-48. The notion that these homorhythmic pieces offered an "entirely novel sound," however, needs some qualification, since numerous sacred and profane works of the period contained passages marked by homorhythmic declamation.

[6]See Peter Bergquist, "Petrus Tritonius," *New Grove*. Some of Tritonius' Horatian odes appeared as lute solos in Hans Judenkünig's *Utilis & compendiaria introductio* (Vienna, c. 1515-19; a few of the settings are transcribed in DTÖ 37:1, 7); though the pieces may have been included because of their simplicity, composers generally intabulated popular tunes. Paul Hofhaimer's similar settings of Horace's odes (1539) found at least one admirer in Spain, for Alfonso Mudarra included Hofhaimer's "Beatus ille" as a vihuela-song (no. 63) in his *Tres libros de música en cifras para vihuela* (1546); Weber's *Musique mesurée* shows that the influence of Tritonius' settings was extensive.

[7]See Rochus von Liliencron, "Die Chorgesänge des lateinisch-deutschen Schuldramas im XVI. Jahrhundert," *VfMW* 6 (1890): 309-87.

[8]Liliencron, "Die Horazischen Metren," 39.

[9]Hans Moser, *Paul Hofhaimer: ein Lied- und Orgelmeister des deutschen Humanismus* (Stuttgart: J. G. Cotta'sche Buchhandlung Nachfolger, 1929), 163.

[10]The entire introduction is printed in Ludwig Senfl, *Sämtliche Werke*, ed. Arnold Geering and Wilhelm Altwegg, 11 vols. (Wolfenbüttel: Möseler Verlag, 1961), 6:119-21. The Latin, based on Quintilian's *Institutio oratoria* I.x.24-25, is rather ambiguous, since Minervius has borrowed phrases originally used to describe oratory and placed them in a musical context. The gist, in any event, seems clear. Applying Quintilian's words about oratory to music seems to

Senfl somehow has that unique ability to inspire with his music (as a great poet inspires with his words, [affecting] both the bearing and the mental state of the listeners), when he sets great things exaltedly, moderate things mildly, pleasing things sweetly, sad things softly, and harmonizes the emotions with all his skill.

Minervius' comparison of Senfl's musical ability to a great poet's control over his audience – while appropriate simply because it links poetry and music – also suggests that the settings had a deeper purpose than merely to serve as a pedagogical aid. The listeners were to feel transported, inspired, when they heard Horace's odes well set and properly sung. Indeed, the passage calls to mind the rhapsode Ion, who in a state of "divine frenzy" wept when reciting sad passages or recoiled in fear when reciting terrible ones – eliciting like responses from his audience.[11] But whatever Minervius expected from Senfl, the new settings, following the homorhythmic style established by Tritonius, are not likely to create in us the same *frisson* that some of Senfl's dense, text-blurring motets do.[12] We should bear in mind, however, that the goal of such pieces, though admittedly didactic, was not *only* to help schoolchildren learn their Latin prosody; it was also (at least in theory) to bring life to the lyrics and to restore some of their original impact, which would necessarily have diminished with the disappearance of what classicists judged the requisite musical accompaniment.

Two other Teutonic musical humanists deserve mention: Johannes Cochlaeus (1479-1552) and his Swiss-born student Heinrich Glarean (1488-1563), both of whom – propounding humanist ideology the while – taught Latin and music to children.[13] While rector of the St. Lorenz School in Nuremberg, Cochlaeus wrote and published his *Tetrachordum musices* (1511), "written chiefly for instruction of the youth at the church of St. Lorenz, but also for the profitable and uncomplicated instruction of others

have occurred as early as the *Musica enchiriadis* (c. 900); see John Stevens, *Words and Music in the Middle Ages* (Cambridge: Cambridge University Press, 1986), 403-4.

[11]Plato, *Ion* 535B-536D. One thinks also of the story of Timotheus, whose music was reputed first to have put Alexander the Great into a warlike frenzy and then to have calmed him down. See Morrison C. Boyd, *Elizabethan Music and Musical Criticism*, 2d ed. (Philadelphia: University of Pennsylvania Press, 1967), 30.

[12]Senfl's ode-settings in modern clefs and in halved time are in Senfl, *Werke*, 6:71-92; in original clefs and note-values, Liliencron, "Die Horazischen Metren," 49-91. The texts in Senfl's collected works differ slightly from those in Liliencron.

[13]See Clement Miller, "Johannes Cochlaeus" and "Heinrich Glarean," *New Grove*. Richard Marius, in *Thomas More* (New York: Knopf, 1984), points out that Cochlaeus corresponded with More, though their exchanges seem to have focused mainly on Luther (310-11). Cochlaeus' *Grammatica* (1515) in several places includes breves and whole-notes, without melodies, to illustrate poetic meters (see, for example, fol. 78).

who are beginners in the art of music," as its title page tells us. Near the
end of the treatise is a homorhythmic setting of an elegiac couplet that may
serve as a setting for several other elegiac couplets culled from Ovid and
included after the setting. Cochlaeus also sets Christian hymns. Both classical
and Christian settings show the probable influence of Tritonius' odes, though
Cochlaeus' melodies have greater rhythmic variety.[14] His attitude toward
setting the text is illuminating:

> Iucundum est . . . carmen melo coniungere antiquitatisque simula-
> crum referre. . . . Nonne lyrica carmina ad lyrae strepitum verba
> iungebant? Quid ille Phemius Homeri. Ioppasque vergilii? Nonne
> ad doctissima heroum carmina harmonicos concentus applicuere?
> Non ab re itaque hos metris donamus concentus. Veruntamen pedum
> quantitates non ubique custodivimus / melodiae hic potius quam
> metrice indulgentes. (Sig. Fii)

> it is pleasant to join poetry and music, and to recreate a conception
> of antiquity. . . . Did not lyric poems join their words to the sound
> of the lyre? What about Phemius in Homer and Ioppas in Vergil?
> Did not they apply harmonious strains to the most distinguished
> heroic poems? Therefore, it is with good reason that we present
> these metrical compositions. But we have not observed the metric
> feet in every place, favoring the melodies rather than the meters.[15]

Then follows the elegiac song (Ex. 1.2).

Ex. 1.2, Cochlaeus, "Da mihi"

He sets sacred texts in a similar way, perhaps showing that impulse so
common in the Renaissance to join the Christian and classical worlds;[16]

---

[14]*Tetrachordum musices*, trans. and ed. Clement Miller (n.p.: AIM, 1970), 6, 11, 12. The
Latin text is based on the 1514 edi tion, published in Nuremberg.

[15]Ibid., 83.

[16]Ibid., 84.

similarly, Baïf would later apply his theories about quantitative verse in French to a set of his translations of the psalms.

Heinrich Glarean was a more important figure than his teacher Cochlaeus. Maximilian I, impressed with Glarean's poetic ability, crowned him with a laurel wreath in 1512.[17] A friend of Erasmus for many years,[18] Glarean also knew Budé. Like his learned friends, Glarean helped to bring antiquity to the present by publishing scholarly editions of ancient authors – Tacitus, Livy, Horace, and others.[19] In his *opus magnum*, the *Dodecachordon* (1547), Glarean expresses many opinions deriving from classical authorities. He is critical of the four-voice settings of Horace discussed earlier, arguing that they will not sufficiently move the listeners or the singers, and proposes instead monophonic settings:

> Ego Tenorem requiro, quem unus vel solus secum personet, vel aliis accinet, vel quem multi simul, sed unum intonent, quemadmodum in Choro sacri Hymni ac Psalmi adsolent. Praeterea eum requiro, qui brevibus longisque syllabis sua det tempora, quod in Choro hodie mirum cur non observetur, olim, ut puto, non neglectum, unde adhuc puto esse, ut nonnunquam unilongae syllabae plures datae fuerint notulae, quanquam posteri hoc ita deinde neglexerunt, ut brevibus pariter ac longis promiscue plureis dederint notulas.[20]

> I am looking for a tenor which one may sing either by himself or to others, or which many may sing together, but as one, just as is customary with hymns and psalms in the choir. Moreover, I am looking for one which gives the long and short syllables their own time values, which certainly cannot be observed in a choir today, but which I believe was not neglected in former times; therefore, I believe that hitherto it happened that sometimes single long syllables were given more notes, although posterity has so neglected this thereupon, that they have given many notes indiscriminately to both long and short syllables.[21]

He gives a few of his own settings of Horace's odes, his approach being more expressive than that of Tritonius and the other pedagogues. Glarean, for example, does not always use the same music to serve for each stanza, since the words generally demand different music – even if the meter does

---

[17]Introduction to *Dodecachordon*, trans. and ed. Clement Miller, 2 vols. (n.p.: AIM, 1965), 1:6.

[18]Miller's translation of *Dodecachordon* 1:129.

[19]Ibid., Introduction, 1:16.

[20]*Dodecachordon* (1547; New York: Broude Brothers, 1967), 179.

[21]Miller's translation of *Dodecachordon*, 1:210.

not. So in his setting of "Cum tu Lydia" (*Odes* 1.13), we find, in the first
stanza, that the exclamation "*vae*" ("ah!") jumps up a fifth to suggest the
singer's sudden outburst of passion, and "*fervens*" ("burning") is placed in the
upper register of the piece (Ex. 1.3).

Ex. 1.3, Glarean, "Cum tu Lydia"

In the last stanza, Glarean allows himself increased rhythmic and melodic
freedom when he stretches out the first syllable of "*Felices*" ("happy") by
adding a short, felicitous melisma to it, while the b-flat in "*querimoniis*"
("complaints") adds a sad note appropriate to the word (Ex. 1.4).

Ex. 1.4, Glarean, "Felices ter"

Glarean also includes a homorhythmic, Tritonian setting of "Ut queant laxis"
(bk. 3, ch. 25), the famous poem in Sapphic stanzas from which our solfeggio
system derives; but he adduces the piece to illustrate modes, not prosody.

In Germanic countries, then, a growing interest in understanding and
teaching quantitative verse, and in restoring lyrics to their original splendor,
led some humanists to experiment with settings that made the scansion clear

and the words easily discernible. But for most of the sixteenth century, Teutons made little attempt to write quantitative verse in their mother tongue. The sporadic essays at German verse in antique meters – rhymed Sapphics and the like – were based on accent rather than on real quantity and had a negligible influence on Teutonic poetry of the Renaissance.[22]

The Pléiade and Baïf's Académie

The great French savant Lefèvre d'Étaples furthered the cause of musical humanism in his *Musica libris demonstrata quattuor* (1496), one of the earliest printed treatises on music. The content of his book is generally Boethian, differing little from earlier works on speculative music.[23] But at the end of the treatise, he criticizes those modern musicians who have polluted the ancient modes with their new ones and who indulge in excesses that render the music impotent – unlike those older musicians, such as Orpheus, who drew men away from savage customs and recalled them to the path of virtue (*"virtutis callem revocabant,"* sig. [h6v]). Lefèvre's humanism shows in his scorn for modern music and in his praise of and faith in ancient music. Widely read in the sixteenth century,[24] his treatise serves as an apt prelude to the many discussions about music and poetry that sixteenth-century France would produce.

In 1514, Lazare de Baïf (d. 1547) – a disciple of the humanist Budé, and the father of Jean-Antoine, who played a key role in the development of French musical humanism – set out for Italy.[25] There, inspired by the revival of interest in all things Greek, he became skilled in the language of Sophocles and Euripides (and eventually translated into his mother tongue plays by both tragedians). Baïf returned to France a Grecophile. Later made ambassador to Venice, he came to know many of the leading Italian humanists of the day. He was called to Germany in 1540; his six-year-old son, Jean-Antoine, he committed to the care of one of Budé's former pupils, Jacques Toussaint, who tutored the boy in Latin and Greek. Lazare de Baïf had as secretary in his German mission a precocious sixteen-year-old who eventually

[22]Indeed, Walter Bennet in *German Verse in Classical Metres* (The Hague: Mouton, 1963), goes as far as to suggest that "in the 16th century no one had any idea of the *length* of German syllables . . ." (21). See, however, some of Weber's examples in *Musique mesurée*, 2:635-37, which are genuine attempts at quantitative verse in the vernacular. They are atypical.

[23]In his *Lutes, Viols and Temperaments* (Cambridge: Cambridge University Press, 1984), however, Mark Lindley notes that Lefèvre incorporated some of Euclid's methods when working out his proportional formulas (23-24).

[24]Clement Miller summarizes this passage in his introduction to Glarean's *Dodecachordon*, 2 vols. (n.p.: AIM, 1965) 1:3.

[25]The facts in this paragraph are drawn from Henri Chamard's *Histoire de la Pléiade*, 4 vols. (Paris: Henri Didier, 1939-40), 1:57-61. See also Lucien Pinvert, *Lazare de Baïf* (Paris: Ancienne librairie Thorin et Fils, 1900), 64, 83.

became the most famous exponent of that coterie first called the Brigade, later the Pléiade: Pierre de Ronsard.

Whether Ronsard and Lazare de Baïf spoke to the leading German humanists about setting quantitative verse is unknown; but Binet, in his *Discours de la vie de Pierre de Ronsard* (1586), makes it clear that Baïf enjoyed intellectual intercourse with the "most learned men of Germany" during his stay.[26] Although no firm connection has been established between the compositions of Tritonius and his followers and the experiments of Jean-Antoine de Baïf's circle, the 1540 embassy of Lazare de Baïf seems a possible point of contact.[27]

The members of the Pléiade who contributed most to the advancement of musical humanism were Jean-Antoine de Baïf and Pontus de Tyard. Nevertheless, both Joachim Du Bellay and Ronsard took part to a degree in the polemics that would lead to further experimentation with classical meters in the vernacular and with *musique mesurée*.[28]

Du Bellay's *Deffence et illustration de la langue francoyse* (1549), though only marginally concerned with musico-poetic relations, acts as a stepping stone toward later theorizing and experimentation.[29] Du Bellay makes several points worthy of our attention. For Du Bellay (as for many of his contemporaries), *"l'immitation des Grecz & Romains"* is the key to elevating the vernacular.[30] He considers the work of the Middle Ages, with few exceptions, unworthy of imitation (33) but does not condemn rhyme, which he compares to musical consonance; nevertheless, he warns against insipid rhyming, recommending instead blank verse such as that written by Luigi Alamanni (47).[31] Du Bellay himself, however, seems to have felt no urge to write in

---

[26]Claude Binet, *La vie de P. de Ronsard (1586)*, ed. Paul Laumonier (Paris: Librairie Hachette, 1909), 6-7.

[27]Kenneth J. Levy comments on the possibility that the German settings of quantitative verse influenced the French; see his "Vaudeville, vers mesurés et airs de cour," in Jean Jacquot, ed., *Musique et poésie au XVIe siècle* (Paris: CNRS, 1954), 199.

[28]The second and third volumes of D. P. Walker's "Vers et Musique Mesurés à l'Antique," diss., Oxford, 1940, 4 vols., offer the most thorough examination of the relations between French polemical tracts and *musique mesurée*. For convenience' sake I have limited my discussion to works written by members of the Pléiade and of Baïf's Academy; but, as Walker makes clear, the quantitative-verse movement touched a large number of other French writers, several of whom wrote *vers mesurés rimés*, a popular (though less classical) variety of vernacular quantitative verse.

[29]I shall treat the ideas expressed in the *Deffence* as Du Bellay's own, though some were drawn from Sperone Speroni's *Dialogo delle lingue* (1542), which I discuss in the next chapter. Pierre Villey, in *Les sources italiennes de la "Deffense et illustration de la langue françoise" de Joachim du Bellay* (Paris: Librairie Honoré Champion, 1908), lists Du Bellay's borrowings.

[30]Du Bellay, *Oeuvres françoises de Joachim Du Bellay*, ed. Ch. Marty-Laveaux, 2 vols. (Paris, 1866-67), 1:33. All further references to the *Deffence* are to volume 1 of this edition and will be incorporated into the text.

[31]Living in exile in France, Alamanni "was interested in those problems of the transfer of the classical genres to the modern tongues and of the reproduction of classical prosody in modern

classical meters; he says outright that the French have not *"cet usaige de Piez comme eux* [the Greeks and Romans]" but have rather a system based on *"un certain nombre de Syllabes"* coupled with rhyme (46). Ficino's influence perhaps shows up in Du Bellay's passing reference to that *"fureur divine"* that sometimes moves and fires poetic spirits, and without which there is no hope of creating a work of lasting value (53-54).[32]

Urging would-be poets to imitate classical models, to use blank verse rather than hackneyed rhymes (though well-chosen rhymes are still laudable), and to esteem poetic frenzy, Du Bellay is the first member of the Pléiade to raise – in print, at least – a number of arguments to be defended and augmented or gainsaid and slighted by later polemicists. Though at one point Du Bellay mentions the ability of the ancient Gallic bards to calm the rage of opposing armies (48), his treatise generally avoids philosophical notions of the wondrous effects of poetry and music. Du Bellay's advice is largely for the practical, rather than for the philosophical, poet.

In marked contrast to the *Deffence* stand Pontus de Tyard's two *Solitaires,* both dealing extensively with music and philosophy. Although Tyard spent much of his earlier career in Lyons, members of Ronsard's circle in Paris knew him through his writings (if not through personal acquaintance) and regarded him as a member of the Pléiade.[33] His *Solitaire premier* (1552; reprinted and revised 1587) – a work heavily indebted to Ficino, Giraldi, and Leo Hebraeus[34] – popularizes neo-Platonic thought for those unable to read such recondite matter in Latin or Greek.[35]

Lute-songs begin and end the work. The Solitaire, at the beginning of the book, chances upon Pasithée, who sings – or rather "measures"[36] – an ode (Italian in the first edition, French in later ones). The ode seems to ravish him *"comme d'une celeste harmonie"* (5). Yates sees this opening scene as emblematic of the blending of music and poetry, with music already having the special meaning it was to have in Baïf's academy – an encyclopedic term

---

vernacular poetry . . . ," as Frances Yates observes in *The French Academies of the Sixteenth Century* (London: Warburg Institute, 1947), 7.

[32]Thomas Sebillet also linked divine inspiration (*"Enthousiasme"*) and poetry in his *Art poetique Françoys* (1555; Geneva: Slatkine Reprints, 1972), fols. 3-4v. The preface *"Au lecteur"* is dated 1548.

[33]Kathleen Hall, in *Pontus de Tyard and his "Discours Philosophiques"* (London: Oxford University Press, 1963), explores the possibility that Tyard might not have come to Paris until 1570; indeed, he might not have met the other members of the Pléiade till then (17-27).

[34]Hall, 69. See also Yates: "The Platonic theory of the four kinds of enthusiasm is mediated to Tyard *via* Marsilio Ficino's commentaries on Plato which he often reproduces word for word" (81).

[35]*Oeuvres: Solitaire premier,* ed. Silvio F. Baridon (Geneva: Droz, 1950), xix-xx. Citations throughout are to this text.

[36]On the meaning of "measures" here, see Yates, 51.

embracing "all the arts and sciences."[37] We do not know whether the song Pasithée "measures" is supposed to be something on the order of the *musique mesurée* produced about two decades later in Baïf's *Académie,* but comments that Tyard makes in his *Solitaire second* suggest that he had at least thought of such matters. Poetry and music merge with marvelous effect in Pasithée's song, which serves as a preamble to a discourse on divine frenzy (17).[38]

The human soul, which originated in heaven, where there is celestial harmony at all times, must endure discord in its earthly existence; through poetic frenzy, however, the music of the soul is reawakened, and the soul is recalled to the sovereign One (19-20). This marks the first step in the soul's heavenward climb. Music and poetry thus have an edifying effect on the listener. Song, moreover, is the *"propre exercice"* of the muses and the particular *"industrie"* attributed to Apollo (45); indeed, the muses spend their time dancing and singing hymns of praise to the gods (48-49). Again like Du Bellay, Tyard defends the French language against those detractors who believe it incapable of expressing the lofty thoughts found in Greek and Latin poetry; to bolster his case, he mentions the new sonnets, epigrams, and odes of (presumably) the Pléiade (66-67). At the end of the dialogue, Pasithée – pointing out that poetic verses, not sung, lose much of their grace (74) – coaxes the Solitaire into singing a Pindaric ode to the lute. Singer and auditor find themselves moved to a melancholy state of mind after hearing the ode – another reference to the powerful effects of poetry and music.

This early philosophical work, then, seems a pivotal point in French musico-poetic theory. Not only Ficino's ideas on divine frenzy but also his seriousness toward musico-poetic relations are evident in the *Solitaire premier.* Music and poetry can elevate (or debase) one's soul; Baïf will later argue that, having this power, music and poetry need to be correctly harnessed. The next stage in the progress of French musical humanism concerns the nature of contemporary music and poetry; Tyard broaches this subject in his second Solitaire.

Tyard's *Solitaire second* (1555) borrows freely from Boethius' *De institutione musicae,* Gaffurius' *De harmonia* (1518) and *Theorica* (1492), and Glarean's

---

[37]Yates, 25, 79. Chapter 4 of Yates's book is devoted to this concept. Klaus W. Niemöller also discusses the topic in "Zum Einfluss des Humanismus auf Position und Konzeption von Musik im deutschen Bildungssystem der ersten Hälfte des 16. Jahrhunderts," in Walter Rüegg and Annegrit Schmitt, eds., *Musik in Humanismus und Renaissance* (Weinheim: Acta Humaniora, 1983), 77-97 (see esp. 89-90).

[38]Tyard's discussion is deeply indebted to Plato's *Phaedrus* 243E-245C and the seventh *oratio* (chap. 14) of Ficino's *De amore;* see Raymond Marcel's edition and translation of Ficino's work, *Commentaire sur le Banquet de Platon* (Paris: Société d'Édition "Les Belles Lettres," 1956), 258.

Dodecachordon (1547);[39] it concerns itself primarily with speculative music. Though painfully overtechnical to the modern reader uninterested in proportional formulas, Tyard's book contains a number of observations and comments showing the general direction in which French musical-humanist thought was moving. As in the *Solitaire premier,* music, *"vrey image de Temperance,"* is a term embracing all branches of knowledge (8).[40] It has the power to temper the soul, making it move toward laudable ends, as the ancient philosophers knew:

> La Musique servoit d'excercice pour reduire l'ame en une parfette temperie de bonnes, louables, & vertueuses meurs, emouvant & apaisant par une naïve puissance & secrette energie, les passions & affeccions, ainsi que par l'oreille les sons estoient transportez aus parties spirituelles. (11)

> Music served as an exercise to bring the soul to a perfect balance of good, praiseworthy, and virtuous qualities, moving and assuaging the passions and emotions by an innate strength and secret energy, as the sounds were transported through the ears to the spiritual parts.

Tyard declares that the *"propre suget"* of music is a song in which words are pronounced well (*"bien dites"*), measured in some graceful cadence of rhyme, or balanced in an unequal equality (*"une inegale egalité"*) of long or short syllables (12-13). So music is best employed in the service of song. He is aware of the difference between modern rhyming verse and ancient quantitative verse, and he knows that ancient songs were monophonic (13). Both ideas are developed later in the treatise.

Showing some knowledge of antique musical symbols, he presents the reader with a French rhymed ode, first in an ancient notation, then in his own modern transcription (Ex. 1.5).[41] Tyard observes that the Greek system needed no rhythmic signs, for each note would have been long or short, depending on the length of the particular syllable – the shorts lasting half the length of the longs.[42]

---

[39]Tyard's sources are listed and discussed in Hall, 82-88.

[40]Page numbers and citations are to the 1555 Lyons edition, *Solitaire second, ou prose de la musique.*

[41]Some of Tyard's symbols correspond to those in Boethius (bk. 4); others resemble those given in Gustave Reese, *Music in the Middle Ages* (New York: Norton, 1940), 27. Walker, however, points out that "only one of the texts [of ancient Greek music that] we now have had been discovered [in the sixteenth century] and this had not been transcribed"; it was published, moreover, only in 1581 ("Musical Humanism in the 16th and Early 17th Centuries," *The Music Review* 2 [1941]: 2).

[42]Walker, in "Musical Humanism," *Music Review* 2 (1941): 300-2, observes that Mersenne, Bergier, and Salinas had discovered ancient sources refuting the theory that only two note-values had been used in the songs of antiquity.

⌐E	W	λ	⊖	W	⌐E	⌐E
	Z	7	N	Z		
Plus,	*d'u-*	*ne*	*paix*	*re-*	*bel-*	*le,*

⌐E	W	λ	⊖	W	⌐E	⌐E
	Z	7	N	Z		
Vo-	*tre*	*dou-*	*ceur*	*cru-*	*el-*	*le*

λ	λ	λ	⊖	W	⊖	⊖
7	7	7	N	Z	N	N
Au	*tra-*	*vail*	*me*	*dis-*	*po-*	*se,*

λ	⊖	W	⌐E	W
7	N	Z		Z
Plus	*je*	*re-*	*po-*	*se.*

Plus   d'une   paix   re- bel- le   Au   tra- vail me
Vo-   tre dou- ceur cru- el-   le

dis- po- se   Plus   je   re- po- se.

Ex. 1.5, Tyard, "Plus d'une paix"

The French language, of course, "*moins parfette que la Grecque ou la Latine,*" requires signs to mark both pitch and duration. Like Du Bellay, Tyard hopes that someone will lay down rules distinguishing longs from shorts in French (27); he would clearly like to have a system of versification in French comparable to that in ancient quantitative verse. Much later in the work, the Solitaire explains how the ancient lyric poets, "marrying music and poetry," managed to achieve their desired effects, whereas he has trouble getting a "*seul chant propre*" from modern musicians: no wonder modern music works no marvels (132-33). The difficulty lies not in the impossibility of making effective polyphonic settings of verse or in the age itself, but in the language – not yet measured in longs and shorts – and in the scant care given by musicians, most of them lacking knowledge of letters and poetry, as indeed most poets lack knowledge of music (133).

Yet on the question whether a text should receive a polyphonic or a monophonic setting, the Solitaire sides with the humanists, who want their

words intelligible, not lost in a confusion of polyphony, which is bound to
frustrate the effects the poets want to bring about, since "elaborate music
most often sounds like nothing more than a great noise" ("*la Musique figuree
le plus souvent ne raporte aus oreilles autre chose qu'un grand bruit*") (132). Earlier
in the treatise (112-15), Tyard gives the standard catalogue of the legendary
effects of music and, more important, includes an example drawn from
contemporary life. He tells us of a performance of the "divine" Franceso da
Milano (114-15),[43] whose expressive lute-playing captivated his audience –
indeed, seemed to to put them in a state of "*divine fureur.*"[44]

Tyard, then, deals with several issues soon to become the subject of serious
investigation in France: whether one should write in traditional syllabic verse
or in quantitative verse, whether one should set texts polyphonically or
monophonically, and whether modern music and poetry can elicit the same
responses as did ancient song. To all these questions, Tyard gives the proper
humanist answer: modern song, if composed as was ancient song, can indeed
have the same effect on the listener. But Tyard is still only a theorist: his
French poetry rhymes, and his attempts to have his poems set effectively
have come to naught – so his story goes – because of insensitive and ignorant
musicians.[45]

The poetic careers of Pierre de Ronsard and Jean-Antoine de Baïf are
closely related. After the death of Ronsard's father, Lazare de Baïf offered
to pay for Ronsard's education. As a result, the twenty-year-old Ronsard
found himself a fellow student of the twelve-year-old Jean-Antoine de Baïf.
Both studied under the arch-humanist Jean Dorat, himself later counted as
a member of his pupils' coterie, the Pléiade.[46] The two students had been
surrounded by the classics since childhood: Ronsard's home bore inscriptions
in Latin; Baïf's, inscriptions in Greek.[47] Though Ronsard was Baïf's senior
by eight years, the two got along well, studying Greek models – as Horace
had advised (*Ars poetica* 268-69) – day and night.[48]

Ronsard's father, himself a classicist, thought of poetry as something
musical and developed theories about the alternation of masculine and feminine endings.[49] Ronsard also seems to have regarded lyric poetry as words
to be sung. Though partially deaf from 1540 onward, Ronsard apparently

---

[43]This passage, translated into English by Joel Newman, is given in Piero Weiss and
Richard Taruskin, eds., *Music in the Western World* (New York: Schirmer, 1984), 159-60.

[44]See Walker, "Musical Humanism," *Music Review* 2 (1941): 112-13. In this article, Walker
describes other passages that deal with similar contemporary musical wonders.

[45]Yates, 85-88, discusses several aspects of the *Solitaire second* marginally related to my
thesis.

[46]Chamard, 1:84.

[47]Ibid., 1:67; Yates, 16.

[48]On the intense study habits of Ronsard and Baïf, see Binet, 11; Yates, 14-15; Chamard,
1:100.

[49]Chamard, 1:67.

enjoyed music.[50] He could perhaps play the guitar[51] and more than once argued that lyric poetry was gravely deficient without music. Discussing Sapphics, for example, he asserts that they will not please "if they are not sung by voices, or at least [sung] to the accompaniment of instruments" ("*s'ils ne sont chantez de voix vive, ou pour le moins accordez aux instruments*").[52] On standard French lyric poetry in general, Ronsard's views are more or less the same:

> La Poësie sans les instrumens, ou sans la grace d'une seule ou plusieurs voix, n'est nullement agreable, non plus que les instrumens sans estre animez de la melodie d'une plaisante voix.

> Poetry without instruments, or without the grace of one or several voices, is not at all pleasing – no more than instruments are when not animated by the melody of a pleasant voice.

Thus writes Ronsard in 1565, in his *Abbregé de l'art poëtique françois* (47), which gives practical advice on writing poetry in the vernacular – imitation of the ancients being *de rigueur*. Always aware of the musical side of poetry, Ronsard recommends that aspiring poets recite (or, better yet, sing) their verses aloud (60-61); doing so, they will be able to judge the words as sounds, as music – not just as clusters of letters on paper.

In a discussion of neologisms, Ronsard expresses the opinion that explanatory notes may be useful in clarifying difficult coinages (65). Ronsard's friend, Marc-Antoine de Muret (1526-85), in fact annotated many poems in Ronsard's *Amours*. A leading humanist scholar in Ronsard's time and also a competent composer, Muret set two of Ronsard's poems to music. His setting of "Las, je me plain" appeared, along with other composers' settings of Ronsard's poems, in the musical supplement to the 1552 edition of the *Amours*.[53] The piece begins homorhythmically (Ex. 1.6), but the voices soon

---

[50]Works dealing with Ronsard and music include the outdated but still useful book by Julien Tiersot, *Ronsard et la musique de son temps* (Paris: Librairie Fischbacher, [c. 1902]) and Raymond Lebègue's "Ronsard et la musique," in Jacquot, ed., *Musique et poésie*, 105-19.

[51]Lebègue, 105. Ronsard's poem "A sa guittare" may well not be addressed to a literal guitar. Brian Jeffery, in "The Idea of Music in Ronsard's Poetry," from Terence Cave, ed., *Ronsard the Poet* (London: Methuen, 1973), 209-39, argues that Ronsard was little interested in practical music and that his poetry uses music as a metaphor for writing poetry. See also Frank Dobbins' article on Ronsard in the *New Grove*.

[52]"Les Oeuvres de P. de Ronsard Gentil-homme Vandomois" (1587), in Paul Laumonier, ed., *Pierre Ronsard, Oeuvres complètes*, 8 vols. (Paris: Librairie Alphonse Lemerre, 1914-19), 7:75. All subsequent references to Ronsard's prose works are to volume 7 of this edition and will be incorporated into the text. Agrippa d'Aubigné also felt that vernacular quantitative verse had to be sung to be pleasing: "*tels vers [vers mesurés] de peu de grace à les lire & prononcer, en ont beaucoup à estre chantés. . .*" (d'Aubigné, *Oeuvres complètes*, ed. Réaume and de Caussade, 6 vols. [Paris, 1873-92], 3:273); see Walker, "Vers et Musique Mesurés," 2:92.

[53]Tiersot, 12. My reduction is based on the transcription in Tiersot, 52-54, and the facsimile in Ronsard, *Oeuvres complètes* 4:224-29.

become more independent, breaking into short melismas here and there (Ex. 1.7).

Ex. 1.6, Muret, "Las, je me plain"

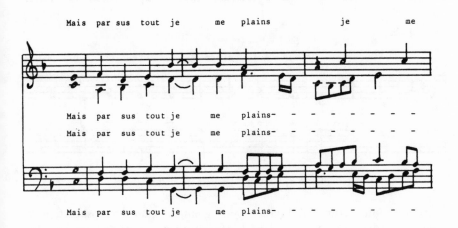

Ex. 1.7, "Mais par sus"

At measure 21, where each voice sings a different word, the text becomes unintelligible. From Muret, we might have expected a more "humanist" setting, one that would not obscure the text with polyphony: something like Pierre Certon's almost completely homorhythmic setting of "J'espere & crains," included in the same supplement to the *Amours* (Ex. 1.8).[54]

Ex. 1.8, Certon, "J'espere & crains"

Certon's homorhythmic and syllabic setting employs, for the most part, only two note-values, one half the length of the other – traits that suggest the possible influence of German quantitative-verse settings.[55] Certon's style, in any case, influenced the later French chanson, marked by homophony and syllabic treatment of the text.[56] In one respect, incidentally, Certon's piece is distinctly contrary to the goals of most musical humanists, for the supplement tells us that the setting will serve for fourteen other sonnets by Ronsard.[57] This argues a rather cavalier attitude toward the relations between music and text.

---

[54]Tiersot, 34-37, and Ronsard, *Oeuvres complètes* 4:190-95.

[55]The influence of humanist settings on the later chanson is hard to gauge; see Levy's "Vaudeville, vers mesurés et airs de cour," 185-201.

[56]See Aimé Agnel, "Pierre Certon," *New Grove*.

[57]Ronsard, *Oeuvres complètes* 4:194-95. Other settings in the supplement are also marked as suitable for more than one text; Janequin's "Qui voudra voyr comme un Dieu" can supposedly accommodate ninety-two sonnets (4:248-49).

Ronsard seems to have wanted his lyrics set to music, and composers of the day were wholly willing to comply: over two hundred settings of his poems had appeared in print by 1600. Naturally, Ronsard had little influence on most composers who used his texts, but I suspect that the potentially distracting polyphony of Muret's settings did not bother Ronsard, who expressed his admiration for contrapuntists like Josquin, Mouton, Richafort, Janequin, and Orlando di Lasso.[58] Though Ronsard advocated emulating the classics, he wrote rhymed verse and savored contrapuntal music. Jean-Antoine de Baïf, however, joined theory and practice in his quest to revive antiquity.

Baïf was not only a member of the Pléiade but also the founder of the *Académie de Poésie et de Musique*, given the support of Charles IX in 1570.[59] Although humanists in France and Italy had attempted to write quantitative verse in the vernacular already in the fifteenth century,[60] Baïf viewed himself as the one who "left the beaten track and first discovered a new path [and] showed ancient song to France" (*"laissa / Les chemins frayés, et premier decouvrit / Un nouveau sentier, à la France montra / L'antique chanson"*).[61] One can form a good idea of Baïf's method for recreating ancient song by examining the letters patent and the statutes of Baïf's academy.[62]

In the letters patent of 1570, one learns that Baïf and Joachim Thibaut de Courville had been experimenting for three years – with *"grande estude & labeur assiduel"* – in an attempt to raise the level of French music and poetry to that of the ancient Greeks and Romans. But their travail was not merely in the interest of aesthetics; it had social importance also, for where music is disordered, customs are depraved; where music is well ordered, the populace is well mannered (*"bien moriginez"*).[63] Baïf makes clear his desire to render his audience capable of the highest knowledge (*"plus haute connoissance"*), after being purged of any vestiges of barbarism (320).

Of the early experiments with Courville, little survives; this is very likely a result of the academy's statute forbidding the circulation of poems and songs (321).[64] A handful of Courville's songs, however, saw print thanks to his students. The songs are homophonic but not fully homorhythmic, for occasionally a voice will sing a short ornamental passage against the sustained

[58]See the "Preface de P. de Ronsard . . . 26 chansons" (1560), *Oeuvres complètes* 7:20.

[59]D. P. Walker, "The Aims of Baïf's *Académie de Poésie et de Musique*," *Journal of Renaissance and Baroque Music* 1 (1946): 92.

[60]See Derek Attridge, *Well-Weighed Syllables* (Cambridge: Cambridge University Press, 1974), 125; and Yates, 52.

[61]Cited in Yates, 55. Baïf's lines resemble the opening of a poem in Italian quantitative verse by Claudio Tolomei, from his *Versi, et regole de la nuova Poesia Toscana* (Rome, 1539): "Questa novella via, che fuor de l'altro camino / Per si dritta riga girsene Alesso vedi, / Ella per anticquo sentier per ruvido calle / Al puro fonte sacro; al sacro monte mena" (sig. T).

[62]The letters patent are given in full in Appendix I of Yates's *Academies*, 319-22.

[63]Ibid., 319.

[64]See Frank Dobbins, "Joachim Thibault de Courville," *New Grove*.

notes in the other voices, as one can see in Courville's setting of Baïf's
"Lorsque mouroy de t'aymer" (Ex. 1.9).[65] The text is clear because all the
voices declaim simultaneously. The short ornamental notes add musical
variety, and long syllables still last twice the length of the shorts. The meter
thus remains inviolate.

Ex. 1.9, Courville, "Lorsque mouroy"

At some point, musicians writing for Baïf's Academy apparently decided
that using only two note-values to mark longs and shorts was musically
wanting. Sometimes, therefore, longs are marked by dotted half-notes, shorts
by quarters. Giving themselves even more freedom, later composers like Le
Jeune and Mauduit treated a long here as a whole-note, there as a half –
making sure, however, that the note immediately following (when a short)
was at most half as long.[66]

Like other classicists who wanted to write quantitative verse in the vernacular, Baïf wrote treatises on orthography and on determining longs and
shorts, both subjects being intimately related to each other. In Latin, diph-
thongs, vowels long "by nature," and any vowels followed by two or more
consonants are, with few exceptions, counted as long syllables. This principle
requires fixed spelling, and the vagaries of Renaissance orthography in the
vernacular often confused matters.[67] Scholars eager to show off their erudition
might add letters – though unpronounced – to a word in order to indicate
its linguistic provenance, and consonant doubling seems often to have been
purely a matter of whim. Baïf's system, however thoroughly worked out,

[65]From François Lesure et al., eds., *Anthologie de la chanson parisienne au XVIe siècle* (Monaco:
l'Oiseau Lyre, 1953), 107; my reduction.

[66]For a further discussion, see Yates, 54.

[67]Attridge discusses problems of orthography in *Well-Weighed Syllables*, 113, n. 1; see also
G. D. Willcock, "Passing Pitefull Hexameters: A Study of Quantity and Accent in English
Renaissance Verse," *Modern Language Review* 29 (1934): 10.

did not catch on; its dependence on non-French letters (like *k*'s) apparently did not appeal to his contemporaries.[68]

Baïf's Academy did not deal exclusively with unrhymed quantitative verse; we have evidence that Ronsard's rhymed poems were also performed. Moreover, according to Mersenne, the "music" of Baïf's Academy was music not only in the modern sense, but also in the encyclopedic sense – a term comprising sciences, languages, music, poetry, geography, and painting.[69] Religion should perhaps be added to this list, for Baïf spent years working on various translations of the psalms (including one complete set in *vers mesurés*), which he hoped would "drive out the metrical psalms which the Huguenots sing every day."[70] We have already seen how Orpheus could be linked with Moses, David, and Christ. The desire to link the pagan world with the Christian was strong throughout the Renaissance, and one more connection was through a supposed similarity between the verse structure of the psalms and that of Greek lyrics.[71] Courville, Le Jeune, and Mauduit – all members of the academy – provided Baïf with music for his new renderings of the psalms.

Strangely, it seems that the French had little desire to experiment with monody, though we know from Pontus de Tyard that French humanists were aware of the monophonic quality of ancient music. On this point, perhaps the anonymous author of the "Preface sur la musique mesurée" (at the beginning of Le Jeune's *Le printemps*) expresses an opinion widely held among the French. According to him, the ancients had perfected rhythm in their music – so much so that it produced miraculous effects – but they possessed only a rudimentary knowledge of harmony and used only the octave, fifth, and fourth. In later times, men lost control over rhythm but developed skill in harmony. Now Claude Le Jeune has combined the best of both approaches, rendering the music "not only equal to that of the ancients, but far more excellent" (*"non seulement egale à celle des antiens, mais beaucoup plus excellente"*).[72]

---

[68]Mathieu Augé-Chiquet, in his *La vie, les idées et l'oeuvre de Jean Antoine de Baïf* (1909; Geneva: Slatkine Reprints, 1969), reconstructs Baïf's system for determining longs and shorts (347-52).

[69]Yates, 24. See, however, D. P. Walker's review of Yates's *Academies* in *Musica Disciplina* 2 (1948): "The encyclopedic character of Baïf's academy should . . . be asserted more tentatively. The evidence rests solely on one passage in Mersenne, who, though he was closely connected, through Mauduit, with Baïf's movement, was writing fifty years later" (261).

[70]Yates, 65, 70-71.

[71]Ibid., 65, n. 1. See also Israel Baroway, "The Hebrew Hexameter: A Study in Renaissance Sources and Interpretation," *English Literary History* 2 (1935): 66-91.

[72]Le Jeune, *Le printemps*, ed. Henry Expert, Les Maîtres Musiciens de la Renaissance Française 12-14 (Paris: Alphonse Leduc, 1900-1), 3 (facsimile preceding the text proper in each volume).

So in France, the development of musico-poetic theory – at least among the members of the Pléiade and of Baïf's *Académie* – derived from a desire to imitate the lyrics of antiquity and to reject medieval "barbarisms," which drained modern song of its potency. Petrarchan sonnets and Pindaric odes appeared, and musicians readily set them. As classicists tried harder and harder to reproduce the splendor of antiquity, they advocated radical innovations: the adoption of quantitative verse in the vernacular and the rejection of text-obscuring polyphony. These experiments were neither disastrous nor greatly successful; they did, however, affect musico-poetic relations in the last decades of the sixteenth century and may well have inspired Campion to write his own piece of *musique mesurée*.[73]

[73]Walker, in "Vers et Musique Mesurés," vols. 2 and 3, studies the movement into the 1630s.

Chapter 2
Italy

Quantitative Verse and "Measured" Music

Italian humanists keenly felt the influence of their forebears, the ancient Romans, whose ruins provided a constant reminder of the civilization that had thrived magnificently until the Goths, Vandals, and other barbarians invaded the empire and (in the humanists' view) polluted its art, poetry, music, and mores. Vasari lamented the deterioration of the Roman Empire when he examined the sculpture and architecture produced under Constantine – works that he felt already betrayed crude sensibilities.[1] For neoclassicists, Gothic art – the very word *Gothic* being strongly derogatory – provided further evidence of the northern invaders' malignant influence.

In the sixteenth century, some saw the Italian language itself as a corruption of Latin, unfit for serious literature. By writing his three-volume *Prose* (1525) in defense of the Italian language, Pietro Bembo became its recognized champion.[2] In the *Dialogo delle lingue* (1542) – from which Du Bellay translated passages word for word in the *Deffence,* and which Claude Gruget translated into French in 1551[3] – Sperone Speroni presents the Latinists' arguments and Bembo's counter-arguments. Although Speroni's work appeared near the middle of the century, the ideas expressed in it had been current throughout the early decades of the 1500s. The main argument takes place between Bembo, who defends his mother tongue, and Lazaro, a classical philologist with decided reservations about the capacity of the Italian lan-

---

[1]Giorgio Vasari, *The Lives of the Painters, Sculptors and Architects,* trans. A. B. Hinds, rev. and ed. William Gaunt, 4 vols. (1927; London: Dent, 1963), 1:7. The most thorough study of Italian polemical works devoted to literary theory is Bernard Weinberg's comprehensive *History of Literary Criticism in the Italian Renaissance,* 2 vols. (Chicago: University of Chicago Press, 1961); Weinberg does not, however, deal with the quantitative-verse movement except in passing. Claude Palisca's *Humanism in Italian Renaissance Musical Thought* (New Haven: Yale University Press, 1985) presents the fullest account of musical humanism in Italy.

[2]Bembo began work on his *Prose* in 1502, according to Villey, *Les sources italiennes* (cited chap. 1, n. 29), intro. xxii. The intense disdain that some Italians felt for the vernacular can be traced to the late 1300s, as Hans Baron shows in *The Crisis of the Early Italian Renaissance,* rev. ed. (Princeton: Princeton University Press, 1966), 273-90.

[3]Villey, 19.

guage to attain great literary heights. Lazaro severely criticizes the vernacular:[4]

A me pare . . . che tale sia la volgar thoscana per rispetto alla lingua latina, quale la feccia al vino; perochè la volgare non è altro che la latina guasta et corrotta hoggimai dalla lunghezza del tempo, o dalla forza de barbari; o dalla nostra viltà. (113)

It seems to me . . . that the Tuscan vernacular is to Latin what the dregs are to wine; for the vernacular is nothing but Latin spoiled and corrupted today by the passage of time or by the power of barbarism – or by our own baseness.

He continues to condemn the Italian language as the product of barbaric peoples: it is Latin ruined by those whom the Romans most hated, the *"Francesi"* and *"Provenzali,"* "from whom not only [our] nouns, verbs, and adverbs are derived, but also [our] art of composing oratory and poetry" (*"da quali non pur i nomi, i verbi et gli adverbi di lei, ma l'arte anchora dell'orare et del poetare si derivò"*). Huns, Goths, Vandals, Lombards – barbarians deprived of humanity – invaded the empire and spoiled its culture; how can we expect a language debased by such barbarians to produce a Virgil or a Cicero? Indeed, Italian to Lazaro is "an indistinct confusion of all the barbarisms of the world" (*"una indistinta confusione di tutte le barbarie del mondo"*) (117-18).

Bembo, of course, finds much to admire in Italian, especially in the works of Petrarch and Boccaccio. To Bembo, Italian is not at all so barbarous, so deprived of number and harmony as Lazaro has insisted (119). And the examples of Petrarch and Boccaccio should be an adequate warning against writing today in Latin: "Behold the Latin work of Petrarch and Boccaccio and compare it with their vernacular writings; of the former you will judge nothing worse, of the latter nothing better" (*"vedete le cose latine del Petrarca et del Boccaccio, et agguagliatele alle loro volgari; di quelle niuna peggiore, di queste niuna migliore giudicarete"*) (121). In defense of Italian poetry, Bembo maintains that vernacular verses have their feet, their harmony, and their numbers; and in prose, one uses the same rhetorical devices in both languages: if the words differ, the art of joining them is the same (121-22).

Unconvinced, Lazaro asserts that Italian is wanting in feet, number, ornament, and consonance (122); moreover, he argues, rhyme and a fixed number of syllables cannot make up for the lack of true – that is, classical – poetic feet (126-27). Neither side of this argument emerges victorious, though Lazaro's extremism looks suspect beside Bembo's common sense. But the argument presents us neatly and concisely with a key linguistic and aesthetic problem of the day: whether to write serious literature in Latin or in Italian.

---

[4]References are to the 1542 edition as given in Villey, 111-46.

Even late in the sixteenth century, we find debates revolving around the question whether Italian or Latin poetry is preferable. In Stefano Guazzo's dialogue "Del Paragone della Poesia Latina, et della Thoscana" (1586), the interlocutors quarrel over the respective difficulties involved in writing Italian and Latin poetry.[5] Tomaso Paolucci takes the side of the Latinists, maintaining that Italian, as one's mother tongue, naturally presents fewer difficulties than Latin, a "foreign language" that requires long and continued labor on the part of aspiring neo-Latin poets (fol. 66). And of course Latin, with its longs and shorts, has a complex metrical system,

> il qual intoppo non si truova nel verso Thoscano, ove si pongono confusamente tutte le voci senza obligo di ricercare nè di sapere se le sillabe siano lunghe, ò brievi, & per questo è cosa facilissima il comporre il verso. . . . (66v)

> the which difficulty is not found in Tuscan verse, where all the vowels are placed confusedly, without the need of finding or of knowing whether the syllables are long or short, and thus it is a simple matter to compose verse [in the vernacular]. . . .

Stefano Ruffa defends the vernacular by pointing out the restrictions one must deal with when writing Italian poetry. Finding a suitable rhyme, for instance, has sometimes taken him so long that he could have composed fifty Latin verses in the same amount of time (66v). Furthermore, the various forms – ottava rima, the sestina, the sonnet – present the problem not only of finding rhymes but also of saying what one wants to say in a limited space: the Greeks and Romans, in contrast, could make their poems as long as they pleased (68r-v). Tomaso, invoking the name of Claudio Tolomei, condemns the sonnet's limitations and compares the form to the bed of Procrustes. (Campion uses the same simile in his Observations.) Tomaso further adduces two Latin sonnets – just to show that one can write them in Latin – but Stefano, though mildly impressed, says that a third would be one too many; he is also critical of Italian hexameters, less so of Italian Sapphics (69-69v). But at the end of Guazzo's dialogue – in which, by the way, the interlocutors are more friendly and playful than those in Speroni's dialogue – Tomaso is convinced that "Tuscan verse is of a far stricter religion than Latin" ("ch'el poema Thoscano è d'una religione assai più stretta di quel che sia il latino . . .") (71).

One solution to the problem of writing respectable poetry in the vulgar tongue was simply to "elevate" the Italian language to the level of Latin by composing quantitative verse in the vernacular. Claudio Tolomei presumably had this in mind when he established his Accademia della nuova Poesia around

---

[5] In Guazzo's Dialoghi piacevoli del Sig. Stefano Guazzo (Venice, 1586), fols. 64v-71v.

1538. [6] Though Leonardo Dati and Leon Battista Alberti had composed
Italian quantitative verse in the preceding century, Tolomei had the distinc-
tion of being the first poet to establish and to publish rules determining longs
and shorts in the vernacular.[7] The *regolette* appeared at the end of the *Versi,
et regole de la nuova Poesia Toscana* (Rome, 1539), a large collection of Italian
quantitative verse to which over twenty poets contributed. Cosimo Pallavicino prefaces the anthology in a somewhat apologetic tone, explaining that
the poems were composed in a short space of time – eight to ten months –
but are nevertheless "*nobili versi*"; he grants that pastoral lyrics may
overabound in the collection yet reminds us that Virgil too began with
pastoral (sig. [a3]). These weaknesses notwithstanding, he feels that the
collection deserves the highest praise:

> Et questo essempio basterebbe a mostrar, che questa non è cosa
> biasimevole, ma degna di somma lode, mostrandosi con essa
> l'incredibil forza, la mirabil virtù, & il gran poter de la nostra volgar
> favella, laquale in questo modo si conosce atta, non solo ad esprimer
> tutto quello, che esprimeva la Latina; ma anchora à dirlo con tutto
> quello obligo di piedi, et di numeri, che fece quell altra. . . . ([aiiiv])

> And this anthology ought to suffice to show that this is not a
> blameworthy thing, but one worthy of the highest praise, showing
> the incredible force, the wondrous strength (*virtù*), the great power
> of our vernacular language, which is here shown to be apt not only
> to express all that Latin has expressed, but to do so with the same
> requirement of feet and numbers that the other language uses. . . .

Pallavicino's stress on the *power* of words ("*l'incredibil forza,*" "*mirabil virtù,*"
"*il gran poter*") seems at once to hark back to Ficino's notions about the
strength of certain words (*De vita,* bk. 3, chap. 21) and to look forward to
the claims of later musical humanists, such as Mei and Galilei, whose ideas
we shall examine before long. (Of course, Pallavicino's hyperbolic words
may be intended more to promote sales of his friends' book than to advance
the cause of humanism.) Although Tolomei's experiments did not enjoy great
popularity, his poetry found champions in the middle and late sixteenth
century. Antonio Minturno, for example, praises Tolomei in 1563 for his
admirable examples of vernacular quantitative verse.[8] In 1574, Contile argues
that if some find little pleasure in Tolomei's poetry, their ears are at fault,

[6]See Michele Maylender, *Storia delle accademie d'Italia,* 5 vols. (Bologna: Licinio Cappelli,
1926-30) 4:86; and Luigi Sbaragli, *Claudio Tolomei: Umanista senese del cinquecento* (Siena: Accademia per le arti e per le lettere, 1939), 53ff.

[7]Sbaragli, 53.

[8]Minturno, *L'arte poetica* (1564; Munich: Wilhelm Fink Verlag, 1971), 110.

not the verse.[9] And in 1586, Stefano Guazzo, through his mouthpiece Stefano Ruffa, asserts that Tolomei (along with such luminaries as Petrarch, Sannazaro, Ariosto, and Bembo) deserves two crowns: one for his Italian, the other for his Latin, poetry.[10]

Curiously, the verses of the Tolomei circle were not, to my knowledge, set to "measured" music.[11] In fact, the Italians seem to have contributed little to the great number of Renaissance settings of quantitative verse that used long and short notes to illustrate a poem's verse structure. This is all the more perplexing when we turn to Pescennius Franciscus Niger's *Grammatica* (Venice, 1480), which shows, at an early date in Italy, an interest in relations between music and classical verse. The book contains perhaps the earliest printed secular music in the West – monophonic settings of poems by Virgil, Lucan, Ovid, and Horace.[12] In his chapter "Harmonia," Niger underscores the importance of actually *singing* lyric poetry:

> Decet enim vatem habile poeticae instrumentum habere: quo modulante carmina condat: ad priscorum imitationem poetarum: qui sine melo nullum versum componebant: Carmina enim a canendo ideo dicta sunt: quia nisi decantata fuerint: divinum nomen: in turpissimum foedissimumque convertunt. (fol. 207)

It is truly fitting for the poet to have an apt instrument with which he may melodiously compose his songs in imitation of the ancient poets, who wrote no poem without a melody. Indeed, *carmina* [poems] are said for that reason to come from *canendo* [singing]: unless they were sung, they transformed the divine name [*vates?*] into a name most ugly and most foul.

He then presents some settings of classical Latin verses. We do not know who composed the music, but two aspects of it seem especially relevant. First, although the composer has used mainly breves and whole-notes – with the apparent intention of illustrating the meter of the poems – the long and short notes do not correspond to the long and short syllables. Second, the

[9]L. Contile, *Ragionamento . . . sopra la proprietà delle imprese* (Pavia, 1574), cited in Sbaragli, 64-65.

[10]Guazzo, *Dialoghi piacevoli*, 71v.

[11]Tolomei's "Questi soavi fiori," however, received a nonhumanist setting by Jacques Buus, published first in 1542; see Don Harrán, *The Anthologies of Black-Note Madrigals*, 5 vols. in 6, CMM 73 (Neuhausen-Stuttgart: AIM, 1978-81) 1[2]:138-42.

[12]See Henry Thomas, "Musical Settings of Horace's Lyric Poems," *Proceedings of the Musical Association*, 46th Session (1919-20): 79; and Peter Bergquist, "Franciscus Niger," *New Grove*. Karl-Günther Hartmann discusses Niger's *Grammatica* at great length in *Die humanistische Odenkomposition in Deutschland: Vorgeschichte und Voraussetzungen*, Erlanger Studien 15 (Erlangen: Palm und Enke, 1976).

music for the "heroic and grave harmony," suitable for epic verse (in this case, Virgil's *Aeneid* 1.522-23), uses repeated notes to effect speechlike declamation (Ex. 2.1).[13]

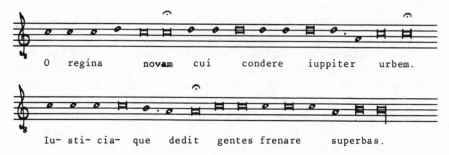

Ex. 2.1, Niger (1480), "O regina"

It seems likely that the composer considered a declamatory style appropriate specifically for epic verse, since his settings of other kinds of verse – "heroic and warlike," "elegiac," "Sapphic," "lyric" – all have livelier melodies. In the Basel edition of the *Grammatica* (1500),[14] moreover, the composer (apparently a different one) has provided new settings, most of them following the meter of the poems, and again the setting for epic verse is more declamatory than the rest. Unlike the 1480 settings, which treat "heroic and grave" and "heroic and warlike" as two different species of "harmony," the epic settings of 1500 place both Virgil's and Lucan's words beneath the same melody. Neither text quite fits the music – Lucan's lines (the opening of the *Bellum civile,* somewhat mangled) are especially ill served – but the composer has manifestly tried to illustrate dactyllic hexameters (Ex. 2.2).[15]

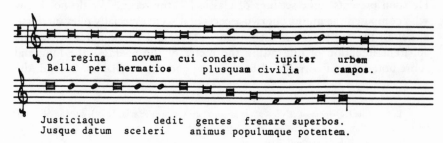

Ex. 2.2, Niger (1500), "O regina"

[13]Fols. 207r-v; no staff lines in the 1480 edition.

[14]Hartmann, whose research is scrupulous, writes that a 1499 edition was published in Basel and that the musical examples differ from the those of the 1500 edition only in foliation (192, n. 48); I have not, however, been able to locate any 1499 edition. Several editions listed as such in *NUC Pre-1956* have proved to be from a different date.

[15]Fol. LXXVIII.

In the music provided for the Sapphic stanza, however, the composer of the
later settings uses accent, rather than quantity, as a prosodic guide. Horace's
words (*Odes* 1.32.13-16) are thus given a kind of pseudo-quantitative setting
(Ex. 2.3).[16]

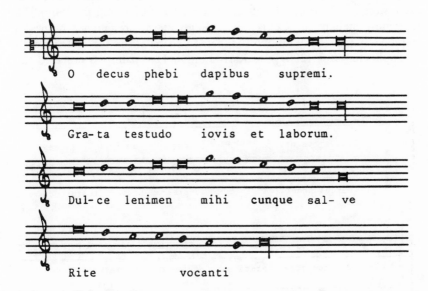

O   decus   phebi   dapibus   supremi.

Gra-ta   testudo   iovis   et   laborum.

Dul-ce   lenimen   mihi   cunque   sal- ve

Rite   vocanti

Ex. 2.3, Niger (1500), "O decus phebi"

Almost all of Horace's Sapphic hendecasyllables fit accentually into this
pattern, and throughout the sixteenth century we find pseudo-quantitative
settings, sometimes even homorhythmic, using this pattern to represent the
Sapphic meter (Ex. 2.4):[17]

Ex. 2.4, Common rhythmic pattern for the Sapphic hendecasyllable

[16]Fols. LXXVIII^V-LXXIX.

[17]In addition to those mentioned later, see the anonymous "Hanc io lucem" (1509-10),
published in Wolfgang Osthoff, *Theatergesang und darstellende Musik in der italienischen Renaissance
(15. und 16. Jahrhundert)*, 2 vols. (Tutzing: Hans Schneider, 1969) 2:64; Marchetto Cara, "Quis
furor tanti" (1517), and Bartolomeo Tromboncino, "Integer vitae" (1517), both published in
Andrea Antico's *Canzoni sonetti strambotti et frottole, libro tertio (1517)*, ed. Alfred Einstein (Northampton, Mass.: Smith College, 1941), 40-42, 37-39.

Perhaps Niger's book encouraged the trend, since the *Grammatica* is the first authoritative printed source stating that this particular rhythm distinguishes the eleven-syllable Sapphic line.[18]

One piece published early in the sixteenth century was certainly related to the setting in both the 1480 and the 1500 editions: a chorus sung at the conclusion of the third act of Conrad Celtis' *Ludus Dianae* (1501). The uppermost melody for Celtis' text, "Regis eternas resonemus omnes" (a Sapphic stanza), closely follows the melodic shape of the 1480 setting of "O decus phoebi," (fol. [208v]), as Karl-Günther Hartmann has observed (Ex. 2.5).[19]

[The dots beneath (a) and (b), though distant from the notes they affect, seem intentional; the dot under (c) should probably precede the c' it follows; all appear to be examples of the *punctus divisionis*.]

Ex. 2.5, Celtis, "Regis eternas", and Niger (1480), "O decus phoebi"

[18]Most editions of the *Grammatica* that I have examined reproduce, with varying degrees of fidelity, the earlier settings, though Hartmann writes that before World War II, the editions of 1499 and 1500 were in numerous libraries (192, n. 48), so they may have circulated widely in their day.

[19]Hartmann, 42. Celtis' piece is given in Liliencron, "Die Chorgesänge des lateinisch-deutschen Schuldramas" (cited chap. 1, n. 7), 359. Peter Bergquist, in "Conradus Protucius Celtis," *New Grove*, suggests that "the unknown composer of these choruses [i.e., those of the *Ludus Dianae*] might even be Celtis himself."

Celtis' setting, however, uses the rhythm given in the 1500 edition of the *Grammatica,* and the melody for the first line of "Regis eternas" almost duplicates the melody that serves, with little variation, for all three hendecasyllables in the 1500 setting of "O decus phebi." It seems likely that the musician who composed the new settings for Niger's book had some connection with the Celtis circle; indeed, a single composer might easily have written both the music for Celtis' play and the new settings in the *Grammatica.*

Another possible link with the *Grammatica* presents itself in Petrucci's first book of frottole (1501). Here, Michele Pesenti sets Horace's "Integer vitae" in the strict homorhythmic style later used by Tritonius; but Pesenti's rhythm, perhaps inspired by Niger's recent setting of a Sapphic stanza, is also based on accent, not quantity (Ex. 2.6).[20]

Ex. 2.6, Pesenti, "Integer vitae"

It is ironic that the homorhythmic style of composition, associated with attempts to teach correct scansion, produced such a pedagogically unsound result. And, consciously or not, other composers followed Pesenti's lead. Arcadelt, for example, wrote three settings for Sapphic stanzas in which he joined the "classical" chordal style with the nonclassical rhythm in Niger's 1500 *Grammatica.*[21] These two elements, incidentally, appear even in some nineteenth-century settings. Giuseppe Baini (1775-1844), who studied Renaissance music and was familiar with Hofhaimer's homorhythmic settings of quantitative verse, composed music for three poems written in

---

[20]A modern edition of this piece using original clefs and barred differently from mine is in Rudolf Schwartz, ed., *Ottaviano Petrucci Frottole, Buch I und IV* (1935; Hildesheim: Georg Olms, 1967), 34. My transcription is based on the facsimile reproduction in Benvenuto Disertori's *La frottola nella storia della musica* (Cremona: Athenaeum Cremonese, 1954), [p. 4]. Pesenti's piece, arranged for voice and lute, was also included in Franciscus Bossinensis' *Tenori e contrabassi . . . Libro primo* (1509; Geneva: Minkoff, 1977), 36r-v. On some of the connections between the frottole and musical humanism, see the third chapter of Francesco Luisi's *La musica vocale nel Rinascimento: Studi sulla musica vocale profana in Italia nei secoli XV e XVI* (Torino: Rai Radiotelevisione Italiana, 1977), 319-438.

[21]See Jacobus Arcadelt, *Opera omnia 9,* ed. Albert Seay, CMM 31 (n.p.: AIM, 1968), 1-3.

Sapphic meter using the chordal style and Niger's later rhythm.[22] And Frie-
derich Flemming's famous setting of "Integer vitae" (1811) also combines
these two traits (Ex. 2.7).[23]

Ex. 2.7, Flemming, "Integer vitae"

By the time Franchinus Gaffurius printed his *Harmonia* (Milan, 1518),
however, one can find Sapphics correctly set in Italy. Gaffurius writes: "Lyric
poets sing such a Sapphic song by giving long syllables a complete measure
of time beating. We notate them as breves and short syllables as semibreves
containing exactly half of the breves."[24] He then presents a setting of a
Sapphic stanza (Ex. 2.8); the long and short syllables in the poem (by
Gaffurius' contemporary, Lancius Curtius) translate into their musical equivalents.

Ex. 2.8, Gaffurius, "Musices septemque"
(original note-values halved; editorial bar-lines removed)

[22]Given in the musical supplement to Adrien de la Fage, *Essais de diphthérographie musicale*,
2 vols. in 1 (1864; Amsterdam: Frits A. M. Knuf, 1964) 2:38-39.

[23]In *Göpel's deutsches Lieder- und Commers-Buch* (Stuttgart, [1847]), 167.

[24]Gaffurius, *De harmonia*, trans. and ed. Clement Miller (n.p.: AIM, 1977), 192. Gaffurius
also discusses ancient prosody in book 2 of his *Practica musicae* (1496), trans. and ed. Clement
Miller (n.p.: AIM, 1968), 69-72; he draws on Diomedes, Augustine, Aristides, Quintilian, and
others in this chapter. His annotated copy of Ficino's works (including the commentary on the
Timaeus) exists; see Otto Kinkeldey, "Franchino Gafori and Marsilio Ficino," *Harvard Library
Bulletin* 1 (1947): 379-82. See also Palisca, "Gaffurio as a Humanist," *Humanism in Italian
Renaissance Musical Thought*, 191-225.

Although the Italian quantitative-verse poems of Tolomei and his compeers were not given neoclassical homorhythmic settings, Andrea Gabrieli
in 1585 used musical-humanist methods to set some choruses in Orsatto
Giustiniani's blank-verse translation of *Oedipus Rex*.[25] The *Accademia Olimpica*
had chosen Giustiniani's rendition of Sophocles' masterpiece as the play to
inaugurate the new *Teatro Olimpico*.[26] The performance and translation were
clearly meant to appeal to the most noble and exacting denizens of Vicenza
and its environs. Gabrieli's choruses show many of the traits associated with
sixteenth-century musical humanism: strict homorhythmic counterpoint,
close attention to speech rhythm, and at times striking harmony to underscore
a strongly emotional text. Although the translation is not written in modernized quantitative verse, the choice of blank verse for a tragedy, from
Trissino's *Sofonisba* (1515) onward, represented a standard humanist compromise between ancient and modern poetic meters. One occasionally finds
rhythms in Gabrieli's settings that suggest ancient meters; dactyllic movement, for example, seems present in parts of the chorus "O del gran Giove"
(Ex. 2.9).[27]

Ex. 2.9, Gabrieli, "O del gran Giove"

But the arrangement of two short notes after a longer one is used only
occasionally and was probably suggested more by the immediate rhythm of
the modern Italian than by any supposed classical meter in the vernacular.[28]

From Polyphony to Monody

Robortello's important Latin translation of (and commentary on) Aristotle's
Poetics appeared in 1548, followed shortly thereafter by a large number of
other Latin and vernacular translations and commentaries that greatly affected

[25]See Leo Schrade's introduction to his edition of *La représentation d' "Edipo tiranno"* au
Teatro Olimpico (Paris: CNRS, 1960) and his "L' 'Edipo tiranno' d'Andrea Gabrieli et la renaissance de la tragédie grecque," in Jacquot, ed., *Musique et poésie* (cited chap. 1, n. 27), 275-83.

[26]Schrade, "L' 'Edipo tiranno,'" 275.

[27]Schrade, *La représentation,* 163-64; my reduction.

[28]Schrade comments that Gabrieli usually composed these settings phrase by phrase, or
theme by theme (*La représentation,* 70).

poetic and musical theory.[29] In the area of musical humanism, Claude Palisca has seen a move away from Plato's *Timaeus* and toward Aristotle's *Poetics*; that is, late Italian musical humanists aimed less at writing "mathematically perfect" music and more at eliciting pity and terror from the audience.[30] Gioseffo Zarlino (1517-90) and his student Vincenzo Galilei (late 1520s-1591) perhaps best represent these differing points of view.

Zarlino's encyclopedic and influential study, *Le istitutioni harmoniche* (1558), presents a thorough examination of speculative and practical musical theory. Well acquainted with the Latin and the translated Greek treatises available to him, Zarlino praises the music of antiquity and of recent times but scorns that of the Middle Ages.[31] In his chapter "Della battuta" (bk. 3, chap. 48), he shows his awareness of humanist settings of quantitative verse by telling the reader to use whole-notes and halves to represent the long and short syllables of feet like the dactyl and the anapest.[32] This chapter, however, seems to have been included perfunctorily, for Zarlino is concerned chiefly with contemporary polyphonic music. Modern music, for him, already produces powerful *effetti*; as we see in our own times,

> la Musica induce in noi varie passioni, nel modo che anticamente faceva: imperoche alle volte si vede, che recitandosi alcuna bella, dotta, & elegante Poesia al suono di alcuno istrumento, gli ascoltanti sono grandemente commossi, & incitati a fare diverse cose, come ridere, piangere, overo altre cose simili. (75)

> music induces in us various passions, in the manner that it did of old: so at times we see that when some beautiful, learned, and elegant poetry is recited to the sound of an instrument, the listeners are greatly moved and incited to do various things – to laugh, to cry, and the like.

But ancient music was more moving than many modern pieces insofar as it was monodic and thus allowed the words to be heard clearly – unlike

---

[29]See Weinberg, *A History of Literary Criticism*, 388-418 and all of chapters 10 and 11; and Gary Tomlinson, "Rinuccini, Peri, Monteverdi, and the Humanist Heritage of Opera," Ph.D. diss., University of California at Berkeley, 1979, 136-37.

[30]Claude V. Palisca, "The Beginnings of Baroque Music; Its Roots in Sixteenth Century Theory and Polemics," Ph.D. diss., Harvard, 1953, 198. Many of the ideas in Palisca's dissertation appear again in his introduction to Girolamo Mei, *Letters on Ancient and Modern Music to Vincenzo Galilei and Giovanni Bardi*, ed. Palisca (n.p.: AIM, 1960).

[31]Strunk *SR*, 228. For Zarlino's knowledge of ancient sources, see Palisca's introduction to Zarlino's *On the Modes*, trans. Vered Cohen (New Haven: Yale University Press, 1983), vii-xiii.

[32]*Le istitutioni harmoniche* (1558; New York: Broude Brothers, 1965), 208. I am indebted to D. P. Walker's "Musical Humanism in the 16th and Early 17th Centuries," *Music Review* 2 (1941): 295-308, for many of my points about Zarlino.

contemporary settings that obscure the text by treating it polyphonically. Such music, sometimes sounding like nothing more than "a din of mingled voices" ("*un strepito de voci mescolate*"), cannot have any effect on us worthy of memory (75). But if we moderns sing our songs to the lyre, the lute, or other such instruments (which provide harmony without obscuring the words), we too shall witness wondrous effects. This is not to say that contrapuntal music cannot move the listener, but such music must be simple, and the words must be declaimed together (75).

Despite his humanist pronouncements, Zarlino himself wrote complex polyphonic pieces based on the precepts set forth in the last two books of the *Istitutioni*; his musical works and his later admissions betray his allegiance to the contrapuntal school. Mathematical formulas fill Zarlino's *Istitutioni* and represent the mathematical perfection of the Timaean universe. When criticized for his inaccuracies concerning ancient music, Zarlino responded in his *Sopplimenti musicali* (1588) that it was never his intention to write about the practice of the ancients, Greek or Roman, but to discuss "that manner of ours of having many parts sing together with diverse modulations and diverse melodies" ("*questa nostra maniera, nel far cantar insieme molte parti, con diverse Modulationi, & diverse Aria* [sic]").[33] The man who attacked Zarlino and thus provoked the *Sopplimenti* was Vincenzo Galilei, one of Zarlino's former pupils. And two men had a considerable influence on Galilei: Giovanni de' Bardi (1534-1612) and Girolamo Mei (1519-94).

Around 1563, the Florentine nobleman Giovanni de' Bardi sent his protégé Galilei to study with Zarlino – to learn counterpoint from a great master and perhaps to discover something about ancient music.[34] By the early 1570s, Bardi's house was frequented by such soon-to-be important musicians as Caccini, Strozzi, and of course Galilei, who was still studying ancient music. In effect, these gatherings constituted an informal academy, which we, following Caccini and Pietro de' Bardi, now call the Florentine Camerata.[35] Other such musical coteries existed in parts of Italy. Although the groups were all under the influence of humanism, they did not necessarily agree with one another on how to revive the music of the ancients, insofar as it was possible to do so at all.[36] But new ideas emerged, especially from Bardi's Camerata – ideas that would radically change the approach to setting serious lyric poetry.

---

[33]*Sopplimenti musicali* (1588; Ridgewood, N.J.: Gregg Press, 1966), 9.

[34]Claude Palisca, "Giovanni de' Bardi," *New Grove*.

[35]See Claude Palisca, "The 'Camerata fiorentina': A Reappraisal," *Studi Musicali* 1 (1972): 203-22.

[36]Nino Pirrotta, "Temperaments and Tendencies in the Florentine Camerata," *Musical Quarterly* 40 (1954): 170.

Nino Pirrotta suggests that music formed only a part of the discussions held under Bardi's roof; and, to be sure, Bardi – who became a member of the Alterati in 1574 and of the Accademia della Crusca in 1585 – had a strong interest in literature. Himself a poet, he took the side of Ariosto (in 1583 and 1585) in the controversy over Ariosto and Tasso.[37]

Bardi wrote a discourse, addressed to Caccini, on "Ancient Music and Good Singing" ("Sopra la musica antica, e'l cantar bene") around 1578.[38] In it, he speaks about the ancient modes (or *tonoi*), about singing, and about the place of counterpoint in contemporary song.[39] For Bardi, music and poetry are interrelated; indeed, he scorns the contrapuntists who garble their texts and "spoil" ("*guastar*") the verse (112-13), for "just as the soul is nobler than the body, so the text is nobler than the counterpoint. . ." ("*così come l'anima del corpo è più nobile, altresì le parole più nobili del contrapunto sono . . .*") (114-15).

Most of the ideas in the *Discorso* find amplification and intensification in Galilei's *Dialogo della musica antica, et della moderna* (1581), chiefly "a violent attack on the very foundations of Zarlino's teachings."[40] After studying with Zarlino, Galilei came into contact with Girolamo Mei, a classical philologist who discovered (with a fellow apprentice) the text of Euripides' *Electra* and worked on editions of – among other texts – Aeschylus' *Agamemnon* and *Choephoroi* as well as the *Argonautica* of Apollonius of Rhodes.[41] In 1540, Mei became a member of the *Accademia de' Umidi,* later to become the *Accademia fiorentina*; and as a member he produced several erudite discourses. Though not a musician, Mei knew almost "every theoretical source known to present day specialists on Greek music"[42] and worked for many years on an important book on the modes, in which he proved that the modes handed down from the Middle Ages (and discussed by such theorists as Glarean and Gaffurius) were not same as those of antiquity. This was a crucial point for those who wanted to revive the ancient effects, since each mode had its own supposed effect on the listener. A sixteenth-century musical humanist could hardly expect the Mixolydian and Lydian modes to make the listener despondent (as those modes were said to do in Plato's *Republic* 398B-399C) if the modes consisted of sequences of notes different from the sequences in Plato's day. Mei, with his deep learning, knew far more about ancient treatises than did

[37]Palisca, "Bardi," *New Grove*; and Weinberg, *History of Literary Criticism,* 985.

[38]Now reprinted in a reliable text, with a facing translation, in Claude Palisca, ed. and trans., *The Florentine Camerata* (New Haven: Yale University Press, 1989), 90-131. Further references, included parenthetically in the text, are to this edition and translation.

[39]The discussion of contemporary music for several parts is found on 110-19.

[40]Strunk *SR,* 303, n. 3.

[41]Palisca, Introduction to Mei's *Letters,* 20. Mei's life is summarized on 18-34.

[42]Ibid., 36.

Zarlino, who relied on Latin translations of a few Greek treatises for his knowledge of ancient Greek musical theory.[43]

In 1562, Mei wrote to Pier Vettori (to whom he had been an apprentice) that he planned to "discover the state of the music of the ancients, about which one reads so many miracles. . . ."[44] He read through the available sources and finally concluded that ancient music, which was monodic, depended largely on high, middle, and low pitches (representing excited, moderate, or humble speech and feelings) to move the audience. Renaissance polyphony – which combined high, middle, and low pitches – would naturally be ineffective since the voices would cancel out one another's effects.[45]

Galilei began corresponding with Mei in 1572.[46] The letters that Mei wrote strongly influenced Galilei, who used several of Mei's ideas in the *Dialogo*. Galilei begins his work with the standard humanist view of cultural history: after the barbarian invasions, learning in Rome suffered for "a long period" (the Middle Ages); music, like other branches of learning, fell into decline, but finally a Renaissance triumvirate – Gaffurius, Glarean, and Zarlino – began "to investigate what music was and to rescue it from the darkness in which it had been buried" (*"ad investigare quello che ella fusse, & à cercare di trarla dalle tenebre ove era stata sepolta"*).[47] Despite their efforts, however, these valient modern masters failed to restore music "to its ancient state" (Strunk *SR*, 303). After a lengthy discussion of modes and intervals,[48] the two interlocutors, Bardi and Strozzi, discuss modern music and its inability to produce the marvelous *effetti* of antiquity. Strozzi wants to know what to say to those who deride ancient music and its fabled effects. This gives Bardi ample opportunity to praise ancient, and to criticize modern, music:

> Vedete quanto costoro siano temerarii, che si ridono degli effetti che faceva una cosa la quale non sanno qual fusse, ne conoscono la natura & proprietà di essa, ne come potesse ciò operare. qual maggiore argumento volete per convincergli, che i miracoli per cosi dirgli, che ella faceva? i quai ci sono raccontati da piu degni & famosi scrittori fuor della professione de Musici, che mai habbia havuto il mondo. . . . (80)

---

[43]Ibid., 40-42.

[44]Ibid., 28.

[45]Ibid., 46-47.

[46]Ibid., 8.

[47]Strunk *SR*, 303; *Dialogo della musica antica, et della moderna* (1581; New York: Broude Brothers, 1967), 1.

[48]Not included in Strunk *SR*.

Observe how bold they are, these men who laugh at the effects of a thing without knowing what it was, or what its nature and properties were, or how its effects could have been produced! What better argument do you wish, in order to convince them, than the miracles, to give them that name, that this music performed, miracles related to us by the worthiest and most famous writers, outside the profession of music, that the world has ever had? (Strunk *SR,* 305)

Bardi argues that "the present manner of singing several airs together has not been in use for more than a hundred and fifty years" (an exaggeration), yet experts claim that music has reached a high point; how much better Greek and Roman music must have been, having had *hundreds* of years to develop (80; Strunk *SR,* 305-06). And in spite of asseverations that modern music is excellent,

> non si ode ò pur vede hoggi un minimo segno di quelli che l'antica faceva, ne anco si legge che ella gli facesse cinquanta ò cento anni sono quando ella non era cosi comune & familiare à gli huomini. di maniera che ne la novità, ne l'eccellenza di essa, ha mai havuto appresso de nostri prattici, forza d'operare alcuno di quelli virtuosi effetti che l'antica operava. . . . (81)

> there is not heard or seen today the slightest sign of its accomplishing what ancient music accomplished, nor do we read that it accomplished it fifty or a hundred years ago when it was not so common and familiar to men. Thus neither its novelty nor its excellence has ever had the power, with our modern musicians, of producing any of the virtuous, infinitely beneficial and comforting effects that ancient music produced. (Strunk *SR,* 306)

Polyphony, Bardi conjectures, arose in ancient Greek instrumental music; but those who invented the rules of counterpoint never intended them to be used in vocal music – music that conveys ideas through words (82-83; Strunk *SR,* 308-12). He brings up the argument that in polyphonic music, the melodies cancel out one another's effectiveness and the differing rhythms work at cross purposes (82; Strunk *SR,* 308). Madrigalisms – various kinds of word-painting typically used by sixteenth-century madrigal composers – are risible. Bardi mocks the excesses of the madrigalists and singers who use obvious devices, like very high notes to connote the heavens: "if Isocrates or Corax or any of the other famous orators had ever, in any oration, uttered two of these words in such a fashion, they would have moved all their hearers to laughter and contempt . . . " (Strunk *SR,* 317) (*"se Isocrate, ò Corace, ò altri piu celebrati oratori, havessero orando profferite una sol volta due di quelle parole*

*si fattamente; haverebbono mosso nell'istesso tempo tutti gli uditori à riso & à sdegno
. . ."* [89]); he advocates instead a theatrical style of declamation.

Galilei himself had performed, in Bardi's Camerata, a declamatory setting of Dante's lament of Count Ugolino, accompanied by viols.[49] More important in the development of monody, however, were the experiments of Caccini and Peri, both of whom set to music a pastoral poem by Ottavio Rinuccini on the theme, appropriately enough, of Orpheus and Eurydice. The two settings found a special place in the history of music, for they became the earliest printed operas.

A member of the *Accademia fiorentina,* Rinuccini (1562-1621) was familiar with the most recent humanist ideas on poetry and drama. He came into contact with some of the most progressive musicians of the day and collaborated with Bardi in 1589 to provide entertainment celebrating the wedding of the Grand Duke Ferdinando I.[50] Already in these early productions, Rinuccini stresses the power of music and poetry.[51] He wrote the libretto of *Dafne,* one of the earliest operas, "solely to make a simple trial of what the music of our age could do," as he tells us in the dedication of *Euridice* (1600).[52] In the same dedication, he expresses his admiration for Peri, whose setting of *Dafne* "gave pleasure beyond belief" (*"incredibilmente piacque"*) to its small audience; this artistic success proved that one could, in modern times, sing a dramatic text from beginning to end, as the ancient Greeks and Romans supposedly did.[53] Modern critics have detected a stronger influence of Renaissance pastoral than of Aristotelian tragedy in the libretti of the early operas, yet Rinuccini and his collaborators clearly wanted to move the members of the audience and make them experience the mysterious catharsis.[54] Jacopo Peri (1561-1633), who knew Bardi and "apparently met with musicians, poets and philosophers at the home of Jacopo Corsi during the 1590s,"[55] set Rinuccini's words in a manner that many others throughout Europe would soon adopt.

In his preface to *Euridice,* Peri admits that he has compromised: like Rinuccini, he believes that ancient tragedies were sung throughout – hence his approach. But he knows that this particular collaboration between poet and composer has not reproduced ancient tragedy; rather, it offers a modern equivalent: "just as I should not venture to affirm that this is the manner of

[49]See Palisca, "The 'Camerata fiorentina,'" 206.

[50]Barbara R. Hanning, "Ottavio Rinuccini," *New Grove.*

[51]Hanning describes these works in *Of Poetry and Music's Power: Humanism and the Creation of Opera* (Ann Arbor: UMI Research Press, 1980), 11-12.

[52]Strunk *SR,* 368.

[53]In Angelo Solerti, ed., *Le origini del melodramma* (Torino: Fratelli Bocca, 1903), 40.

[54]See Hanning, *Of Poetry and Music's Power,* 1-19.

[55]William J. Porter, "Jacopo Peri," *New Grove.*

singing used in the fables of the Greeks and Romans, so I have come to
believe that it is the only one our music can give us to be adapted to our
speech" (Strunk *SR,* 375) (*"si come io non ardirei affermare questo essere il canto
nelle greche e nelle romane favole usato, cosi ho creduto esser quello che solo possa
donarcisi dalla nostra musica, per accomodarsi alla nostra favella"*).[56] In *Euridice,*
Peri generally makes the text govern the music. Recitative constitutes most
of the nonchoral music, and even the choruses are frequently declamatory
(take, for instance, the homorhythmic "Poi che gl'eterni imperi").[57] Peri's
declamatory style is marked by a melody that follows impassioned speech-
rhythm with great care; the style is dramatic rather than lyrical. The melody
often stays within the range of an octave and tends to creep upward or
downward in slow stepwise movement, each step frequently consisting of
repeated notes (though angular melodies may occur if the text demands
them). The repeated notes often fall into the pattern ⌐ 𝄾 ♪♪♪ or some variant
of it. Peri uses unprepared and at times shocking dissonance for emotional
effect, while the accompaniment is simple: chords improvised over a
written-out bass line and played on a lute or a keyboard instrument. One
can see these traits clearly already in the opening measures of Orfeo's famous
aria "Non piango e non sospiro," sung after Orfeo learns of Euridice's death
(Ex. 2.10).[58] Peri's vocal line is notable for its speechlike freedom of movement and its expressive use of dissonance to bring out the pathos in the text.

Ex. 2.10, Peri, "Non piango"

[56]Solerti, ed., *Le origini,* 47.

[57]*Le Musiche sopra l'Euridice* (1600; New York: Broude Brothers, 1973), 39.

[58]*Euridice,* 79. See Hanning's discussion of this piece in *Of Poetry and Music's Power,* 112-17,
and Palisca's in *Baroque Music* (Englewood Cliffs, N.J.: Prentice Hall, 1968), 32-34.

Giulio Caccini (c. 1545-1618), who also set Rinuccini's *Euridice* text, participated in the gatherings at Bardi's house. A more lyrical composer than Peri, Caccini won lasting fame through his *Nuove musiche* (1601; 1602, new style), the first collection of baroque monodic songs. Caccini's introduction to this important book tells us of his indebtedness to Bardi and to the other members of the Camerata, whose discussions taught Caccini – so he says – more about music than did his thirty years of studying counterpoint.[59] He, too, objects to composers who, in focusing on the counterpoint, mutilate the text; surely it would be preferable to conform

> à quella maniera cotanto lodata da Platone, & altri Filosofi, che affermarono la musica altro non essere, che la favella, e'l rithmo, & il suono per ultimo, e non per lo contrario, à volere, che ella possa penetrare nell'altrui intelletto, e fare quei mirabili effetti, che ammirano gli Scrittori, e che non potevano farsi per il contrappunto nelle moderne musiche, e particolarmente cantando un solo sopra qualunque strumento di corde, che non se ne intendeva parola per la moltitudine de i passaggi, tanto nelle sillabe brevi quanto lunghe, & in ogni qualità di musiche. . . .[60]

> to that manner so lauded by Plato and other philosophers (who declared that music is naught but speech, with rhythm and tone coming after; not vice versa) with the aim that it enter into the minds of men and have those wonderful effects admired by great writers. But this has not been possible because of the counterpoint of modern music, and even more impossible in solos sung to one or another stringed instrument, wherein not a single word has been understood for the multitude of *passaggi* [florid passages] on both short and long syllables and in every sort of piece. . . .[61]

Caccini takes credit for having invented the new monody, his solution to the problem of text obfuscation. Since his early songs apparently date from about 1585, his claim seems valid. He calls his settings a "kind of music in which one could almost speak in [harmony]" (Hitchcock, 44) (*"una sorte di musica, per cui altri potesse quasi che in armonia favellare"* [A2v]) above improvised chords played on a lute or a theorbo. But Caccini's harmonious speech will seem far more lyrical than Peri's austere recitative. "Amarilli mia bella,"

---

[59]Giulio Caccini, *Le nuove musiche*, intro. Francesco Vatielli (1601; Rome: Reale accademia d'Italia, 1934), sig. A2v.

[60]Ibid.

[61]*Le nuove musiche*, ed. and trans. H. Wiley Hitchcock (Madison, Wis.: A-R Editions, 1970), 44. This translation will be henceforth referred to as Hitchcock.

which Robert Dowland included already in his *Musicall Banquet* (1610),[62] nicely illustrates Caccini's approach to a text – Guarini's, in this case (Ex. 2.11).[63]

Ex. 2.11, Caccini, "Amarilli"

The melody has more leaps than we find in Peri's "Non sospiro." Caccini uses the rhythm ♩♪♪♪ , but he tends not to use it on one note exclusively and thereby makes the motif lyrical as well as declamatory (Ex. 2.12).

Ex. 2.12, Caccini, "Credilo pur"

Still, in following impassioned speech rhythm, in using unprepared disso-nance for emotional effect, and in making his accompaniments chordal, Caccini resembles Peri.

Thus, among the many theories concerning Italian poetry and music, we note the following significant points: A large number of writers, inspired by ancient treatises on music and poetry, wanted to achieve in modern times what they had read of in classical sources. Poets who believed that modern Italian was simply a corruption of Latin wrote serious works in the older language. Others, fond of their mother tongue but unsatisfied with the poetry

---

[62]Robert Dowland also published Caccini's "Dovrò dunque morire" in the *Musicall Banquet* (no. 18), giving both of Caccini's monodies written-out, intabulated lute-parts. A highly orna-mented setting of "Amarilli" as a viol-song exists in an English MS now in the British Museum (Egerton 2971); Peter Phillips arranged "Amarilli" for the keyboard around 1600.

[63]My examples are based on Hitchcock, [33] (facsimile) and 85-86 (modern transcription).

that had thus far been written in it, tried to alter the poetry by using the supposedly nobler and more dignified meters of the antique world. The vast majority of poets, of course, found the tradition begun by Dante, Petrarch, and Boccaccio – the *tre fontane* of Italian eloquence – great and worthy of imitation. Serious musicians for the first three quarters of the century generally treated texts in a complex, polyphonic way; with the advent of Mei's discoveries and with the musico-poetic experiments produced in the learned coteries, however, monody became an essential part of word-setting.

Chapter 3

England

The English Channel has always been more than a geographical barrier between England and the continent. Ideas from Italy, France, Germany, and the Netherlands gained identifiably English properties when they traversed the channel. With its combined Germanic and Romance roots, the English language itself ensured a change in at least the aural quality of poetic forms borrowed from Italy and France. Though Elizabethan critics like Puttenham and Carew were aware of the Norman and Saxon components of their language and knew that the varied roots could increase its expressive power,[1] one senses that early in the sixteenth century – before Sidney, Spenser, and Shakespeare – a number of English authors struggled to find a direction for their poetry. Some early Tudor poets wrote Chaucerian lyrics; but Chaucer, the greatest English poet of their past, wrote in a language foreign to sixteenth-century Englishmen. True, Gascoigne and Webbe, defending the vernacular in the last quarter of the sixteenth century, respectively described Chaucer as "our Mayster and Father" and as "the God of English Poets"; Puttenham, however, had the last word: "Our maker . . . shall not follow *Piers plowman* nor *Gower* nor *Lydgate* nor yet *Chaucer,* for their language is now out of use with us. . . ."[2] Yet what did the early Tudor "courtly makers" have to offer in place of Chaucerian verse? Skeltonics, with their short lines and rambling rhymes, could hardly fit the bill. Wyatt and Surrey anglicized the Italian sonnet, but their sonnets did not stimulate the kind of creative response that Sidney's did in the 1590s.

Poets, of course, were not the only artists who needed assistance or guidance during the first half of the sixteenth century. One often imagines the musical activities in Henry VIII's England to have been widespread and strong: after all, the king himself was a music lover – a composer, no less. Yet recent studies suggest that serious music-making in early Tudor times

---

[1]George Puttenham, *The Arte of English Poesie,* ed. Edward Arber (1906; Kent, Ohio: Kent State University Press, 1970), 92-93. For the reader's convenience, references to Puttenham will be both to this edition and to the substantial excerpts in G. Gregory Smith, ed., *Elizabethan Critical Essays,* 2 vols. (Oxford: Clarendon Press, 1904), henceforth referred to as Smith. See Smith 2:82-83 (Puttenham) and 2:285-94 (Carew).

[2]Smith 1:56 (Gascoigne), 1:241 (Webbe) 2:150 (Puttenham); *Arte of English Poesie,* 157. See also Thomas Wilson, *Wilson's Arte of Rhetorique 1560,* ed. G. H. Mair (Oxford: Clarendon Press, 1909), 162: "The fine courtier wil talke nothing but *Chaucer.*"

took place chiefly in the homes of a few well-to-do officials and noblemen, and in the church. In general, moreover, musical literacy was rare.[3] We should not assume that the picture Thomas Morley paints in 1597 – of a gentleman ridiculed for his inability to sight-sing – presents a wholly reliable portrait of the early Tudor courtier.[4]

The political and religious difficulties that would trouble England for much of the sixteenth and seventeenth centuries (and later) – difficulties that mounted in 1533 with Henry's excommunication and persisted throughout Elizabeth's reign – certainly affected the music and poetry of the mid-to-late sixteenth century. The dissolution of the monasteries put a number of professional musicians out of work.[5] A growing distrust of elaborate church music – indeed, an open attack on it – placed professional composers in an awkward position, for one of their most important accomplishments was their ability to create magnificent polyphonic motets and masses, often around simple cantus firmi. Reformers preferred their plainsong plain. They wanted the words of devotional songs to be "plainly understanded."[6] Similarly, critics like Stephen Gosson (in the 1570s) seized on and inveighed against the lascivious qualities of plays and romances in particular and of poetry in general – hardly encouraging artistic growth for writers.[7]

The Petrarchan sonnet sequence had a significant impact in England in the 1590s – decades after the French had produced some of their most important sequences, and centuries after the composition of Petrarch's *Rime sparse*. Of course, many English distrusted all things Italian. Ascham, while encouraging the young to read *Il cortegiano*, sees no need for them to *visit* Italy, a land full of "Circes" and "Sirens" ready to corrupt unwitting, upright English travelers.[8] Webbe tells us that the hint of homoeroticism in the January eclogue of Spenser's *Shepheardes Calender* (1579) – which he curiously identifies as the sixth eclogue – offended some who felt that it was "skant allowable to English eares, and might well have beene left for the Italian

---

[3]On musical literacy in the early Tudor period, see John Stevens, *Music and Poetry in the Early Tudor Court* (1961; Cambridge: Cambridge University Press, 1979), chap. 3; and David Price, *Patrons and Musicians of the English Renaissance* (Cambridge: Cambridge University Press, 1981), chap. 1.

[4]Thomas Morley, *A Plain and Easy Introduction to Practical Music*, ed. R. Alec Harman, 2nd ed. (New York: Norton, 1963), 9.

[5]Price, *Patrons*, 48-65.

[6]Peter Le Huray, *Music and the Reformation in England 1549-1660* (1967; Cambridge: Cambridge University Press, 1978), 1-29. Cranmer's comments on the matter are illuminating (7).

[7]Smith 1:xiv-xxxvi, Introduction. See also J. W. H. Atkins, *English Literary Criticism: The Renascence*, 2d ed. (Oondon: Methuen, 1951), 111-12.

[8]Roger Ascham, *English Works*, ed. William A. Wright (Cambridge: Cambridge University Press, 1904), 218, 223-25.

defenders of loathsome beastlines, of whom perhappes he learned it. . . ."[9]
And Thomas Nashe, in *The Unfortunate Traveller* (1594), reveals what was
doubtless a common English view of Rome as a center of degeneracy and
corruption.[10]

But in spite of the evils that one might encounter on the continent, travel
held an important place in education throughout the sixteenth century. As
the century wore on, the Grand Tour of Europe became an increasingly
important stage in a young gentleman's learning experience. After the defeat
of the Armada in 1588, the number of English who made the Grand Tour
rose noticeably[11] – as did the number of sonnet sequences and Italianate
madrigals written in England.

Another factor inhibiting artistic growth in the middle years of the sixteenth century was a lack of adequate patronage. Puttenham complains of
the indifference among nobles toward poets and musicians; their attitude, he
feels, is indicative of "this iron and malitious age of ours."[12] Still, a number
of wealthy aristocrats retained musicians in their households from the 1540s
onward, and the number increased with the years.[13]

If we look for signs of musical-humanist activity in the early Tudor court,
we shall generally meet with disappointment. Nevertheless, England in the
early sixteenth century had its share of notable humanists – Thomas More
(1478-1535), of course, being the most famous. In the *Utopia* (1516), More
seems aware of the salient ideas expressed by the continental musical humanists. Raphael Hythlodaye mentions music several times while describing the
Utopians' customs. At one point, he praises the Utopians for their expressive
way of singing prayers; in doing so, he touches on issues regularly addressed
by musical humanists:

> In one thinge doubtles they goo exceding farre beyonde us. For all
> their musike bothe that they playe upon instrumentes, and that they
> singe with mannes voyce dothe so resemble and expresse naturall
> affections, the sound and tune is so applied and made agreable to
> the thinge, that whether it bee a prayer, or els a dytty of gladnes,
> of patience, of trouble, of mournynge, or of anger: the fassion of
> the melodye dothe so represente the meaning of the thing, that it
> doth wonderfullye move, stirre, pearce, and enflame the hearers
> myndes.[14]

[9]Smith 1:264.

[10]*The Works of Thomas Nashe,* ed. Ronald McKerrow, rev. F. P. Wilson, 5 vols. (Oxford:
Basil Blackwell, 1958) 2:209-328; for Venice and Rome, 255-328.

[11]Price, *Patrons*, 31.

[12]Smith, 2:22; *Arte of English Poesie*, 36. The authorship of the *Arte of English Poesie* is
uncertain, though George Puttenham is usually regarded as its author; it may have been written
well before 1589.

[13]Price, *Patrons*, 12-14.

that it doth wonderfullye move, stirre, pearce, and enflame the hearers myndes.[14]

Hythlodaye's criticism of contemporary music seems at least partly justified, for much of the music of the early Tudor era was composed without the expressive devices (like word-painting) commonly employed later in the century. This is not to say that a music lover, then or now, would feel no emotion upon hearing masterpieces by Cornyshe or Pygott, and composers of More's day certainly used pitch, rhythm, and harmony to stress some words and phrases. But, in general, the music was meant not so much to create an aural, nonverbal equivalent to the text as to provide a harmonious setting for it – which could, of course, be profoundly moving in its own right.[15]

In his *De fructu qui ex doctrina percipitur* (1517), Richard Pace (c. 1483-1536), another English humanist, also recalls ideas brought up by continental musical humanists. Pace studied in Padua, Bologna, Ferrara, and Venice; he was a friend of Erasmus and More.[16] In the *De fructu*, a defense of the liberal arts, music naturally comes up as a topic for discussion. Pace presents us with the standard *laus musicae* catalogue (39-45), such as one can find in innumerable medieval and Renaissance tracts, but he also metes out some interesting (though vague) criticism of modern music:

> Omnia quae musici nostri faciunt hodie, sunt fere trivialia, si cum his quae fecerunt antiqui, comparentur, adeo ut vix unus aut alter reperiatur, qui quid sit harmonia (quam semper habent in ore) intelligat. Huic itaque restituendae, quum Romae essem, nactus in bibliotheca summi Pontificis magnam librorum copiam, quos in hac scientia multi & summi Philosophi scripserunt, magna & miranda continentes, vacare coepi. . . . Sed repentina Cardinalis Angliae defuncti morte . . . impeditus, & Romam relinquere coactus, institutum prosequi non potui. (44, 46)

Everything our musicians do today is insignificant if we compare it with what the ancients did. There are hardly one or two people today who know what harmony is, though they are always talking about it. When I was in Rome, I came across a great number of books in the Vatican Library that many eminent philosophers wrote on music. They had great wonders in them, and . . . I began to

---

[14]*Utopia with the 'Dialogue of Comfort'*, trans. (*Utopia* only) Raphe Robinson (London: Dent, [1910]), 110.

[15]See John Stevens, *Music and Poetry in the Early Tudor Court*, 58-65.

[16]See the introductory essay to Pace's *De fructu qui ex doctrina percipitur (The Benefit of a Liberal Education)*, ed. and trans. Frank Manley and Richard Sylvester (New York: Frederick Ungar, 1967), ix-xxiv. References to the text and translation are to this edition.

devote my leisure time to the revival of music. But I was hindered
by the sudden death of the late English Cardinal . . . and forced to
leave Rome. So I was not able to carry out what I had begun. (45,
47)

Pace and More notwithstanding, musical humanism had few exponents
in early Tudor England. Vernacular experiments in ancient poetic meters are
also wanting. Surrey's blank-verse translation of two books from the *Aeneid*
represents a compromise that one greater classicist, Milton, settled for. Being
used to unrhymed iambic pentameter as the standard English verse-form for
much dramatic and narrative poetry, the modern reader may find it hard to
see Surrey's foray into the field of blank verse as an example of classicizing.
But Roger Ascham did not – though he considered Surrey's work not entirely
satisfying. In *The Scholemaster* (1570), Ascham's comments on and criticisms
of Surrey's work have the true humanist ring to them; he vehemently berates
the barbaric practices handed down from the Middle Ages:

> Now, when men know the difference, and have the examples, both
> of the best, and of the worst, surelie, to follow rather the *Gothes* in
> Ryming, than the *Greekes* in trew versifiyng, were even to eate
> ackornes with swyne, when we may freely eate wheate bread
> emonges men. . . .
>   The noble Lord *Th.* Earle of Surrey, first of all English
> men, in translating the fourth booke of *Virgill*: and *Gonsaluo Periz*
> that excellent learned man . . . , in translating the *Ulisses* of *Homer*
> out of *Greke* into *Spanish,* have both, by good judgement, avoyded
> the fault of Ryming, yet neither of them hath fullie hite perfite and
> trew versifiyng. In deede, they observe just number, and even feete:
> but here is the fault, that their feete: be feete without joyntes, that
> is to say, not distinct by trew quantitie of sillables. . . .[17]

In the Elizabethan period, a large number of poets and critics – Stanyhurst,
Spenser, Webbe, Sidney, Puttenham, Harvey, to name some – theorized
about quantitative verse in English and adduced original poems to support
or illustrate their theories. Derek Attridge has published a fine study ana-
lyzing a large chunk of this relatively neglected body of English poetry;[18]
there is thus no need to present a survey of the quantitative-verse movement
in England. But those theorists whose ideas Samuel Daniel and Thomas
Campion surely would have known demand our attention. Moreover, we

---

[17]Ascham, *English Works,* 289, 291. Like Puttenham, apparently, Ascham found it hard to
distinguish between Thomas Wyatt and Henry Howard: hence "*Th.* Earle of Surrey." Webbe
oddly describes Surrey's *Aeneid* translations as an example of *Hexametrum Epicum* (Smith 1:283);
but he may simply be following Ascham, whose ideas he parrots several times.

[18]Attridge, *Well-Weighed Syllables* (cited chap. 1, n. 60), esp. 129-35.

ought to try to determine how much of the outpouring of continental musical humanism spilled over into England.

Although England produced no formal academies such as those in France, Germany, and Italy, we know that various *cénacles* existed, the most tantalizing of these being the Areopagus, a group referred to (perhaps jokingly) in the Spenser-Harvey correspondence.[19] We know little about this circle of friends, though it seems to have been an informal gathering of poets and scholars, chief among whom were Sir Philip Sidney, Edmund Spenser, Gabriel Harvey, Sir Edward Dyer, and Fulke Greville. (Daniel Rogers and George Buchanan seem also to have figured in the group.)[20] Sidney and Spenser, two of the leading writers in Elizabethan England, would be important influences on contemporary poets in any case; as it happens, Samuel Daniel received kind words from Spenser and much-needed support from the Sidney family, specifically from Mary, Countess of Pembroke.[21]

Quantitative verse in the vernacular is among the topics discussed in the letters exchanged between Spenser and Harvey. In his 1579 letter to Harvey, Spenser writes that the Areopagus has proclaimed a "generall surceasing and silence of balde Rymers, and also of the verie beste to: in steade whereof, they have, by authoritie of their whole Senate, prescribed certaine Lawes and rules of Quantities of English sillables for English Verse. . . ."[22] Harvey and Spenser come back to the subject of quantitative verse several times in their letters, offering each other examples (neither contemptible nor impressive) of their own poetic experiments in ancient meters. Sidney, Ascham, and Drant – all of whom wanted reforms in vernacular poetry – are mentioned as modern authorities on the matter.[23] Harvey brings up the tricky problems of accent and orthography in English (1:99-107) and makes a number of commonsensical criticisms of Spenser's neoclassical poetry. But the discussions of quantitative verse in the Spenser-Harvey correspondence are strictly

---

[19]See *The Works of Gabriel Harvey, D.C.L.,* ed. Alexander Grosart, 3 vols. (London, 1884-85) 1:7-8, 20.

[20]See the articles on the Sidney circle by James Phillips: "Daniel Rogers: A Neo-Latin Link between the Pléiade and Sidney's 'Areopagus,'" *Neo-Latin Poetry of the Sixteenth and Seventeenth Centuries* (Los Angeles: University of California, 1965), 5-28; and "George Buchanan and the Sidney Circle," *Huntington Library Quarterly* 12 (1948-49): 23-55. John Dee, who also had contact with the Sidney circle, owned copies of Zarlino's *Istitutioni harmoniche* and Glarean's *Dodecachordon*; see Peter J. French, *John Dee: The World of an Elizabethan Magus* (London: Routledge and Kegan Paul, 1972), 139.

[21]See Joan Rees, *Samuel Daniel* (Liverpool: Liverpool University Press, 1964), chap. 3; and Pierre Spriet, *Samuel Daniel (1563-1619): Sa vie – son oeuvre* ([Paris]: Didier, 1968), 59-71.

[22]Harvey, *Works* 1:7.

[23]Ibid. 1:9, 36, 75-76. Drant's rules for establishing longs and shorts in English are lost, but Sidney's have survived and are reproduced in *The Poems of Sir Philip Sidney,* ed. William A. Ringler, Jr. (Oxford: Clarendon Press, 1962), 391.

literary and give no indication that either poet cared to have his verses set to *musique mesurée à l'antique.*

Sir Philip Sidney (1554-86), through a number of poets in his circle of friends (Daniel Rogers, George Buchanan, Paul Melissus Schede), must have known of the quantitative-verse settings in France and Germany. He draws connections between music and poetry, in passing, throughout the *Defence of Poesie.* And in the *Old Arcadia* (1580), which contains a large number of English poems in classical meters as well as in standard rhyming forms, he offers a sustained discussion of the importance of music relative to verse. At the end of the First Eclogues, Dicus and Lalus raise an issue that reveals Sidney's interest in musico-poetic relations:[24]

> Dicus said that since verses had their chief ornament, if not end, in music, those which were just appropriated to music did best obtain their end, or at least were the most adorned; but those must needs most agree with music, since music standing principally upon the sound and the quantity, to answer the sound they brought words, and to answer the quantity they brought measure. So that for every semibreve or minim, it had his syllable matched unto it with a long foot or a short foot, whereon they drew on certain names (as dactylus, spondeus, trocheus, etc.), and without wresting the word did as it were kindly accompany the time, so that either by the time a poet should straight know how every word should be measured unto it, or by the verse as soon find out the full quantity of the music.

With humanistic enthusiasm, Dicus inveighs against "such hives full of rhyming poets, more than ever there were owls at Athens," but Lalus presents a cogent counter-argument:

> Since music brought a measured quantity with it, therefore the words less needed it, but as music brought time and measure, so these verses brought words and rhyme, which were four beauties for the other three. And yet to deny further the strength of his speech, he said Dicus did much abuse the dignity of poetry to apply it to music, since rather music is a servant to poetry, for by the one the ear only, by the other the mind, was pleased.

Sidney was in an optimum position to soak up the newest theories on musico-poetic relations held by continental poets and savants. He was familiar with Claudio Tolomei's letters.[25] In 1572, he visited the court of Charles IX

---

[24]The debate between Dicus and Lalus appears in *The Countess of Pembroke's Arcadia (The Old Arcadia)*, ed. Jean Robertson (Oxford: Clarendon Press, 1973), 89-90.

[25]See John Buxton, *Sir Philip Sidney and the English Renaissance* (London: Macmillan, 1954), 72.

and must have become acquainted with some of the key men of letters in France; while there, he made a favorable impression on Ramus, whose influence is perhaps detectable in Sidney's rules for establishing longs and shorts in English.[26] It seems likely that Sidney would have met members of the *Académie de Musique et de Poésie*.[27] Unfortunately, we have no concrete evidence showing that Sidney came directly in touch with Ronsard or Baïf; but Daniel Rogers, who knew Sidney, Harvey, Spenser, and other important writers, attended Baïf's meetings and addressed several poems to Baïf and Ronsard. In a poem to Baïf, Rogers describes his delight at hearing the French poet's works recited (or perhaps sung):[28]

> O quae lux adeo mihi benigna
> Fulsit, sorte adeo mihi benigna
> Nuper, quum peterem tuos Baifi
> Penates, legeres mihi tuae quum
> Musae delicias venustiores.

O what light, so pleasing to me, shone, through such kind fortune, when recently I sought out your dwelling, Baïf, [and] you read me the lovely delights of your muse.

Another link between Sidney and the continental musical humanists may exist in Rogers' friend George Buchanan (1506-82), whom Sidney praises in his *Defence of Poesie*.[29] Buchanan's friends and acquaintances were spread throughout Europe. Ascham seems to have been on amicable terms with the Scottish humanist, and Gabriel Harvey "praised Buchanan as a 'divine' poet. . . ."[30] For a while, Buchanan lived with Lazare de Baïf and may at the same time have tutored Jean-Antoine.[31] In 1566, Henri Estienne published Buchanan's psalm paraphrases (written in Latin and employing classical meters), which met with great popularity. Plantin's edition of them, also published in 1566, included an appendix of *Carmina genera* that explained

---

[26]On Sidney's 1572 trip to France, see Buxton, 44-56. Buxton mentions Ramus' influence on Sidney (46), as does Attridge (*Well-Weighed Syllables*, 122).

[27]See Bruce Pattison, *Music and Poetry of the English Renaissance*, (1948; Folcroft, Penn.: Folcroft Press, 1969), 62.

[28]See J. A. van Dorsten, *Poets, Patrons, and Professors: Sir Philip Sidney, Daniel Rogers, and the Leiden Humanists* (Leiden: Sir Thomas Browne Institute at the University Press, 1962), 100, 214. Most of Rogers' text, from a manuscript in the Huntington Library (HM 31188, fol. [291r-v]), is included in Anne L. Prescott, *French Poets and the English Renaissance* (New Haven: Yale University Press, 1978), 260.

[29]In *Prose Works*, ed. Albert Feuillerat, 4 vols. (1912; Cambridge: Cambridge University Press, 1962) 3:41.

[30]Phillips, "Buchanan," 28, 47.

[31]Ian McFarlane, *Buchanan* (London: Gerald Duckworth, 1981), 102.

the various meters; thus the paraphrases could be used to teach classical prosody.[32] Jean Servin set some of Buchanan's psalms to music already in 1579; and in 1585, shortly after Buchanan's death, the psalms were set in the Tritonian manner by Statius Olthof.[33] Olthof's settings, which taught schoolchildren proper scansion without abandoning the Judeo-Christian tradition, took a firm hold in the curriculum of the German *Lateinschule*.[34] One cannot know whether Buchanan wished to have his translations set to music; but keeping in mind Baïf's opinions on the psalms (widely held among humanists), one would not be surprised if Buchanan also wished to join his devotional lyrics with music.[35]

If Buchanan's ties with music are questionable, Paul Melissus Schede's are not. Schede (1539-1602) practiced both poetry and music in the best humanist tradition. Already in 1559, he became cantor in Königsberg, and shortly thereafter the emperor crowned him poet laureate in Vienna.[36] By 1567, he had made his way to Paris, where he soon became friends with such intellectual notables as Ramus, Dorat, and Ronsard; he later gained the friendship of Muret and Baïf.[37] Writing poetry in German, Latin, and Greek, he set his verses with due attention to metrics; in France, he was inspired to write settings and German rhyming translations of the psalms, published in Heidelberg in 1572.[38] Later, he returned to Germany and became the librarian to the elector Palatine. In 1577, Schede published a poem addressed to Sidney that suggests that the two poets enjoyed each other's company.[39] Impressed with Schede's poetry and music during his visit to England in 1586, Eliza-

---

[32]Ibid., 257, 263. Buchanan's psalm paraphrases were also published in England.

[33]Benedikt Widmann, "Die Kompositionen der Psalmen von Statius Olthof," *VfMW* 5 (1889): 291. Widmann reproduces the four-voice settings at the end of his article.

[34]See Klaus W. Niemöller's *Untersuchungen zu Musikpflege und Musikunterricht an den deutschen Lateinschulen* (Regensburg: Gustav Bosse Verlag, 1969), 203, 215, 298, 624.

[35]According to Drummond of Hawthornden, Ben Jonson told James I that Buchanan – the king's tutor – "had corrupted [James's] eare when yoūng & learned him to sing Verses, when he soūld have read them" (*Ben Jonson*, ed. C. H. Herford, Percy Simpson, and Evelyn Simpson, 11 vols. [Oxford: Clarendon Press, 1925-52] 1:148).

[36]Exactly when Schede was crowned poet laureate, and by whom, seem difficult questions to answer. Pierre de Nolhac, in *Un poète rhénan ami de la Pléiade: Paul Melissus* (Paris: Librairie ancienne Honoré Champion, 1923), states that the Emperor Ferdinand crowned Schede (5); Paul Bergmans, in "Deux amis de Roland de Lassus: les humanistes Charles Utenhove et Paul Melissus Schede," *Académie royale de Belgique, Bulletin de la classe des beaux-arts* 15 (1933), writes that "en 1564, l'empereur Maximilien le [Schede] nomma *poeta laureatus*" (107); and Ferdinand Haberl, in "Paul Melissus Schede," *New Grove*, tells us that Schede was "crowned poet in Vienna in 1561, raised to the rank of hereditary nobleman in 1564 and given the titles 'Comes Palatinus', 'Eques Auratus', and 'Civis Romanus' in Italy in October 1579."

[37]Nolhac, 11-19, 32-38, 59-63.

[38]Haberl, "Schede."

[39]Buxton, *Sidney*, 90-91.

beth I tried to convince Schede to remain in her country.[40] He is thus a likely point of contact between the humanist musico-poetic experiments in Germany and France and those (such as they were) in England.

As an important artistic catalyst, then, Sidney could well have spread continental humanist ideas about the relations between poetry and music to those learned friends forming part of his circle. William Byrd (1543-1623), probably the greatest of the Elizabethan composers, set several of Sidney's lyrics and may have been influenced by the musico-poetic theories of the Sidney coterie. In 1588, Byrd published his *Psalms, Sonets & songs of Sadnes and pietie*, which includes two pieces of *musique mesurée*. One of them, "Constant Penelope" (no. 23), is a translation from Ovid's *Heroides* (1.1-8) into English hexameters; the other, "Come to me, grief" (no. 34), written in English Aristophanics, is the first of two funeral songs to Sidney included at the end of the collection.[41] At first sight, neither piece looks much like *musique mesurée*, for only the upper voice follows the meter of the poem by matching long and short syllables with long and short notes, and the voices do not declaim at once. But Byrd himself tells us that the songs were "originally made for Instruments to expresse the harmonie, and one voyce to pronounce the dittie";[42] this arrangement, highlighting the upper voice, makes the words and meter clear to the listener.[43] Byrd's two settings of English quantitative verse prevent us from writing off such neoclassical experiments in poetry and music as dull and unexpressive. For example, when the soprano first declaims the text in "Constant Penelope" (m. 5), the difficulty of remaining "constant" is underscored by the sudden shift from b-natural to b-flat in the accompaniment (Ex. 3.1).[44]

[40]Haberl, "Schede."

[41]See Byrd's *Psalms, Sonnets and Songs (1588)*, ed. Edmund Fellowes, rev. Philip Brett (London: Stainer and Bell, 1965), 117-23, 190-93. A connection between the Sidney circle and Byrd is suggested in the introduction to that edition (xxxiv). Derek Attridge, in *Well-Weighed Syllables*, points out that "Come to me Grief" is written in Aristophanics (131, n. 1).

[42]*Psalms, Sonnets and Songs*, ix.

[43]Joseph Kerman, in *The Elizabethan Madrigal: A Comparative Study* (New York: American Musicological Society, 1962), 103, suggests that Byrd texted the lower voices to attract a public eager to sing a-cappella madrigals.

[44]My reduction, based on Fellowes' transcription, treats the piece as an accompanied solo-song. (Oxford University MS 439, dating from the early seventeenth century, carries on fol. 58 a version of this piece for solo voice and bass accompaniment, an arrangement that emphasizes the dactyllic-hexameter verse scheme.)

Ex. 3.1, Byrd, "Constant Penelope"

Apart from the two pieces by Byrd, the only "measured" setting of English quantitative verse in the Renaissance is Campion's "Come, let us sound," which I shall discuss in the chapter devoted to Campion's songs. But in Thomas East's collection of four-voice, homorhythmic settings of *The Whole Book of Psalms* (1592), one can perhaps detect the influence (however indirect) of the Tritonian school. Ldith Weber cogently argues that the Tritonian settings of Latin secular poetry gave reformers a model on which to base their musical arrangements of hymns and psalms.[45] The melodies of the Geneva Psalter (completed in 1562), which were set contrapuntally by Protestants throughout Europe, use two note-values, one twice the length of the other. In the eleven-syllable lines, the most commonly used rhythm is the one humanists and nonhumanists often employed when setting Sapphic

[45]Weber, *La musique mesurée* (cited chap. 1, n. 3), chap. 14 and *passim*.

hendecasyllables (see Ex. 2.4).[46] Claude Goudimel, who in 1555 wrote settings of Horace's odes (no longer extant, but perhaps composed in the
Tritonian manner), arranged one of his three collections of settings of the
Geneva Psalter in a simple, four-part, homorhythmic way. This collection
(1565) remained popular for centuries and inspired Protestants in other countries to write similar arrangements. We find the melody of the fiftieth psalm
in the tenor of Goudimel's setting, which for each line uses a rhythm almost
identical to that mentioned above, though the ending is masculine rather
than feminine (Ex. 3.2).[47] Edward Blancks' setting of the Sternhold and
Hopkins version of the fiftieth psalm uses the same melody as Goudimel's;
it is also in the tenor. Like the other settings in East's 1592 collection,
Blancks' is strictly homorhythmic (Ex. 3.3).[48] And in Richard Alison's
arrangements of the *Psalmes of David in Meter* (1599) for four voices (or for
one voice and various stringed instruments), also homorhythmic for the most
part, the melody is also placed in the soprano line (Ex. 3.4).[49]

Ex. 3.2, Goudimel, "Le Dieu"

[46]Waldo S. Pratt, *The Music of the French Psalter of 1562* (New York: Columbia University
Press, 1939), 43. This rhythm is used sixty-nine times; the next most popular rhythm is used
only eleven times.

[47]Claude Goudimel, *Oeuvres complètes*, ed. Pierre Pidoux, 13 vols. to date (New York:
Institute of Medieval Music, 1967-), 9:43.

[48]My reduction is based on the version in Edward Rimbault's edition of Thomas Este,
pub., *The Whole Book of Psalms* (London, 1844), 26-27.

[49]My reduction is based on the text in the facsimile edition of Richard Alison's *Psalms of
David in Meter* (1599; Menston: Scolar Press, 1968), sigs. Hv-H2.

Ex. 3.3, Blancks, "The mighty God"

Ex. 3.4, Alison, "The mighty God"

Though Goudimel almost certainly knew that he was using a style associated with humanist settings of quantitative verse, I doubt that the English
composers had humanist goals in mind; the simple, homorhythmic style
appealed to reformers because it allowed the words to be heard clearly and
would probably not alienate any members of the congregation who might
find syncopations and complex polyphony confusing. Nevertheless, the four-
part settings of Horace's odes at the beginning of the sixteenth century seem
to have indirectly influenced the Protestant hymns at the end of it.

But, in general, how widespread was musical humanism in England?
Certainly the movement affected mainstream English poetry only to a slight
degree. Thomas Whythorne (1528-96) – a poet, though a middling one,
and a professional musician who traveled throughout Europe in the mid
1500s – strikes us as someone who would be fully receptive to new musico-

poetic experiments.[50] Indeed, Whythorne was the first Englishman to publish a set of his own original part-songs (1571); moreover, he promoted spelling reform by using a more systematic orthography than that commonly in use in the sixteenth century. But despite the generous sprinkling, throughout his autobiography, of quotations from Aristotle, Plato, and other *auctores*, Whythorne seems to have found little inspiration among the continental musical humanists. His verses, which occasionally please by their matter, are for the most part doggerel. His music, in contrast, is competent, charming, and at times even moving. Some of his songs are almost completely homorhythmic ("Though choler cleapt the heart about," for example), and others have homorhythmic passages; but he has not illustrated classical verse patterns, and he is capable of having several voices declaiming different texts simultaneously (as in the expressive "It doth me good when Zeph'rus reigns").[51] I would hesitate to attribute his simpler style to humanist experimentation; simple songs, after all, existed throughout the Renaissance. Still, his concern for expressing the text and for making the words audible may owe a small debt to the humanist polemics revolving around the proper way to set poetry to music.

Another Renaissance writer who left an autobiography was Edward, Lord Herbert of Cherbury (1583-1648). Like Whythorne, Herbert wrote poetry (decidedly better than Whythorne's) and occupied himself with music. In his personal lute-book, one finds pieces written for both Renaissance and baroque tuning; Herbert clearly kept up with the important changes in the music of his day.[52] About the year 1608, Herbert traveled throughout the continent with the polyglottal Aurelian Townsend (whose *Tempe Restored* is an adaptation of Beaujoyeulx's *Balet comique de la reine*, a work influenced by Baïf's *Académie*).[53] In Paris, Herbert applies himself "much to know the use of [his] arms, and to ride the great horse, playing on the lute, and singing

---

[50]Thomas Whythorne, *Autobiography*, ed. James Osborn (Oxford: Clarendon Press, 1961); see especially 60-71 for Whythorne's European travels. One would like to have the book (now lost) that Whythorne wrote specifically about his travels (mentioned on 65-66), which might throw more light on the acquaintances he made.

[51]"Though choler cleapt" and "It doth me good" are transcribed and edited by Peter Warlock in the series *The Oxford Choral Songs from the Old Masters* (London: Oxford University Press, 1927), nos. 354 and 360. For a good discussion of Whythorne's songs, see Edward Doughtie, *English Renaissance Song* (Boston: Twayne, 1986), 46-61.

[52]See Thurston Dart, "Lord Herbert of Cherbury's Lute-Book," *Music and Letters* 38 (1957): 136-48.

[53]For Townsend's masque, see Stephen Orgel and Roy Strong, *Inigo Jones: The Theatre of the Stuart Court*, 2 vols. (Berkeley: University of California Press, 1973) 1:61; for Beaujoyeulx's *Balet comique*, see Yates, *French Academies* (cited chap. 1, n. 31), chap. 11; and Baltasar de Beaujoyeulx, *Le balet comique de la royne 1581*, trans. Carol and Lander MacClintock (n.p.: AIM, 1971).

according to the rules of the French masters."[54] In Italy, he is enchanted by
various singing nuns and mentions music several times in passing.[55] But he
does not give us any hint that he is interested in the "humanist" side of
music, and his own poetry is written in rhyming forms of the day.

So some sixteenth-century Englishmen interested in poetry and music paid
little if any attention to musical humanism. But as we have seen, Ficino's
De vita, printed at least twice in England during the 1560s, had its share of
readers (John Dee, as one might expect, being one of them).[56] And a number
of ideas held by the musical humanists could reach those unskilled in Latin
and Greek through the anonymous *Praise of Musicke* (1586), dedicated to Sir
Walter Ralegh and often attributed to John Case. This work begins with a
mammoth *laus musicae* catalogue, in which the author dredges up nearly
every instance of music's beneficial effect on humankind from antediluvian
times onward in order to declare, as the subtitle tells us, "the sober and
lawfull use of the same [i.e., music] in the congregation and Church of
God."[57] Although the *Praise* is lengthier by far than the standard medieval
lists of musical miracles, it resembles them in content for the first eight
chapters, after which the author argues in favor of music in the church.
While searching through history and mythology for musical *exempla*, the
author makes a number of points that smack of musical humanism. The
author, who believes that music comes partly from "som divine & hevenly
inspiration" (34) and that "poetrie . . . is but a part of Musicke" (37), links
music to the soul:

> . . . Musicke . . . hath a certaine divine influence into the soules
> of men, whereby our cogitations and thoughts . . . are brought into
> a celestiall acknowledging of their natures. For as the Platonicks &
> Pythagorians think al soules of men, are at the recordation of that
> celestial Musicke, whereof they were partakers in heaven, before
> they entred into their bodies so wonderfuly delighted, that no man
> can be found so harde harted which is not exceedingly alured with
> the sweetnes thereof. And therfore some of the antient Philosophers

[54]Edward, Lord Herbert of Cherbury, *Autobiography*, ed. C. H. Herford (n.p.: Gregynog
Press, 1928), 38.

[55]Ibid., 56-59, 80, 82.

[56]See French, *John Dee*, 50.

[57]References are to the 1586 edition (STC 20184). One John Case (c. 1539-c. 1599)
received compliments for a *Praise of Musicke* from Thomas Watson and Thomas Ravenscroft,
but Case wrote an *Apologia musices* (Oxford, 1588), to which Watson and Ravenscroft might
have referred. Howard Barnett attempts to prove Case the author of both works in "John Case
– An Elizabethan Music Scholar," *Music and Letters* 50 (1969): 252-66. See, however, J. W.
Binns's rebuttal, "John Case and 'The Praise of Musicke,'" *Music and Letters* 55 (1974): 444-53.
Ellen Knight, in *"The Praise of Musicke*: John Case, Thomas Watson, and William Byrd," *Current
Musicology* 30 (1980): 37-51, again argues for single authorship of the two books.

attribute this to an hidden divine vertue, which they suppose naturally to be ingenerated in our minds, & for this cause some other of
them . . . thought that the soule was nothing else, but a Musical
motion, caused of the nature & figure of the whole body, gathering
thereof this necessary conclusion, that wheras things that are of like
natures, have mutual & easy action & passion betweene themselves,
it must needs be, that Musical concent being like that Harmonical
motion which he calleth the soule, doth most wonderfullie allure,
& as it were ravish our senses & cogitations. (40-41)

The effects of the various modes are described (53-65) and other anecdotes
enumerated. So even a musician with a weak (or nonexistent) grasp of ancient
languages could become familiar with the most important musical marvels
attributed to music in classical and biblical lore – and, in addition, gain some
knowledge of the philosophical issues connected with music.

John Case's *Apologia musices* (1588), a shorter book aimed at a more learned
audience, also deals with the antiquity and marvelous effects of music.[58] It
covers some of the same topics as the *Praise* but, as Binns has shown, is a
separate work, not a translation (as earlier critics supposed). Perhaps most
interesting to us is Case's reference to Ficino in a discussion of the *spiritus*:

Marsilius Ficinus pulchrè hanc rem declarat. Concentus inquit per
aeream naturam in motu insitam corpus movet, per agitatum aerem
concitat spiritum (qui est aereum animae & corporis vinculum) per
affectum sic impressum afficit sensum animi, tandèm per amicam
quasi significationem, in ipsam mentem agit, postremò per subtilioris
aeris motum vehementius penetrans, conformem qualitatem & quasi
consortem imprimit, miráque quadam voluptate perfundit naturam,
non hanc simplicem animi solùm, sed etiam corporis illam natur-
alem, totumque sibi rapit & vendicat iure hominem. (21-22)

Marsilio Ficino explains this nicely. Through its airy nature, he says,
music, being innately in motion, moves the body; through the agi-
tated air, it excites the *spiritus* (the airy bond of the soul and body),
which in turn affects the feeling of the soul. Finally, through
meaning – a friend, so to speak – it goes into the mind itself,
penetrating at last through the movement of the more rarefied air.
[There] it creates a similar and, as it were, a sharing quality; imbues
one's very nature with the same wonderful pleasure (not only the
pure nature of the soul but also the natural [i.e., physical] nature of
the body); and justly seizes and claims for itself the entire man.

---

[58]See the summary of Case's work in Binns, 447-48.

Although Case does not cite Ficino's work, the passage corresponds closely to one in Ficino's commentary on the *Timaeus*.[59] We may assume, then, that Ficino's ideas on music would have been familiar to the select group of scholars to whom Case addressed his *Apologia*. Thomas Watson (c. 1557-92) liked Case's book enough to write "A gratification unto Master John Case, for his learned booke, lately made in the praise of Musicke," a poem praising Case and set by William Byrd.[60] In his *Hekatompathia* (1582), Watson presents several poems on music, one of which seems related to Ficino's ideas about music and the *spiritus*. Watson provides the following commentary before the fourteenth Passion of his sequence:

> Whilest he [the poet] greedelie laied open his eares to the hearing of his Ladies voice, as one more then halfe in a doubt, that *Apollo* him selfe had beene at hand, Love espiyng a time of advantage, transformed him selfe into the substance of aier, and so deceitfullie entered into him with his owne great goodwill and desire, and nowe by mayne force still holdeth his possession.[61]

Here, as the poet listens to his lady's song, Love transforms itself into air and thus enters into the poet's mind, much as music – "through its airy nature" ("*per aeream naturam*"), according to Ficino – can enter the body and affect the human *spiritus*.[62] Though the *Hekatompathia* appeared several years before Case published his *Apologia*, Case and Watson appear to have been friends and may well have shared thoughts on music and poetry. And in any event, Watson could have read Ficino on his own.

A work directed toward a less literary audience, Thomas Morley's *Plaine and Easie Introduction to Practicall Musicke* (1597) proves that one Englishman was well acquainted with most of the works on music theory that we have examined. Morley (c. 1557-1602) quotes from earlier sources throughout his *Introduction*; he certainly read the important treatises by Boethius, Lefèvre d'Étaples, Gaffurius, Glarean, and Zarlino, and no doubt works by many

---

[59]Marsilio Ficino, *Opera omnia*, intro. Paul O. Kristeller, 2 vols. (1576; Torino: Bottega d'Erasmo, 1959) 2:1453. D. P. Walker cites this passage in "Ficino's *Spiritus* and Music," *Annales musicologiques* 1 (1953): 137-38. In "The Musical Theory and Philosophy of Robert Fludd," *Warburg* 30 (1967): 199, 219. Peter Ammann points out an explicit reference to this passage in Robert Fludd's *De templo musicae*. For a discussion of the *spiritus* in England, see Gretchen L. Finney, *Musical Backgrounds for English Literature: 1580-1650* (New Brunswick: Rutgers University Press, 1962), chapters 5 and 7.

[60]See Boyd, *Elizabethan Music and Musical Criticism* (cited chap. 1, n. 11), 32.

[61]Thomas Watson, The *Hekatompathia or Passionate Centurie of Love (1582)*, intro. S. K. Heninger, Jr. (Gainesville, Fla.: Scholars' Facsimiles and Reprints, 1964).

[62]Ficino, *Opera omnia* 2:1453.

other authorities.[63] Although Morley was probably better versed in musical theory than most of his peers, one can at least infer that names like Faber Stapulensis and Glareanus still had some currency among musicians contemporary with Campion and the brothers Daniel.

Some of the finer points of humanism insinuate themselves even into popular literature. If the orthographic reforms suggested by Trissino, Baïf, Whythorne, and others seem unrelated to mainstream literature, we should recall that in *Love's Labour's Lost,* the pompous Holofernes comments on Don Adriano de Armado:

> He draweth out the thread of his verbosity finer than the staple of his argument. I abhor . . . such rackers of ortography, as to speak "dout," fine, when he should say "doubt"; "det," when he should pronounce "debt" – *d, e, b, t,* not *d, e, t. . . .* (5.1.16-22)

Shakespeare does not present Holofernes as a character one would wish to emulate: he is a tiresome pedant. But he must have represented a type recognizable to the average Elizabethan theater-goer.

In *Pericles,* Shakespeare gives us a scene illustrating the therapeutic effect of music. When some gentlemen of Ephesus take a coffin to the Lord Cerimon, we have learned that he has studied many of the occult aspects of medicine (3.2.31-38). After the gentlemen remove the apparently dead body of Thaisa, Cerimon applies some of his "secret art" to the corpse and relies heavily – chiefly, it seems – on the curative powers of music:

> The rough and woeful music that we have,
> Cause it to sound, beseech you.
> The viol once more. How thou stir'st, thou block!
> The music there! I pray you give her air.
> Gentlemen, this queen will live. (3.2.88-92)[64]

Another suggestive passage on music appears in *Cymbeline,* when Cloten tries to win Imogen's favor:

> I would this music would come. I am advis'd to give her music a' mornings; they say it will penetrate.
> *Enter* Musicians
> Come on, tune. If you can penetrate her with your fingering, so; we'll try with tongue too. (2.3.11-15)

---

[63]Specific references are indexed in Harman's edition of Morley's *Plain and Easy Introduction,* 323-25.

[64]Finney, in *Musical Backgrounds,* 117, also calls attention to this passage and to the passage from *Cymbeline* (Finney, 259-60, n. 55). Though the *Riverside Shakespeare* uses *vial* rather than *viol* in line 90, F. D. Hoeniger's argument for *viol* in the Arden *Pericles* (London: Methuen, 1963) is, I think, incontestable (91, n. 92).

The word *penetrate* allows – almost urges – Shakespeare to play with its sexual connotations, but he may have chosen it for another reason. Just *who* says, "It will penetrate"? The odd word is *penetrate*. Ficino, however, writes that "*Concentus . . . penetrat*" in his commentary on the *Timaeus* (*Opera omnia* 2:1453) – in the passage that Case paraphrases. (Case uses the present participle, *penetrans*.) While it is improbable that Shakespeare, with his "small Latin," spent much time reading through Ficino (or through Case), the idea of music's penetrating force may have gained enough currency in Shakespeare's England that the playwright could discover a pun in the lewd and learned meanings of *penetrate*.[65]

The influence of Italian poets and theorists on the English Renaissance has never been questioned. In general, moreover, the Elizabethan poets were familiar with, and often translated, the poetry of the most important French poets.[66] It is difficult to say whether French theorists were as influential as the French poets. The peroration of Richard Mulcaster's *Elementarie* (1582) may owe something to Du Bellay's *Deffence,* but so many ideas were expressed over and over in the sixteenth century that one hesitates to use the word *influence* unless word-for-word translation has taken place or the theorist's debt to another author is frankly admitted. In James VI's "Ane schort Treatise" (1584), for example, the future king of England mentions Du Bellay as an authority.[67] But we cannot so easily pinpoint the source of Puttenham's reference to "some divine instinct – the Platonicks call it *furor.*"[68]

A number of ideas and attitudes expressed by the French critics we have studied appear in Puttenham's *Arte of English Poesie* (1589). When speaking of ancient poetry, Puttenham tells us that "all other [than dramatic] kinde of poems, except *Eglogue . . .* , were onely recited by mouth or song with the voyce to some melodious instrument,"[69] which recalls Ronsard's comments on lyric poetry – though Ronsard was by no means the only writer of the time to express this notion. And, like Du Bellay, Puttenham believes that "Poesie is a skill to speake & write harmonically: and verses or rime be a kind of Musicall utterance, by reason of a certaine congruitie in sounds

---

[65]The verb *penetrate* was often used to describe music's effects; the Utopians' music is, as we have seen, so expressive that "it doth wonderfullye move, stirre, pearce ['*penetret*'], and enflame the hearers myndes" (*Utopia,* 110); for the Latin, see the facsimile of the 1518 Basel edition in *L'Utopie de Thomas More,* ed. André Prévost (Paris: Mame, 1978), 155; Caccini, in *Le nuove musiche* (cited chap. 2, n. 59), hopes that his music will penetrate ("*penetrare*") the intellect of those who hear it (sig. A2v). Surely both passages have connections with musical-humanist thought.

[66]See Prescott, *French Poets,* and Smith 1:lxxi-xcii, Introduction

[67]See the prefatory note to the facsimile edition of Mulcaster's *First Part of the Elementary, 1582* (Menston: Scolar Press, 1970), [5]; and Smith 1:209.

[68]Smith 2:3; *Arte of English Poesie,* 20.

[69]Ibid., 2:36; *Arte of English Poesie,* 50.

pleasing the eare. . . ."[70] Although Puttenham spends many pages showing how classical feet can be used in accentual verse, his final verdict is to wish for "the continuance of our old maner of Poesie, scanning our verse by sillables rather than by feete. . . ."[71]

One clear reference to French musical-humanist thought appears in Richard Hooker's massive work *Of the Laws of Ecclesiastical Polity*, published in several books beginning in 1594. The chapter "Of musique with psalmes" in the fifth book (1597) contains borrowings from Tyard's *Solitaire second*:[72]

> Aylthough we lay altogether aside the consideration of dittie or matter, the verie harmonie of soundes beinge framed in due sorte and carried from the eare to the spirituall faculties of our soules is by a native puissance and efficacie greatlie availeable to bringe to a perfect temper whatsoever is there troubled . . . , able both to move and to moderate all affections.[73]

Hooker has not only drawn the concept from Tyard: in phrases like "*native puissance*" and "perfect temper," he has translated Tyard's "*naïve puissance*" and "*parfette temperie*" with the nearest English cognates. But despite this obvious link with Tyard's work, the influence of the French theorists upon English writers remains hard to determine.

Also difficult to gauge is the importance of Orpheus to the Elizabethans. In England, he represented not so much a figure having supernatural powers and divine knowledge as one possessing great oratorical skill, and his legendary ability to tame wild beasts was often allegorized to illustrate how an eloquent speaker could control his audience, how learning could civilize brutish men, and so on.[74] The allegorists denied outright Orpheus' miraculous deeds and sought a more down-to-earth reading of the myth, a typical example of which presents itself already in Thomas Wilson's *Arte of Rhetorique* (1553, revised 1560):

> . . . Poets doe declare that Orpheus the Musition and Minstrell, did stirre and make soft with his pleasaunt melodie, the most harde

[70]Ibid , 2:67; *Arte of English Poesie*, 79. Cf. Du Bellay, *Deffence*, 47, in vol. 1 of *Oeuvres françoises* (cited chap. 1, n. 30), discussed in chap. 1 of this study.

[71]Smith 2:134; *Arte of English Poesie*, 141. Cf. Du Bellay, *Deffence*, 46, discussed in chap. 1 of this study.

[72]Finney, *Musical Backgrounds*, 65.

[73]Hooker, *Of the Laws of Ecclesiastical Polity*, ed. W. Speed Hill, 3 vols., The Folger Library Edition of The Works of Richard Hooker (Cambridge: Belknap Press of Harvard University Press, 1977–81) 2:152. Compare with Tyard's *Solitaire second*, 11, discussed in chap. 1 of this study.

[74]Kirsty Cochrane discusses the transformation of Orpheus in England from miracle-worker to eloquent spokeman in "Orpheus Applied: Some Instances of His Importance in the Humanist View of Language," *Review of English Studies*, n.s. 19 (1968): 1-13.

Rockes and stones. And what is their meaning herein? Assuredly
nothing els, but that a wise and well spoken man, did call backe
harde harted men, such as lived abrode like beastes from open
whoredom, & brought them to live after the most holy lawes of
Matrimonie.[75]

Francis Clement, in *The Petie Schole* (1587), written for children, also challenges a literal interpretation of the story of Orpheus:

Thou hast hard, I am sure, of the mervelous sweete harmony of
Orpheus his harpe, how it moved mountaines and hard rockes, it
shooke the blockish and senseless trees, it stayed the wilde, cruell
& savage beastes, all were ravished with the wonderfull delectation
and pleasure of his melodie: but trowest thou it was his wooden
harpe that made that golden stirre? no, no child, it was his gallant,
eloquent and learned tongue.[76]

Such readings of the myth naturally do little to advance the cause of musical
humanism. Even more generally, the Orpheus myth suffered from what
might be called myth-inflation, for so many sixteenth-century writers compare contemporary poets and musicians with Orpheus that the compliment
scarcely makes an impression on the reader. I doubt that anyone will think
more highly of Daniel upon reading the following comparison in Francis
Meres's *Palladis Tamia* (1598): "As every one mourneth, when hee heareth
of the lamentable plangors of *Thracian Orpheus* for his dearest *Euridice*: so
every one passionateth, when he readeth the afflicted death of *Daniels* dis-
tressed *Rosamond.*"[77]

Thomas Campion, however, seems to have taken the Orpheus myth more
seriously than did most of his compeers. Of course, he too will slip in an
ineffectual allusion to Orpheus in the interest of maintaining a hyperbolic
style,[78] but he twice treats Orpheus as a figure of real power: in *The Lords'
Masque* and in his longer poem to the great lutenist John Dowland.

Orpheus, a key character in *The Lords' Masque* (1613), has the noble task
of freeing Entheus ("Poeticke furie," as Campion tells us) from the throng
of "Franticks" held in thrall by Mania. When she hears Orpheus' music,
Mania "as one amazed" asks, "What powerfull noise is this importunes me,

[75]Thomas Wilson, *Arte of Rhetorique*, 47.

[76]Passage from Clement cited in Cochrane, 9.

[77]*Palladis Tamia* (1598), intro. Don C. Allen (New York: Scholars' Facsimiles and Reprints,
1938), fol. 280v.

[78]See, for example, the references to Orpheus and Arion in "The Lord Hayes Masque,"
in *The Works of Thomas Campion,* ed. Walter R. Davis (1967; New York: Norton, 1970), 220.

/ T'abandon darkenesse which my humour fits?" (249).[79] Orpheus demands
to have Entheus – "whose rage is exempt / From vulgar censure" (250) –
separated from the crowd of Frantics; Mania fears that the others will break
loose if she sets Entheus free. Orpheus assures her that his divine music will
keep the others in their place:

> Let not feare in vaine
> Trouble thy crazed fancie; all againe,
> Save *Entheus,* to thy safeguard shall retire;
> For *Jove* into our musick will inspire
> The power of passion, that their thoughts shall bend
> To any forme or motion we intend. (250)

I. A. Shapiro writes that Campion's audience "might wonder why
Orpheus, rather than Mercury or another of Jove's usual messengers, should
be employed to release Entheus . . . from Mania's cave, though it is possible
that he meant us to infer that Entheus could be released only by that Orphean
music which could tame wild beasts and move trees, rocks, and rivers. . . ."[80]
It strikes me as more than just "possible" that Campion had this in mind.
The opening pages of his masque, though full of the fantastic ideas one
would encounter in almost any masque of the period, illustrate Campion's
genuine interest in Orpheus' powers and in the notion of *furor poeticus,*
inspired here by his playing. Campion, whose writings reveal a skeptical
mind, probably would have allegorized away the miracles that attached
themselves to the Orphean myth. But he was a musician and a lyric poet
with an ear of the greatest sensitivity; and although his shorter poem to
Dowland rather perfunctorily mentions Orpheus, his longer poem to the
greatest Elizabethan lutenist reveals Campion as a musician deeply moved
by his friend's playing:

> Dolande, misero surripis mentem mihi,
> Excorsque cordae pectus impulsae premunt.
> Quis tibi deorum tam potenti numine
> Digitos trementes dirigit? is inter deos
> Magnos oportet principem obtineat locum.
> Tu solus affers rebus antiquis fidem,
> Nec miror Orpheus considens Rhodope super
> Siquando rupes flexit et agrestes feras.

---

[79]All quotations from Campion's works are based on Davis' edition, henceforth referred
to as *Works.* See David Lindley's discussion of this masque in *Thomas Campion* (Leiden: E. J.
Brill, 1986), 190-210.

[80]In the introduction to his edition of *The Lords' Masque,* from Terence Spencer and Stanley
Wells, eds., *A Book of Masques in Honour of Allardyce Nicoll* (1967; Cambridge: Cambridge
University Press, 1970), 98.

At, o beate, siste divinas manus,
Iam, iam, parumper siste divinas manus!
Liquescit anima, quam cave exugas mihi.

Dowland, you steal away my reason in my misery, and the chords
[i.e., strings] you strike overwhelm my foolish heart. Which of the
gods guides your trembling fingers with his powerful spirit? He
should hold first place among the mighty gods. You alone bring
truth to ancient history, nor do I now find it marvelous that Orpheus
sitting upon Rhodope moved the rocks and beasts of the field. But,
O blessed one, stay your divine hands, now, now for a moment,
stay your divine hands! My spirit melts within me, take care lest you
exhaust me completely.[81]

Again, hyperbole colors Campion's account of Dowland's lute playing. But
the immediacy and intensity of emotion, particularly at the end of the poem,
suggest that Campion's reaction to a great musical performance was profound.

Campion was the last Elizabethan to make a serious attempt to establish
rules for quantitative verse in English. Daniel soon afterward defended his
mother tongue and the Middle Ages; moreover, while respecting Greece and
Rome, he rejected the tyranny that overzealous classicists threatened to
impose on modern literature. The struggle between these two forces – the
ancient versus the modern, the classical versus the nonclassical – is evident
in most of the writings of Daniel and Campion. Our chief concern is with
lyric poetry, either read or sung, and in the following chapters we shall study
in detail the differences between Campion's aesthetic creed and that of the
brothers John and Samuel Daniel, examining the way these differences man-
ifest themselves in song and verse.

[81]*Works,* 442-43; Davis' translation.

Part Two

Polemic and Song

Chapter 4
Campion's *Observations* and Daniel's *Defence*

I n 1591 an important collection of English lyric poetry appeared before the public: Thomas Newman's edition of Sir Philip Sidney's *Astrophel and Stella*. Sidney's sonnets and songs constituted the better part of the book, followed by twenty-eight sonnets by Samuel Daniel, most of which appeared the next year in *Delia*; five poems (ending with the cryptic phrase *"finis. CONTENT."*), one of which is definitely Campion's work;[1] and two individual poems: "Faction that ever dwelles," attributed here to "E. O." (Earl of Oxford) but elsewhere to Fulke Greville, and the anonymous "If flouds of teares." It is fitting that the poems of Daniel and Campion made their debut, albeit in a pirated work, along with those of the recently deceased Sidney, for he must have influenced them both. Perhaps more than any of his contemporaries, Sidney, who experimented with almost every kind of verse form then imaginable, inspired both neoclassicists and Petrarchan sonneteers to produce the great quantities of poetry – often first rate – written in late sixteenth-century England.

Ben Jonson in 1619 traveled to Scotland and there visited Drummond of Hawthornden, who took notes on Jonson's conversations with him. These notes begin with some comments touching on the debate between Campion and Daniel; Jonson, we learn, had planned an epic in couplets, "for he detesteth all other Rimes, said he had written a discourse of Poesie both against Campion & Daniel especially this Last, wher he proves couplets to be the bravest sort of Verses. . . ."[2] Unfortunately, Jonson's "discourse of Poesie" is lost. But Drummond's notes reveal that as late as 1619, Jonson, a highly influential poet, still regarded as controversial the issues about which Campion and Daniel had debated in 1602 and 1603.

As a number of scholars have pointed out, Campion's treatise marks the last significant attempt to justify quantitative verse in English. Campion's arguments have their antecedents in the humanist tracts discussed in the previous chapters. Like Tolomei in his *Regolette* and de La Taille in his

---

[1] Christopher R. Wilson, in "Words and Notes Coupled Lovingly Together" (Ph.D. diss., Oxford University, 1981), 14-18, cogently argues that four of the five Cantos are probably not by Campion. Only *Canto Primo* ("Harke all you Ladies that doo sleepe") can be attributed to Campion with certainty.

[2] *Ben Jonson*, ed. C. H. Herford, Percy Simpson, and Evelyn Simpson, 11 vols. (Oxford: Clarendon Press, 1925-52) 1:132.

Manière,[3] Campion in his *Observations in the Art of English Poesie* (1602; entered in the Stationers' Register, however, in 1591) suggests ways to determine quantity in the vernacular; and like many other continental and English humanists, he disparages rhyme as a medieval barbarism. Campion dedicated his treatise to Thomas Sackville, who himself had contributed to the classicizing of English poetry by co-writing *Gorboduc* (1561), a classical tragedy (the first in English) written in blank verse.[4] But Sackville also furthered the medieval strain in English poetry, for he wrote the rhyme-royal Induction to the *Mirror for Magistrates* (1563), a work designed as a continuation of Boccaccio's *De casibus* in Lydgate's English translation, *The Fall of Princes*.[5] Thus, even in the dedication one senses that Campion will eventually run into trouble, since his addressee not only classicized but also rhymed in a medieval genre – a genre, in fact, that Samuel Daniel exploited successfully in his *Complaint of Rosamund* (1592).

After presenting a neoclassical poem addressed to his book, Campion begins his argument. He starts out by linking music and poetry in a discussion of number:

> As in Musick we do not say a straine of so many notes, but so many sem'briefes (though sometimes there are no more notes then sem'briefes), so in a verse the numeration of the sillables is not so much to be observed, as their waite and due proportion.[6]

Soon he gives us the humanist view of cultural history that we have come to expect:

> Learning, after the declining of the *Romaine* Empire and the pollution of their language through the conquest of the *Barbarians*, lay most pitifully deformed till the time of *Erasmus*, *Rewcline*, Sir *Thomas More*, and other learned men of that age, who brought the Latine toong againe to light, redeeming it with much labour out of the hands of the illiterate Monks and Friers. . . . In those lack-learning times, and in barbarized *Italy*, began that vulgar and easie kind of

---

[3] See Jacques de la Taille, *La manière*, ed. Pierre Han, University of North Carolina Studies in Romance Languages and Literatures 93 (Chapel Hill: University of North Carolina Press, 1970).

[4] See Walter R. Davis's prefatory note on the *Observations* in his edition of *The Works of Thomas Campion* (1967; New York: Norton, 1970), 291; henceforth *Works*.

[5] Lydgate's rhyme-royal translation was itself based on an amplified translation of *De casibus* into French prose by Laurent de Premierfait; Lydgate added to his already expanded source. See Derek Pearsall, *John Lydgate* (London: Routledge and Kegan Paul, 1970), 232-33.

[6] From *Works*, 292-93. All subsequent references to the *Observations* are to this edition; page numbers will be incorporated into the text.

Poesie which is now in use throughout most parts of Christendome,
which we abusively call Rime and Meeter. . . . (293)

Pointing out "the unaptnesse of Rime in Poesie" (293), he argues that
modern rhyming is an ill custom to be abolished and that writing in quantitative verse, an older and better practice, ought to be recalled. Rhyme, a
rhetorical device like alliteration, becomes absurd when overused and thus
cannot serve as a serious constructive device in poetry. Proportion is lacking,
moreover, in modern English poetry: "The eare is a rationall sence and a
chiefe judge of proportion; but in our kind of riming what proportion is
there kept, where there remaines such a confusd inequalitie of sillables?"
(294).[7] Rhymers, he feels, confuse short and long syllables; in contrast, the
ancient Greeks and Romans, "whose skilfull monuments outlive barbarisme,
tyed themselves to the strict observation of poeticall numbers . . ." (295).
He mentions Thomas More, who wrote an epigram in "learned numbers"
and in "rude rime"; like More, Campion is disheartened that the rhymed
version met with greater success. Rhymed forms in general and the sonnet
in particular are criticized in a passage that may owe something to Guazzo's
dialogue "Del Paragone della Poesia Latina, et della Thoscana" (1586). In
both passages, the sonnet is likened to the bed of Procrustes:

> But there is yet another fault in Rime altogether intollerable, which
> is, that it inforceth a man oftentimes to abjure his matter and extend
> a short conceit beyond all bounds of arte: for in *Quatorzens* me thinks
> the Poet handles his subject as tyrannically as *Procrustes* the thiefe
> his prisoners, whom when he had taken, he used to cast upon a bed,
> which if they were too short to fill, he would stretch them longer,
> if too long, he would cut them shorter. (295-96)

> Mi pare che'l Sig. Claudio Tolomei havesse ragione di dire che'l
> sonetto era simile al letto di Procuste. Fù questo Procuste cosi
> fantastico, & bestiale, che tutti i forestieri che capitavano al suo
> albergo, faceva coricar in un certo letto, & à quelli che con la
> lunghezza della persona sopravanzavano il letto, tagliava le gambe
> conforme alla misura d'esso; ma à quelli ch'erano più corti, tirava
> con le corde il collo, & le gambe siche giungevano egualmente à
> quella misura. Et però essendo quasi quasi impossibile il trovar
> soggetto che giustamente capisca nel corpo del sonetto conviene per
> lo più ò aggiungervi parole otiose, troncar i concetti in cosi fatta

---

[7]See Seth Weiner, "Renaissance Prosodic Thought as a Branch of *Musica Speculativa*,"
Ph.D. diss., Princeton, 1981, 259-60, for possible meanings of *proportion* in Campion's treatise.

guisa che'l componimento riesce ò languido, ò oscuro. . . . (fol. 68v)[8]

Perhaps Campion knew Guazzo's dialogue; though it did not exist in a contemporary English translation, Guazzo's other work enjoyed considerable popularity in England.[9] If Campion had read Guazzo's dialogue, he would have known something about Claudio Tolomei, apparently famous for using the conceit of the Procrustean bed to malign the sonnet. (Daniel, who had less reason than Campion to be interested in Tolomei, refers specifically to him in the *Defence*.) In any case, this passage may indicate a conscious continuation, on Campion's part, of the experiments by continental humanists in quantitative vernacular verse.

Criticizing the unserious quality of rhyme, Campion asks, "What Devine in his Sermon, or grave Counseller in his Oration, will alleage the testimonie of a rime?" (296). This reminds one of Vincenzo Galilei's derisive remarks on madrigalisms: if the great orators of antiquity had used such devices, they would have provoked ridicule, scorn, and contempt.[10] In both instances, the modern practice seems ridiculous compared with the ancient.

Although modern rhyming poetry lacks high seriousness in Campion's view, "the devinity of the *Romaines* and *Gretians* was all written in verse" (296); if all the great poets of Italy, France, and Spain could choose between letting their work remain in rhymed verse and having it "translated into the auncient numbers," Campion believes they would take the second option. Now he sets out to free English poetry from the fetters of barbarism by showing how one can write quantitative verse in English.

For Campion, English cannot successfully accommodate dactyllic feet; iambs and trochees best suit the language. He believes, however, that pronouncing an iambic (or trochaic) pentameter line in English takes as much time as pronouncing a dactyllic hexameter line in Latin, and his reasoning has its basis in music:[11]

---

[8]*Dialoghi piacevoli del Sig. Stefano Guazzo* (Venice, 1586). See Sidney Lee, "Ben Jonson on the Sonnet," *Athenaeum* 4002 (9 July 1904): 49, for an English translation of Guazzo's passage. Lee, Herford and the Simpsons (*Ben Jonson* 1:155), and Davis (Campion, *Works*, 295, n. 21) all mention this passage in connection with Jonson's comparison of the sonnet to the bed of Procrustes; Davis, like Herford and the Simpsons, mentions Campion's use of the simile but does not comment on the striking similarity between Campion's passage and Guazzo's.

[9]See John Lievsay, *Stefano Guazzo and the English Renaissance 1575-1675* (Chapel Hill: University of North Carolina Press, 1961), 46-53.

[10]*Dialogo della musica antica, et della moderna* (1581), 89; Strunk *SR*, 317, discussed in chap. 2 of this study.

[11]On this theme, see Martha Feldman, "In Defense of Campion: A New Look at His Ayres and *Observations*," *Journal of Musicology* 5 (1987): 226-56.

The cause why these verses differing in feete yeeld the same length of sound, is by reason of some rests which either the necessity of the numbers or the heavines of the sillables do beget. For we find in musick that oftentimes the straines of a song cannot be reduct to true number without some rests prefixt in the beginning and middle, as also at the close if need requires. (298)

After this, the reasoning in Campion's treatise becomes somewhat strained, as his own contemporaries pointed out. He explains that the "pure *Iambick* in English needes small demonstration, because it consists simply of *Iambick* feete" (298); but the "*Iambick licentiate*" – which allows substitutions of iambs by spondees, trochees, dactyls, and so on – requires demonstration. He adduces an original poem in iambic verses, "Goe, numbers, boldly passe, stay not for ayde," to illustrate his theories. Even Alexander Gil, whose *Logonomia Anglica* (1619) contains a chapter that draws heavily upon Campion's *Observations* and who presumably respected Campion's poetic theories, found it hard to regard this poem as anything more than a standard piece of blank verse; to make his point, Gil tacked rhymes onto the end of several lines and said that then they did not differ at all from everyday English poetry:[12]

> Tell them that pitty or perversely skorne
> Poore English Poesie as the slave to rime,
> You are those loftie numbers that revive
> Triumphs of Princes, and sterne tragedies. . . . (*Works*, 299)

> Tell them, that pity or perversely scorn
> Poor English poesy, as the slave to rhyme;
> You are those lofty numbers which adorn
> Triumphs of princes, and their happy time. . . . (Gil, 141)

Campion discusses various ways to substitute one foot for another, but his system for determining longs and shorts seems confused, based partly on stress, partly on classical criteria.[13] Five chapters present neoclassical verse forms that he considers fit for the English language, with original poems as illustrations. The last chapter contains rules for determining quantity in English that resemble the rules given in the treatises of Tolomei and de La Taille. Campion concludes with an apology: "there is no Art begun and perfected at one enterprise" (317).

How much of Campion's treatise owes its existence directly to continental humanism? One cannot answer this question with any real certainty. Sidney,

---

[12]Gil's passage is based on the text in the second edition of *Logonomia Anglica* (1621; Menston: Scolar Press, 1968); I have modernized Gil's unusual orthography.

[13]See Attridge, *Well-Weighed Syllables* (Cambridge: Cambridge University Press, 1974), 219-27.

Drant, Spenser and others tried to establish rules for determining length in English and of course wrote poems using ancient meters in the vernacular. Campion's treatise, however, with its carefully worked out rules and examples, resembles the work of continental humanists far more than do the classicizing attempts of the Sidney circle. Campion appears to have fought in France on the side of Henri IV for several months from 1591 to 1592.[14] There he might have had first-hand contact with French writers involved in classicizing contemporary music and poetry, though the conditions of war would not have allowed much time for leisurely discussions of the arts. In any case, we know little about this period in Campion's life and must rely on conjecture to fill up the gaps in our knowledge.

Daniel's *Defence of Ryme*, a direct response to Campion's treatise, appeared in 1603, a year after the *Observations* saw print – also the year that James I, a fellow rhymer who had written his own treatise on vernacular poetry, assumed the throne (an event to which Daniel alludes in his dedication). Another commentary on Daniel's famous polemic is hardly necessary.[15] But we ought to examine those passages in which Daniel questions the authority of antiquity and praises the best works of the Middle Ages, for there lie issues that closely touch this study.

Wisely dedicating the *Defence* to his former pupil William Herbert – whose uncle, Sir Philip Sidney, furthered the cause of quantitative verse in English – Daniel expresses his wonder at being "tolde how that our measures goe wrong, all Ryming is grosse, vulgare, barbarous, which if it be so, we have lost much labour to no purpose."[16] Since Campion, "a man of faire parts, and good reputation" (130), has seen fit to attack rhyme, Daniel will come to its defense.

Campion's attacks on rhyme, rather than his attempts at quantitative verse, prompt Daniel's *Defence*: "We could well have allowed of his numbers had he not disgraced our Ryme" (131). Daniel asserts that English verse has components comparable to those of Greek and Latin verse:

> For as Greeke and Latine verse consists of the number and quantitie of sillables, so doth the English verse of measure and accent. And though it doth not strictly observe long and short sillables, yet it

[14]See Percival Vivian's introduction to his edition of *Campion's Works* (1909; Oxford: Clarendon Press, 1966), 31-34, and Edward Lowbury, Timothy Salter, and Alison Young, *Thomas Campion: Poet, Composer, Physician* (New York: Barnes and Noble, 1970), 22-23.

[15]See especially the commentaries by J. W. H. Atkins, *English Literary Criticism: The Renascence*, 2nd ed. (London: Methuen, 1951), 195-205; Joan Rees, *Samuel Daniel* (Liverpool: Liverpool University Press, 1964), 83-88; Pierre Spriet, *Samuel Daniel*, 556-65; Seth Weiner, "Renaissance Prosodic Thought," 344-62.

[16]Samuel Daniel, *Poems and A Defence of Ryme*, ed. Arthur C. Sprague (1930; Chicago: University of Chicago Press, 1965), 129. All subsequent references to the *Defence* are to this edition; page numbers will be incorporated into the text.

most religiously respects the accent: and as the short and the long
make number, so the Acute and grave accent yeelde harmonie: And
harmonie is likewise number, so that the English verse then hath
number, measure and harmonie in the best proportion of Musike.
Which being more certain & more resounding, works that effect of
motion with as happy successe as either the Greek or Latin. (132)

Indeed, rhyme has such a force "in nature, or so made by nature, as the
Latine numbers notwithstanding their excellencie, seemed not sufficient to
satitsfie the eare of the world thereunto accustomed, without this Harmo-
nicall cadence" (133). In the two passages just cited, Daniel argues that
rhymed verse is not only as good as quantitative verse – if not better – but
also more musical. Here he attacks Campion on his own territory; for, as
we know, Campion was always attentive to the musical side of his lyrics.
When Daniel says, "[C]ould our Adversary hereby set up the musicke of our
times to a higher note of judgement and discretion, . . . it were a happy
attempt" (135), we ought to be sensitive to the added barb contained in the
musical conceit. And Daniel had every right to discuss the musical aspect of
rhyme, since he too wrote lyrics to be sung. (On the title page of the *Defence*,
Daniel writes that "Ryme is the fittest harmonie of words that comportes
with our Language"; the word "harmonie" is significant.) Nevertheless,
Daniel's last words on the aural side of poetry reveal his preference for sense
over sound:

> The most judiciall and worthy spirites of this Land are not so delicate,
> or will owe so much to their eare, as to rest uppon the out-side of
> wordes, and be intertained with sound: seeing that both Number,
> Measure, and Ryme, is but as the ground or seate, whereupon is
> raised the work that commends it. . . . (154-55)

He believes that we read Greek and Roman poetry chiefly for its content
and often finds the tortuous syntax confusing (136). His criticism of the
varying metrical patterns in odes smacks almost of Philistinism: "The striving
to shew their changable measures in the varietie of their Odes, have beene
very painefull no doubt unto them, and forced them thus to disturbe the
quiet streame of their wordes, which by a naturall succession otherwise desire
to follow in their due course" (137).

As to the sonnet, Daniel admits that he has "wished there were not that
multiplicitie of Rymes as is used by many in Sonets, which yet we see in
some so happily to succeed, and hath beene so farre from hindering their
inventions, as it hath begot conceit beyond expectation, and comparable to

the best inventions of the world. . ." (137).[17] The sonnet is "neither too long for the shortest project, nor too short for the longest, being onely imployed for a present passion" (138) – in other words, anything but a Procrustean bed. Daniel may have associated Campion's conceit against the sonnet with Tolomei, whom he mentions a few paragraphs later. In fact, Daniel sees Campion marching in line with other unsuccessful humanist verse reformers like Tolomei; after pointing out that Petrarch's Italian poems are more valued than his Latin works, Daniel maintains that the Italians who wrote great rhymed works would certainly *not* rather have them in quantitative verse (though Campion insisted they would): "Nor could this very same innovation in Verse, begun amongst them by C. *Tolomaei*, but die in the attempt, and was buried as soone as it came borne, neglected as a prodigious & unnaturall issue amongst them . . ." (141).

Daniel not only attacks the weaknesses of classical and neoclassical poetry but also defends, several times, the Middle Ages. As we have seen, classicists – hundreds of years before Daniel wrote – had viewed the invasion of the barbarians as perhaps the lowest point in the history of civilization and learning. Daniel challenges this opinion, pointing out that the "*Gothes, Vandales and Longobards* . . . have yet left us still their lawes and customes, as the originalls of most of the provinciall constitutions of Christendome; which well considered with their other courses of governement, may serve to cleere them from this imputation of ignorance" (140). Apparently aware that Petrarch's vernacular poetry is part of the medieval tradition, he points out that long before Erasmus, Reuchlin, and More (those whom Campion mentions as the first to revive learning in modern times), "*Franciscus Petrarcha* (who then no doubt likewise found whom to imitate) shewed all the best notions of learning, in that degree of excellencie, both in Latin, Prose and Verse, and in the vulgare Italian . . ." (140-41). Petrarch, then, not only wrote excellent literature during "those lack-learning times" condemned by Campion, but "no doubt" imitated other excellent authors. Samuel Daniel had probably read about some of the authors, like Arnaut Daniel, Jaufre Rudel, Guittone d'Arezzo, Cino da Pistoia – all praised in Petrarch's *Trionfo d'Amore*.[18] Although we have no reason to suppose that Daniel was familiar with the works of these earlier poets, he surely knew that the themes so often treated by Renaissance sonneteers – himself among them – had antecedents in the Middle Ages.

---

[17]I suspect that Daniel is discussing the Italian, not the English, sonnet; he usually wrote English sonnets and, in the *Defence*, tells us that he favors "alternate or crosse Rime" (156), a characteristic feature of the English sonnet.

[18]Translated into English by Lord Morley in the mid-sixteenth century; see D. D. Carnicelli, ed., *Lord Morley's Tryumphes of Fraunces Petrarcke* (Cambridge: Harvard University Press, 1971), 104. Lord Morley amusingly divides Arnaut Daniel into two separate poets, "Arnolde" and "Daniell."

He commends not only those notable scholars of the past whom we now associate in a general way with humanism – authors like Politian and Pico – but also Bede, Thomas Aquinas, Duns Scotus, and many others who, "though they were not Ciceronians," left many fine writings (142-44). In the final pages of the *Defence*, Daniel makes disparagi ₅ comments about Campion's treatise and its poetry, though he confesses that rhyme does not always satisfy him. Couplets, "used in long and continued Poemes, are very tyresome, and unpleasing" (155), and blank verse best suits tragedy (156). Realizing that everything is mutable, Daniel ends on an unsettling note: "we must heerein be content to submit our selves to the law of time, which in few yeeres wil make al that, for which we now contend, *Nothing*" (158).

Although poets continued to rhyme, we should not assume that Daniel's treatise dealt the death blow to the quantitative-verse movement. Not only did Gil derive a whole chapter of his *Logonomia Anglica* (145-50) from Campion's *Observations*, but Milton (for a time, a student under Gil's supervision) translated Horace's "Quis multa gracilis" (*Odes* 1.5) "word for word without Rhyme according to the Latin Measure, as near as the Language will permit."[19] Milton's versifying, which alternates two iambic pentameter with two iambic trimeter lines, resembles Campion's and yields impressive results: indeed, when he printed his translation, he felt confident enough to include beneath it Horace's original. Although he did not experiment further with "classical" meters, his note on the verse of *Paradise Lost*, included in the 1668 edition, derides rhyme in a way that would have pleased Campion and his humanist predecessors:

> The measure is *English* Heroic Verse without Rime, as that of *Homer* in *Greek*, and of *Virgil* in *Latin*; Rime being no necessary Adjunct or true Ornament of Poem or good Verse, in longer Works especially, but the Invention of a barbarous Age, to set off wretched matter and lame Meter. . . . [M]usical delight . . . consists only in apt Numbers, fit quantity of Syllables, and the sense variously drawn out from one Verse into another, not in the jingling sound of like endings, a fault avoided by the learned Ancients both in Poetry and all good Oratory. (210)

While shunning medieval themes and verse forms, the eighteenth-century Augustan poets accepted rhyme. In this regard, Jonson, who disagreed with both Campion and Daniel and especially favored rhyming couplets, had more followers in the next few generations than did the other two polemicists.

---

[19]John Milton, *Complete Poems and Major Prose*, ed. Merritt Y. Hughes (Indianapolis: Odyssey Press, 1957), 10. Further references to Milton's works are to this edition.

But let us return to Newman's 1591 edition of *Astrophel and Stella*, already relevant to this study in many ways, and make one further observation on it: every known poet included in the book wrote lyrics that appeared in contemporary lute-songs. The songs in Sidney's sequence exist in musical settings by Morley, Lanier, and others;[20] John Daniel set his brother's lyrics (1606) – though he did not choose any included in Newman's edition – and so did George Handford ("An Ode");[21] Campion set his own lyrics (several other composers set them, too); and the last two poems, "Faction that ever dwelles" and "If flouds of teares," appeared in John Dowland's *Second Booke of Songs or Ayres* (1600). The relation between text and tone is especially revealing in the case of the lute-songs written by Thomas Campion and John Daniel, for there we can find a musical extension of the issues debated over in the *Observations* and the *Defence*.

[20]See especially Robert Dowland's *Musicall Banquet* (1610; Menston: Scolar Press, 1969), which includes settings of "Goe my Flocke" (no. 4), "O Deere life" (no. 5), and "In a grove most rich of shade" (no. 7).

[21]See George Handford's manuscript lute-song collection (c. 1609), *Ayres to be Sunge to the Lute*, intro. David Greer (Menston: Scolar Press, 1970), 12.

Chapter 5

Campion's Ayres

Thomas Campion belonged to the intellectual *élite*, writing poetry and masques intended for a fit audience, though few.[1] In 1586, he entered Gray's Inn.[2] Far more than a place to study law, the Inns of Court, in some ways England's answer to continental academies, provided intelligent young men with an opportunity to discuss and produce poems, plays, and music.[3] Gray's Inn, for example, put on an important dramatic work in 1594, the *Masque of Proteus*, to which Campion contributed two lyrics.[4] This masque in some respects foreshadows the serious masques of Jonson and of Campion himself; indeed, Stephen Orgel views the *Masque of Proteus* as "the first one that at all resembles the standard Jacobean masque."[5]

The first authorized edition of Campion's verse was a collection of Latin poems in various genres; Campion seems to have written Latin poetry throughout his life, his *Epigrammatum libri II* (1619) having appeared a year before his death. Roughly a third of Campion's poetic output was in Latin.[6] And while his Latin work appeared in carefully put together volumes of poetry, his English lyrics (with few exceptions) appeared, almost incidentally, as words to songs – mostly of his own composition. He seems to have valued his verses in Latin more than his "eare-pleasing rimes without Arte" in English.

He probably studied medicine in Caen, France, between 1602 and 1605; in 1606 he is described as a "Doctor in Physick."[7] While living in France, he was in a good position to experience and learn about new musico-poetic experiments, and a number of his songs seem at least partly influenced by

---

[1]See Campion's Latin epigram to Charles Fitzgeffrey, in which Campion, with Horatian disdain for the multitudes, urges Fitzgeffrey to publish his verses, "*quales / Nescibit vulgus, scit bona fama tamen*" ("such as the common mob will not know, but good reputation knows"). Text and translation from *Works* (cited chap. 4, n. 4), 430-31.

[2]Lowbury et al., *Thomas Campion* (cited chap. 4, n. 14), 18.

[3]In his study *Music at the Inns of Court* (Ann Arbor: UMI, 1979), Robert Wienpahl discusses the academic nature of the Inns and spends several pages on the *Masque of Proteus* (116-29).

[4]See Lowbury et al., 19-20. The lyrics are in *Works*, 474-75. The masque is reprinted in W. W. Greg, ed., *Gesta Grayorum* (n.p.:Oxford University Press, 1914), 58-67.

[5]*The Jonsonian Masque* (Cambridge: Harvard University Press, 1967), 8.

[6]*Works*, 359.

[7]Lowbury et al., 25.

the *air de cour*.[8] As a aspiring physician, moreover, Campion would surely have read works on the magical effects of music on the body and spirit – perhaps even *De vita*, still being published in 1595[9] – though he expressed reservations about the "far-fetcht" musico-biological "Doctrine" he found in Galen.[10]

In the first two decades of the seventeenth century, Campion published five books of lute-songs; his contribution constitutes over a sixth of the entire English lute-song repertoire. Each collection contains some work obviously indebted to continental musical humanism. Campion's music and poetry have received close scrutiny from several scholars, especially in recent years,[11] and I have benefited from their work. Although there is no immediate need for another survey of Campion's many ayres, examining a relatively small group of songs will reveal certain recurring elements – many of them related to his neoclassical bias – that shed light on Campion's aesthetic goals in general.

Campion's lute-songs first appeared in Philip Rosseter's *A Booke of Ayres* (1601) and made up the first half of the volume, each composer having contributed twenty-one songs. In the anonymous preface "To the Reader" – almost certainly written by Campion[12] – the author immediately establishes a classical precedent for composing ayres and, while attacking the madrigalian approach to text-setting, upholds his own more modest method of composition:

> What Epigrams are in Poetrie, the same are Ayres in musicke, then in their chiefe perfection when they are short and well seasoned. . . . Manie rests in Musicke were invented either for necessitie of the fuge, or granted as a harmonicall licence in songs

---

[8]See Elise B. Jorgens, *The Well-Tun'd Word* (Minneapolis: University of Minnesota Press, 1982), 84-104. Jorgens stresses Campion's "neoclassical approach to the relationship between music and text" (95).

[9]An edition of Ficino's *De vita*, dated 1595 (no place), is listed in the *NUC Pre-1956* 171:436.

[10]*Works*, 323.

[11]The following works, in addition to those already cited, deal particularly with Campion's songs: Miles M. Kastendieck, *England's Musical Poet: Thomas Campion* (New York: Oxford University Press, 1938); David Greer, "Campion the Musician," *Lute Society Journal* 9 (1967): 7-16; Oliver J. Finney, "Thomas Campion, Music and Metrics," Ph.D. diss., University of Kansas, 1975; Stephen Ratcliffe, *Campion: On Song* (Boston: Routledge and Kegan Paul, 1981); Christopher R. Wilson, "Words and Notes Coupled Lovingly Together" (cited chap. 4, n. 1); Elise B. Jorgens, *The Well-Tun'd Word*, 84-126; Edward Doughtie, *English Renaissance Song* (Boston: Twayne, 1986), 142-57; David Lindley, *Thomas Campion* (Leiden: E. J. Brill, 1986); Winifred Maynard, *Elizabethan Lyric Poetry and Its Music* (Oxford: Clarendon Press, 1986), 93-112; Walter R. Davis, *Thomas Campion* (Boston: Twayne, 1987).

[12]In her article on Rosseter for the *New Grove*, Diana Poulton assumes that Rosseter wrote the preface; but the similarities between this and the preface to Campion's *Two Bookes of Ayres*, already noted by Kastendieck (65-66), make Campion a likelier candidate.

of many parts: but in Ayres I find no use they have. . . . And as *Martiall* speakes in defence of his short Epigrams, so may I say in th' apologie of Ayres, that where there is a full volume, there can be no imputation of shortnes. The Lyricke Poets among the Greekes and Latines were first inventers of Ayres, tying themselves strictly to the number and value of their sillables, of which sort, you shall find here onely one song in Saphicke verse; the rest are after the fascion of the time, eare-pleasing rimes without Arte. (*Works*, 15)

The comparison of ayre to epigram appears also in the preface to *Two Bookes of Ayres* (c. 1613): "Short Ayres, if they be skilfully framed, and naturally exprest, are like quicke and good Epigrammes in Poesie, many of them showing as much artifice, and breeding as great difficultie, as a larger Poeme" (*Works*, 55). In both passages, Campion is concerned about the critical reception his ayres will meet. He wants to join the ranks of Catullus and Martial, but his ayres, though wry and pithy, have little else in common with ancient Roman epigrams. Most texts to the secular love songs in his day, of course, relied ultimately on medieval themes and images; Campion, steeped in Augustan verse, surely recognized this – just as he recognized rhyme as a vestige of "barbarous" times. And, just as he distinguishes his neoclassical verse in the *Observations* from the "vulgar and easie" rhymes of his contemporaries, so he has attempted to set off his ayres – by likening them to epigrams (classical, unromantic) – from the Petrarchan plaints and praises usually found in madrigals and lute-songs.[13]

Campion mentions another source of anxiety in the two prefaces – that his songs will be regarded as slight compositions lacking "artifice." In *A Booke of Ayres*, he anticipates such an objection and uses two arguments to defend his craft: first, complexity is inappropriate in a light song; second, since weaknesses are easily spied in a "naked Ayre" (though not in a song "of many parts"), the ayre requires more invention to make it please. His reasoning, though not without precedent,[14] is perhaps overdefensive. Campion seems to have been reluctant to put his songs before the public and did so, according to Philip Rosseter, only because corrupt versions of the songs had begun to circulate; at Rosseter's "entreaty," Campion allowed his friend

---

[13]Thomas Morley in 1597 characterized the madrigal as "a kind of music made upon songs and sonnets such as Petrarch and many poets of our time have excelled in"; see his *Plain and Easy Introduction to Practical Music*, ed. R. Alec Harman, 2nd ed. (New York: Norton, 1963), 294.

[14]In Thomas Hoby's 1561 translation of Castiglione's *The Book of the Courtier* (London: Dent, 1928), "Sir Fredericke" argues that singing to the lute is better than "pricksong" "because all the sweetnes consisteth in one alone, and a man is much more heedfull and understandeth better the feat manner, and the aire or veyne of it, when the eares are not busied in hearing any moe than one voice: and beside every litle errour is soone perceived, which happeneth not in singing with company, for one beareth out an other" (101).

to commit the songs to print.[15] Rosseter's name alone, however, appears on the title page. I have argued elsewhere that the subtle lute accompaniments to Campion's 1601 songs – quite different from the accompaniments found in his next four books of ayres – were in fact composed by Rosseter.[16] Apparently either Rosseter or Campion realized that Campion's skill as a composer did not match that of Dowland, Jones, Cavendish, or Morley (all of whom had published lute-songs before 1601), so Rosseter, a professional musician of considerable ability, provided Campion's songs with lute parts more in keeping with those then most popular. If this theory is correct, it might help to explain the fairly complex writing – which would seem to conflict with the goals outlined in the preface to *A Booke of Ayres* – in songs like "Mistris, since you so much desire" (BA/16).[17]

Campion also speaks scornfully of word-painting. Here he joins the likes of Vincenzo Galilei, who found madrigalisms – and the attendant histrionics of singers – risible and, of course, unclassical: if Isocrates or Corax had ever declaimed their orations in such a manner, "they would have moved all their hearers to laughter and contempt . . ." (*"haverebbono mosso nell'istesso tempo tutti gli uditori à riso & à sdegno . . ."*).[18] In a like vein (perhaps inspired by a similar classicizing motive), Campion ridicules music in which

the nature of everie word is precisely exprest in the Note, like the old exploided action in Comedies, when if they did pronounce *Memini*, they would point to the hinder part of their heads, if *Video*, put their finger in their eye. But such childish observing of words is altogether ridiculous, and we ought to maintaine as well in Notes, as in action, a manly cariage, gracing no word, but that which is eminent, and emphaticall. (*Works*, 15)

---

[15]*Works*, 14.

[16]"Collaboration between Campion and Rosseter?" *Journal of the Lute Society of America* 19 (1986): 13-28. In 1969, Thurston Dart first speculated that Rosseter might have helped his friend Campion with the accompaniments (see "Collaboration," 16, n. 10); David Wulstan has suggested the same in *Tudor Music* (London: Dent, 1985), 32. Richard McGrady, however, while admitting that Rosseter might have assisted Campion, feels that the differing styles between the 1601 songs and the later ones chiefly reflect Campion's changing aesthetic goals; see "Campion and the Lute," *Music Review* 47 (1986/87): 1-15.

[17]The following system identifies Campion's songs: BA = Rosseter's *Booke of Ayres* (1601); 1 and 2 = the first and second parts of *Two Bookes of Ayres* (c. 1613); 3 and 4 = the first and second parts of *The Third and Fourth Booke of Ayres* (c. 1618), published as two volumes in one. Following the abbreviation, after a slash, is the song number given in the particular volume. I have transcribed from the facsimiles of Campion's song books published by Scolar Press, prefaced by David Greer (Menston, 1970), though I have also consulted Fellowes' transcriptions and have sometimes profited from his ideas.

[18]Strunk *SR*, 317; *Dialogo della musica antica, et della moderna* (1581), 89.

Yet Campion himself used some word-painting in all his song books. How can we account for this apparent inconsistency? One point worth noting is that Campion often uses word-painting for a comic or ironic effect. When Josquin des Pres, in his great mass *Hercules dux Ferrariae*, sets the words "ascendit" and "caelum" to rising musical passages, he is seriously – and effectively – conveying the idea of an ascent to heaven (Ex. 5.1).[19]

Et   a-   scen-dit   in   cae- lum

Ex. 5.1, "et ascendit"

Thomas Morley expresses long-recognized rules on this issue when he writes, in 1597, that "you must have a care that when your matter signifieth 'ascending,' 'high,' 'heaven,' and such like you make your music ascend . . . for . . . it will be thought a great absurdity to talk of heaven and point downwards to the earth. . . ."[20] (Galilei, of course, thought it absurd to *depict* an ascension at all.) Among the madrigalists, word-painting is a playful but aesthetically legitimate device; its effect is serio-ludic, not self-subverting. For Campion, however, word-painting – which he finds "childish" and "ridiculous" – often allows for ironic commentary on the text. In "Faire, if you expect admiring" (BA/11), for example, the words "Ile bury my desires," in the first stanza, are set to a descending passage; in the next stanza, the corresponding text is "I'le flie to her againe" (Ex. 5.2).

[1] Ile   bury my   desires
[2] I'le   flie to her againe

Ex. 5.2, "Ile bury"

At first, Campion plays the word-painting game by the rules: "burial" is suggested by the lowering vocal line. But when the same rapidly descending notes carry the words "I'le fly to her againe," the music depicts not only the

---

[19]*Werken van Josquin des Pres*, ed. A. Smijers, 5 vols. and a Supplement (Amsterdam: Vereniging voor nederlandse Musickgeschidenis, 1922-69) 2:27.

[20]*Plain and Easy Introduction*, 291.

speaker's "flight" (in the quickened surface rhythm) but also his self-debasing behavior in continuing to pursue the unyielding "Faire."

A more humorous use of word-painting occurs in "Mistris, since you so much desire" (BA/16). The "place of Cupids fire" does not, according to the speaker, reside in the woman's breast, lips, or cheeks, "but a little higher," in her eyes (Ex. 5.3).

Ex. 5.3, "but a little higher"

Campion's male speakers (some of his female speakers, too) tend to be openly sensual when expressing their desire, so it comes as something of a shock to read, in the lines concluding this poem,

Those eyes I strive not to enjoy,
For they have power to destroy;
Nor woe I for a smile, or kisse,
So meanely triumph's not my blisse;
But a little higher, but a little higher,
I climbe to crowne my chast desire.

Yet the word-painting on "But a little higher" should put us on our guard. If "such childish observing of words is altogether ridiculous," perhaps Campion feels that the sentiments expressed by the speaker are also, in a way, childish and ridiculous. Certainly Campion's own parody of this song, "Beauty, since you so much desire" (4/22), which uses the same ascending passage for the words "But a little higher," has nothing to do with "chast desire":

Beauty, since you so much desire
To know the place of *Cupids* fire:
About you somewhere doth it rest,
Yet never harbour'd in your brest,
Nor gout-like in your heele or toe:
What foole would seeke Loves flame so low?
But a little higher, but a little higher,
There, there, ô there lyes *Cupids* fire.

Thinke not, when *Cupid* most you scorne,
Men judge that you of Ice were borne;
For, though you cast love at your heele,
His fury yet sometime you feele;
And where-abouts if you would know,
I tell you still, not in your toe:
But a little higher, but a little higher,
There, there, ô there lyes *Cupids* fire.

After "I tell you still, not in your toe," the repeated, provocatively rising phrase "But a little higher" turns distinctly bawdy. The parody realizes the potential comedy in the word-painting of the original.[21]

The lute parts of the two versions, incidentally, differ sharply in these parallel passages. The earlier version presents three distinct voices, each with

---

[21]See also "Sweet, exclude mee not" (2/11), which uses similar word-painting, also for comic effect, on the words "yet a little more."

a separate motive repeated in sequence (and interacting with the rising sequence in the vocal line); the later version is chordal. In "Mistris," the busy accompaniment necessitates substantial pauses between the sung phrases to allow the sequence to work itself out. For this section of the piece, at least, I suspect that Rosseter not only composed the accompaniment but also altered the vocal part. Campion's disapproving words about "Manie rests in Musicke" (in the preface to *A Booke of Ayres*), though directed chiefly against madrigals and other "songs of many parts," seem apt here. The later song, "Beauty," separates the phrases with mere quarter rests. I think Rosseter, in "Mistris," has tried to elevate Campion's song – perhaps taking it more seriously than the author himself did – by introducing the active polyphony that informs this passage. "Beauty," surely the work of Campion alone, serves as a satirical gloss on the text while stripping away the intricate part-writing in the accompaniment.

Other revisions of works that appeared originally in *A Booke of Ayres* also suggest that Campion had mixed feelings about his own use of word-painting. The opening measures of "Follow your Saint" are instructive (BA/10, Ex. 5.4).

Ex. 5.4, "Follow your Saint"

The link between the first line and its music is subtle; the music does not actually depict "following" through, say, some kind of motivic imitation (as in "Followe thy faire sunne," discussed below). Yet the ascending bass line and the falling voice part move toward the same point of convergence; the listener, guided by the text, associates this contrary motion with "following," since one voice moves with, and thus seems to follow, the other. The second line ("Haste you, sad noates, fall at her flying feete"), set to the same music, is another matter. Here the music actually consists of hastening notes in the bass and falling notes in the treble; both parts sound "sad" because of the flattened third. When Campion reused this opening in "Love me or not" (4/10), he preserved – in the first stanza, at least – the effect brought about by the word *follow* (now coming after the first measure) but dispensed altogether with the madrigalian effect of "Haste you, sad noates" (Ex. 5.5).

Ex. 5.5, "Love me or not"

Another example of a setting used to accommodate two texts presents itself in "Followe thy faire sunne" (BA/4) and its devotional counterpart, "Seeke the Lord" (1/18). The earlier setting uses word-painting most obviously in two places, first on a rising chromatic passage in the voice, then in an ascending sequence of three falling thirds sung over a rising chromatic line in the bass (Ex. 5.6).

Ex. 5.6, "and she made all of light"

For the first two stanzas, the sung chromatic passage illustrates the words it bears. The line "and she made all of light" works musically through the association of darkness with low notes and brightness with high ones; thus the climax at the word "light" finds a parallel in the high d″. The ascent to this note (the highest in the piece) also serves to depict, in the next stanza, the placing of the loved one in heaven.

In the final lines of the first two stanzas – both beginning with the words "Yet follow" – the music conjures up the notion of following in two ways. First, the vocal part presents three falling thirds, one "following" another in an ascending sequence (see asterisks); second, the chromatic passage in the bass "follows" the one in the voice part. In both cases we have literal following, much as we had literal hastening sad notes in "Follow your Saint."

We might expect a different approach in "Seeke the Lord" – the text of which obliquely criticizes the vain sentiments in "Followe thy faire sunne" – and to some extent we get one. For the chromatic vocal passage, Campion again makes use of the rising line to set "For his steep hill is high" in the first stanza (Ex. 5.7).

Ex. 5.7, "For his steep hill"

The steady climb by half-steps offers, perhaps, an even more vivid picture than that presented by "And she in heaven is plac't." The second stanza of the later song, however, uses subtler devices to express the text. The line "Such sights thy soule shall see," while lifting us aloft, exploits the chromaticism to suggest the wonder of the celestial vision; and although the music rises at this point, it does not illustrate the words at hand: it complements them with an ascent that recalls earlier phrases ("As Eagles flye," "his steep hill is high," "gaine the top").

The music for the final line of the first stanza in each poem uses wordpainting. In "Followe," as we have seen, the music depicts literal following; in "Seeke," the word "top" comes almost at the highest note in the piece (aptly reserved for "triumph"), and the rising sequence of falling thirds illustrates striving well. So, although Campion condemned word-painting –

sometimes revising his songs to eliminate it, sometimes employing it as a comic device – he could also use it effectively in serious songs, as in "Seeke the Lord." The songbooks provide further examples. In "My sweetest Lesbia" (BA/1), "Shall I come, sweet Love" (3/17), and "Leave prolonging" (4/1), Campion has used long notes on words conveying an idea of temporal length – "ever-during," "long," "prolonging" (Ex. 5.8).

Ex. 5.8, "one ever-during night," "Tell the long, long houres," "Leave prolonging"

In one instance, Campion has even inserted word-painting into a revision of an earlier piece; "Lift up to heav'n, sad wretch" (1/12), based on "The Sypres curten of the night" (BA/9), changes the first measure of the earlier version, consisting of three repeated notes, so that it rises steeply, as if lifting itself heavenward (Ex. 5.9). Other instances of word-painting occur in the five books of ayres, and it is only natural to puzzle over Campion's intentions.

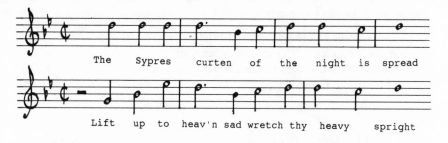

Ex. 5.9, "The Sypres curten" and "Lift up to heav'n"

The problem Campion constantly faced was that he, like other neo-classicists of the Renaissance, had inherited a set of linguistic and musical conventions (and basic building materials) deriving ultimately from nonclassical sources – usually from the despised Middle Ages. Lyric poetry in the vernacular overwhelmingly required rhyme; secular love songs made generous use of advanced counterpoint and of word-painting. Campion was not an antique Roman. He could hardly abandon elements that in large part defined contemporary music and poetry, however much he might berate such elements in his more contentious moods.

Yet musical humanists on the continent had already found two techniques – one based on poetic meter, the other on dramatic expression – for classicizing music in modern times. Campion tried both methods himself. His first overt foray into musical-humanist experimentation, "Come, let us sound," which concludes his half of A Booke of Ayres, is his only attempt at musique mesurée. This "song in Saphicke verse" – the one ayre of the type written by the "Greekes and Latines" (as Campion writes in his preface) – praises "th'omnipotent creator." Like Baïf, who used classical meters to translate the psalms into French, Campion wrote a poem in English Sapphics that is psalmlike in theme and language;[22] the music follows the supposed long and short syllables with half-notes and quarters. It may at first seem perverse for Campion to have chosen the Sapphic meter – with its origin in Pagan secular verse – as a vehicle to carry a text praising the Judeo-Christian deity. Yet Sapphics had been used for hymns throughout much of the Middle Ages, and a number of Renaissance poets believed that the Hebrew psalms had been written according to some quantitative scheme.[23] In the Observations, Campion draws on various traditions – neo-Platonic and Biblical (or pseudo-Biblical) – when he writes "The world is made by Simmetry and proportion, and is in that respect compared to Musick, and Musick to Poetry. . ." (Works, 293). But for Campion, most contemporary poems ("vulgar and easie" rhymes) lack proportion: "What musick can there be," he asks, "when there is no proportion observed?" (293). So Campion's choice of quantitative Sapphics can have cosmic implications, and indeed "Come, let us sound" begins with a stanza reminding us of God's own musical accomplishments:

Come, let us sound with melody the praises
Of the kings king, th'omnipotent creator,
Author of number, that hath all the world in
Harmonie framed.

[22]Davis has in fact called the poem a "free paraphrase of Psalm 19, Coeli Enarrant" (Works, 48, n. 42).

[23]See, for example, Israel Baroway, "The Hebrew Hexameter: A Study in Renaissance Sources and Interpretation," English Literary History 2 (1935): 66-91.

We are to sing praises to God (much as Pontus de Tyard's muses do)[24] in carefully measured verses set to carefully measured music; the perfection of God's harmonic universe should be echoed in both the poetic and the musical meter. Campion's poem and setting subtly bring together Plato's *Timaeus,* the Apocryphal Book of Wisdom (11:20), Augustine's *De musica,* Boethius' *De institutione musica,* and countless other works indebted to these authorities.[25] Christopher R. Wilson has observed, moreover, that Campion's melody in "Come, let us sound" often follows the general movement of Mauduit's "Ode à la reyne," published as a lute-song in 1614 (Ex. 5.10).[26]

Soit que l'oeil pourveu de nou- vel- le clairté

Come, let us sound with me- lo- dy the praises

Ex. 5.10, "Soit que" and "Come, let us sound"

We do not know if either Campion or Mauduit was familiar with the other's work, but the similarities between the two settings tempt one to suspect some influence one way or the other.[27]

---

[24]*Oeuvres: Solitaire premier,* ed. Silvio Baridon (Geneva: Droz, 1950), 48-49, discussed in chap. 1.

[25]Seth Weiner, in "Spenser's Study of English Syllables and Its Completion by Thomas Campion," *Spenser Studies* 3 (1982): 3-56, gives a fascinating account of the possible implications behind Campion's experiments in quantitative verse (esp. 34-48), though I am not wholly persuaded by his numerological interpretation of "Rose-cheekt Lawra."

[26]"Words and Notes Coupled Lovingly Together," 76-78. Wilson feels that the similarities between Campion's piece and Mauduit's demonstrate "a lateral exchange of ideas," but he adds that Campion's setting "measured verse to music cannot be attributed solely to French influences" (78). For Mauduit's piece, see Gabriel Bataille, *Airs de differents autheurs . . . Cinquiesme livre* (1614; Geneva: Minkoff, 1980), fols. 52v-53. For a modern edition, see André Verchaly, ed., *Airs de cour pour voix et luth (1603-1643)* (Paris: Société française de musicologie, 1961), 78-79.

[27]Already in 1546, Alonso Mudarra published "quantitative" settings of Latin verse for vihuela and voice; he arranged Hofhaimer's homorhythmic setting of Horace's "Beatus ille" and offered a setting, apparently his own, of Ovid's "Hanc tua Penelope" (which scans the the first two hexameters correctly but forces the next two less successfully into the same music). See *Tres libros de música en cifra para vihuela,* ed. and transcr. Emilio Pujol, (Barcelona: Instituto espagñol de musicologia, 1949), 108-9. Nevertheless, such "quantitative" settings were uncommon among composers of lute-songs, and the similarities between Campion's song and Mauduit's seem too close for coincidence.

Around 1613, Campion brought out *Two Bookes of Ayres*.[28] In the preface
"To the Reader," he tells us that the songs were "long since composed" and
fall into two distinct categories: "The first are grave and pious; the second,
amorous and light." Like French and Italian musical humanists, Campion
tries to establish a link between modern song and ancient lyric (as we have
seen, he again compares his ayres to epigrams); but he does not feel wholly
satisfied with the new music from Italy and France:

> some there are who admit onely *French* or *Italian* Ayres, as if every
> Country had not his proper Ayre, which the people thereof naturally
> usurpe in their Musicke. . . . In these *English* Ayres, I have chiefly
> aymed to couple my Words and Notes lovingly together, which
> will be much for him to doe that hath not power over both. (*Works*,
> 55)

In the songs presented in *Two Bookes of Ayres* and the next collection, *The
Third and Fourth Booke of Ayres* (c. 1618),[29] we find Campion experimenting
with various native musical idioms (borrowed from folk song, the Protestant
hymn, and other strophic forms) in an attempt to find England's "proper
Ayre." French and Italian elements sometimes appear. But simplicity –
melodic, rhythmic, and harmonic – is the most important recurring characteristic of his last four books of ayres.

The simplicity of certain "grave and pious" songs in *The First Booke*, like
"The man of life upright" (1/2), may owe something to Protestant hymnody;
the rests used to separate short phrases in Campion's song, for example, are
an earmark of the hymn. The simple melody of "To Musick bent is my
retyred minde" (1/7) reinforces the message of the text: the "vaine joyes"
of a "song of pleasure" give the speaker "no comfort," so he turns to "heav'nly
thoughts." The spare music required by the text, which deprecates "earthly
pompe" (intricate songs fall into this category), probably has at least a faint
connection with humanism, in that the straightforward approach to text-
setting used in the Protestant hymn owes some of its method to the humanist
settings of classical odes.

Campion uses a deliberately naïve style to open "Tune thy Musicke to
thy hart" (1/8). On the whole, the words express disdain for artifice in
devotional songs, and the naïve setting springs naturally from the words. Yet
when the second half of the song begins with a rising chromatic passage,
artifice rears its head (Ex. 5.11). The text offers a key to understanding
Campion's use of chromaticism here: "Though Devotion needs not Art, /
Sometime of the poore the rich may borrow." That is, just as the wealthy
may sometimes borrow from those poorer than themselves, so the devout

---

[28]For dating, see *Works*, 52.

[29]For dating, see *Works*, 128.

(spiritually wealthy) may wish to add "Art" (music and poetry) when offering love and praise to God, though art in itself is a "poor" and unnecessary adjunct to love and devotion. The a-natural, the first note to distinguish the rising line as chromatic, appears on the word "Art" – an appropriate joining of text and tone, since the chromaticism is patently more "artificial" (to use the Elizabethan term) than the music preceding it. Campion has used subtle word-painting here; it differs from that in, say, "Seeke the Lord," where the rising chromatic line depicts a steep hill. The desire to couple words and notes together is clear enough in "Tune thy Musicke," but the technique Campion uses to express the text does not depend on madrigalian pictorialism.

Ex. 5.11, "Though devotion"

In "*Jacke* and *Jone*" (1/20), the naïve music is again a response to the text, which castigates the "Courtly Dames and Knights" for their dissembling tongues and "strange delights" while praising the simple life of the "Silly swaine." (In Rosseter's book, Campion had also used a simple setting for "I care not for these Ladies" [BA/3], a text about rural pleasures in the "country

matters" vein.)[30] In the later song books, Campion often plays with the naïve
style for comic effect. The young man in "Pin'd I am, and like to die" (2/14),
for example, opens his plaint with a childishly simple melody (Ex. 5.12).

Ex. 5.12, "Pin'd I am"

Hearing more of his troubles ("If I musing sit or stand, / Some puts it daily
in my hand, / To interrupt my Muse"; "If I sleepe, it seemes to be / Oft
playing in the bed with me"), we understand why Campion has chosen the
ingenuous music. A more complex opening would suggest a more experi-
enced speaker – one like the speaker in Campion's Latin poem "In se" (*Works*,
442-43), a man who with some amusement recalls his alarm when, much
younger, he contemplated his erect penis.

The naïve openings can also deceive us. "Maydes are simple, some men
say" (3/4) – which, like "Young and simple though I am" (4/9), stresses
the word "simple" in the first line – has a fairly artless beginning. But the
speaker is no fool, as we learn soon enough:

> Maydes are simple, some men say:
> They, forsooth, will trust no men.
> But, should they mens wils obey,
> Maides were very simple then.

Her knowledge of the world reveals itself, musically, at the word "obey,"
which carries an unexpected melisma (Ex. 5.13). Flourishes of this kind
appear rarely in Campion's songs,[31] and a florid passage in an otherwise spare

---

[30]See also "Ev'ry Dame affects good fame" (4/5), a simple song stating that "a simple look
is best."

[31]David Lindley, in *Thomas Campion*, has discussed ornamented versions of Campion's
songs preserved in seventeenth-century manuscripts; he feels that these florid versions might
represent a performance style that Campion would have expected (66-72). In "What harvest

song attracts our attention. In demonstrating the singer's skill, the melisma suggests that the woman, who may at first blush seem an untutored youth, is in fact quite "skillful" in the world's false forgeries and will not simply obey men's wills.

But   should they   mens   wils   o-   bey, Maides were very   simple   then.

Ex. 5.13, "But should they"

Campion employed a number of other simple but effective devices for coupling words and notes together. In "Faire, if you expect admiring" (BA/11), the suspended syntax of the opening clauses is matched by the static harmony, which rarely strays from G major; the main clause – "Grace, deere love" – is set apart from the preceding subordinate clauses by the new harmony, by the homorhythmic texture, and by the slower surface rhythm (Ex. 5.14).

Ex. 5.14, "Faire if you expect"

---

halfe so sweet is" (2/10), Campion himself added some ornaments to the original melody, which appeared in "Turne backe, you wanton flyer" (BA/7). Nevertheless, written-in melismas are rare in Campion's melodies and occur mainly at final cadences.

Using these changes in harmony, texture, melody, and rhythm, Campion highlights each of the main clauses in the first section of the setting: *"flie both love* and loves delighting," *"Yield reliefe* by your relenting," *"Helpe to ease* my long lamenting"* (my italics). As author of both lyrics and music, Campion could bring about a pleasing correspondence between the two and maintain the correspondence, as in this instance, throughout the song. Here he has graced the "emphaticall" words of the main clause without resorting to word-painting.

Just as Campion sometimes uses word-painting for comic purposes, so he employs other devices to raise smiles. "If any hath the heart to kill" (4/21), a song about impotence, uses a leap from c″ to f″ – with the f″ slightly lengthened – to stress a key word in the penultimate line of each stanza (Ex. 5.15).

Ex. 5.15, "Yet none alive"

The third stanza, which clarifies the speaker's predicament, slyly places the word "hand" at the salient f″ through a nice chiasmus:

> A Love I had, so fayre, so sweet,
>   As ever wanton eye did see.
> Once by appointment wee did meete;
>   Shee would, but ah, it would not be:
>   She gave her heart, her hand shee gave;
>   All did I give, shee nought could have.

In the first two stanzas, the leap to f″ seems a serious example of rhetorical *exclamatio*. And Campion could use such devices seriously: the beginning of "O Love, where are thy Shafts" (4/13) employs two leaps of a fourth to signify the speaker's indignant outcries (Ex. 5.16). But "If any hath the heart" is one of the "vaine Ditties" at the end of Campion's last book of ayres that we are cautioned about in the preface "To the Reader" (168). Its text conceals the cause of the speaker's distress until the third stanza, at which point the earlier exclamations become retroactively comic as the "vaine" nature of the song exposes itself.

O   Love,   where   are   thy   shafts

Ex. 5.16, "O Love, where are thy Shafts"

John Hollander has written that Campion "never responded to the influence of the new Italian *stilo recitativo* like Alfonso Ferrabosco, or developed
an insistent and personal chromaticism, like John Daniel. . . ."[32] Surely
Hollander has overstated his case. Several of Campion's songs do, in fact,
reveal the influence of Italian monody, and his later songs use chromaticism
expressively. Indeed, Campion sought for a style answerable to what the
composers in France and Italy had developed, and to a degree he succeeded.
We should not forget that Campion was professionally a doctor, not a
composer. His musical talent, though impressive in an amateur, was decidedly
limited, and his attempts to Anglicize monody could be clumsy. Nevertheless,
he did respond to Italy's *nuove musiche*.

The presence of declamatory passages – which occur in lute-songs (and
other genres) throughout the sixteenth century – does not in itself constitute
a link with the Italian monodists. Already in the simple, strophic songs
known as *frottole*, which Francesco Bossinensis arranged for lute and voice
in 1509 and 1511 (they are the earliest printed lute-songs), we can find
passages in which notes in the voice part are repeated for declamatory effect.[33]
If this seems to foreshadow later monody, another aspect of the frottola does
not: for the frottolists rarely had as their goal the profound musical expression
of the text being set; at times, they appear perversely indifferent to correspondences between words and music.[34] A closer analogue to later monodic
experiments presents itself in the songs for vihuela, the guitar-shaped counterpart to the lute in Spain. In Alonso Mudarra's *Tres libros de musica en cifras
para vihuela* (Seville, 1546), a setting of "Dulces exuviae" (*Aeneid* 4.651-65)
– beginning with Dido's last words, often set in the Renaissance – has a

---

[32]*Vision and Resonance: Two Senses of Poetic Form* (New York: Oxford University Press,
1975), 73.

[33]See, for example, in the *Tenori e contrabassi . . . Libro primo* (1509; Geneva: Minkoff,
1977), "Accio chel tempo" (IIII) and "Io cercho pur la insupportabil doglia" (XVIv). Einstein
has used the term "pseudo-monody" to describe the frottola and other similar arrangements of
songs; see *The Italian Madrigal*, trans. Alexander Krappe, Roger Sessions, and Oliver Strunk, 3
vols. (1949; Princeton: Princeton University Press, 1971) 2:836-43.

[34]Einstein has even argued that there is "a contradiction in the frottola between the text
content and music. It really is a contradiction, not merely an indifference toward the text" (*The
Italian Madrigal* 1:79).

striking declamatory conclusion that seems to anticipate by several decades
the early attempts by the Florentine Camerata to capture the sprit of antique
song (Ex. 5.17).[35]

Ex. 5.17, Mudarra, "Dixerat atque"

(That Mudarra has set a classical Latin text in this way is surely significant;
Niger's settings of epic Latin hexameters were also declamatory, with single
pitches being frequently repeated.) And the native English tradition could
also have afforded Campion an immediate source for the declamation and
other rhetorical devices found in his ayres; the consort song, especially when
a lament, favored dramatic, expressive writing. To say (as some have done)
about a song like "Breake now my heart and dye" (3/10) that "in style and
pathos it is comparable with Monteverdi recitative"[36] is to misrepresent both
Campion and Monteverdi. With its steady rhythm and its sharply stylized
moans, the song has more in common with Cara's frottola "Oime il cor
oime la testa"[37] than with Monteverdi's rhythmically flexible recitatives (Exx.
5.18 and 5.19). The declamatory opening of "See where she flies" (BA/13)
and the pathetic yearning in "Author of light" (1/1) may well owe nothing
to Italian monody. And why should they? As Campion tells us in prefatory
remarks to the volumes published around 1613 and 1618, most of the songs
printed in those books had been composed long before their publication and
probably long before Italian monody had had a significant impact on England.
But some songs were written later, and some can even be roughly dated.
"All lookes be pale," the last song in The First Booke of Ayres, shows decided
traces of the new style. And we know that Campion composed this no earlier
than 1612, for it laments the death of Henry, Prince of Wales, who died in
that year (Ex. 5.20).

[35]Tres libros de música en cifra para vihuela, 107-08; I have removed notes added by Pujol.
[36]Lowbury et al., 163-64.
[37]Bossinensis, Tenori e contrabassi (1509), 32.

Ex. 5.18, Cara, "Oime il cor."

Ex. 5.19, "Breake now my heart"

(*Continued,* next page)

Ex. 5.19, "Breake now my heart" *(continued)*

teares must   be.

Ex. 5.20, "All lookes"

At the beginning of the piece, the voice sings an angular melody over slow-moving, simple chords. After a dramatic pause, the singer explains why all looks are to be pale: "For *Hally* now is dead and gone." Here, the emotional agitation implicit in the text is paralleled by the increased speed of the sung notes, which have a jagged shape appropriate to the impassioned text. Campion sweetens the word *sweet* with a melisma, makes the words "all the earth" declamatory by placing them on the same pitch (a'), and stresses the word *late* by having the voice leap a minor sixth to reach it. The setting of "ev'ry eye" – with its quarter rest followed by two rapidly sung d″s and a long f″ – reminds one of many similar passages in Italian monodies. Nicholas Lanier (1588-1666) also used such phrases in the song "Bring away this sacred Tree," which he composed for (and sang in) Campion's masque for the Earl of Somerset, performed in 1613.[38] The next section of "All lookes" (mm. 10-12), with its thrice-repeated phrase "weepe with me," inspires Campion to use a rising chromatic line interspersed with dramatic pauses.

"All lookes be pale," then, contains several earmarks of Italian monody: declamatory and angular melodies, abrupt shifts in rhythm, chordal accompaniment, and expressive use of chromaticism. It is appropriate that Campion employed Italianate devices in his eulogy to Henry, around whom there had gathered a number of musicians and poets instrumental in bringing continental neoclassicism to England. Already in 1607, James Cleland described Henry's household as an "academy":

> Without offence to either of the famous *Universities* here, or our *Colledges* in Scotland, for all sort of good learning, I recommend in particular the *Academie* of our Noble Prince, where young Nobles

[38]Davis, 278. Ian Spink, in his article on Lanier in *New Grove*, writes that "Lanier composed the music for Ben Jonson's masque *Lovers Made Men* (1617) and in doing so was described by Jonson in the printed text of 1640 as introducing *stilo recitativo* into England; in the absence of the music this claim must be accepted guardedly." Clearly Lanier was regarded by his contemporaries as a member of the avant-garde. See McDonald Emslie, "Nicholas Lanier's Innovations in English Song," *Music and Letters* 41 (1960): 13-27.

may learne the first elements to be a *Privie Counseller,* a *Generall* of
an Armie, to rule in peace, & to commande in warre. . . . The nine
Sisters hearing of our ninth Prince Henry accompained [sic] with
his nine *right honorable nobles* left the waters of *Aganippe* to come
here riding upon their *Pegasus,* who with his hoofe hath made a
nother *Hyprocrene* to spring in the midst of his Court. Here are they
making so sweet & harmonious musick at the name of nine, that
Phrix and *Mysius* would daunce to heare them.[39]

Cleland's "harmonious musick," however, is only a metaphor for intelligent
conversation; indeed, although Cleland praises dancing – good exercise – as
a suitable pastime for a young nobleman, he says nothing about music.
Apparently it lacks the utility that Cleland seeks in all amusements. (He
recommends, as light but worthwhile reading, Castiglione's *Cortegiano;* the
young nobleman who has not yet mastered Italian, however, need not despair
– *"Mr. Cleark* hath translated him into verie pure latine" [153].)

Henry himself enjoyed dancing and took part, as a dancer, in Jonson's
Hymenaei (1606).[40] In 1610-12, he counted among the musicians in his
household the Italian Angelo Notari,[41] whose *Prime musiche nuove* (1613)
contains various types of Italian song popular at the beginning of the seventeenth century. The monodies among them use all the standard devices
discussed earlier: expressive chromaticism, declamatory repetitions of one
note, impassioned angular melodies. Campion surely was familiar with
Notari's music and perhaps with Notari himself.

In 1613, Campion collaborated with John Coprario on a book of *Songs
of Mourning* for Prince Henry. Campion wrote the lyrics, Coprario the music.
In the "Elegie upon the untimely death of Prince *Henry,*" preceding the
songs, Campion comments knowingly on Henry's love of music:

To [Henry's] eternall peace wee offer now
Guifts which hee lov'd, and fed: Musicks that flow
Out of a sowre and melancholike vayne,
Which best sort with the sorrowes wee sustaine. (*Works,* 119)

Coprario, who eventually worked for Prince Charles, may have tutored
Henry in music, though no contemporary evidence exists to prove this.[42] As

---

[39]*Hērō-paideia, or the Institution of a Young Noble Man* (Oxford, 1607), 35-37.

[40]Elkin Wilson, *Prince Henry and English Literature* (Ithaca, New York: Cornell University
Press, 1946), 42.

[41]David Price, *Patrons and Musicians of the English Renaissance* (Cambridge: Cambridge
University Press, 1981), 225. In the document given in Price, Notari is referred to simply as
"Signor Angelo." See also Ian Spink's article on Notari in *New Grove* and Roy Strong's *Henry,
Prince of Wales and England's Lost Renaissance* (New York: Thames and Hudson, 1986), 173.

[42]Davis, in *Works,* asserts that Coprario taught music to Prince Henry (114). Christopher
Field, however, points out that "Hawkins [in the eighteenth century] set down the tradition

one might expect from a composer who changed his name from Cooper to Coprario, some of the *Songs of Mourning* betray the influence of Italian monody. The chordal lute-accompaniments are like written-out continuo parts.[43] "O Griefe," the first song in the collection, is especially monodic.[44] Indeed, parts of "O, Griefe" seem to echo phrases in Caccini's "Amarilli, mia bella," well known in England by 1612 (Ex. 5.21).

O Griefe, how di-vers   wherein men languish

A- ma-   ril-li mia   e se ti- mor t'assale

Ex. 5.21, "O Griefe" and "Amarilli mia"

Since Campion published his own songs around the time when the *Songs of Mourning* saw print, we can assume that he respected Coprario musically and perhaps recognized his colleague's superior ability to compose emotionally profound music. They collaborated twice more in 1613; on both occasions, Campion wrote masques to which Coprario contributed music.[45]

In the second of the *Two Bookes* published around 1613, Campion wrote generally in a light vein; but again, the last song of the collection, "Where shall I refuge seeke" (2/21), contains moments of Italianate pathos. The musical phrases are longer than those of the other songs in the collection.

---

that [Coprario] 'taught music to the children of James the First.'" Field himself says nothing about Henry's putative studies with Coprario ("John Coprario," *New Grove*).

[43]In Robert Dowland's *Musicall Banquet* (1610), two of Caccini's songs appeared with a written-out continuo part in tablature. See Joan Myers, "Caccini-Dowland: Monody Realized," *Journal of the Lute Society of America* 3 (1970): 22-34. Other English lute-parts from the early seventeenth century seem little more than worked out continuo parts. See, for example, the accompaniment to the anonymous, but very monodic, setting of Donne's "The Expiration" in André Souris, ed., *Poèmes de Donne, Herbert et Crashaw mis en musique par leurs contemporains* (Paris: CNRS, 1961), 10-11; or the accompaniment to Nicholas Lanier's setting of Campion's poem "Bring away this sacred Tree" (transcribed in *Works*, 278).

[44]Nigel Fortune oddly denies the Italianate element in Coprario's songs: "The songs of Coperario are sometimes said to be Italianate . . . but they are nothing of the kind, although some of them do foreshadow the continuo-songs of the next generation of English composers" ("Solo Song and Cantata," *The Age of Humanism*, ed. Gerald Abraham, The New Oxford History of Music 4 [London: Oxford University Press, 1968], 211).

[45]Coprario contributed at least one piece to *The Lords' Masque* (see Davis' introductory note in *Works*, 233) and three songs to the *Somerset Masque* (*Works*, 280-83).

Particularly striking is the repeated section at the end, which begins with
declamatory repeated notes and uses chromaticism and dramatic pauses
expressively; though stiff beside a comparable passage from Caccini's
"Amarilli mia bella," Campion's writing evinces a clear debt to Italy here
(Exx. 5.22 and 5.23).[46]

Ex. 5.22, "O bitter griefe,"

[46]Caccini, *Le nuove musiche*, ed. H. Wiley Hitchcock (Madison, Wi.: A-R Editions, 1970),
86-87; I have omitted Hitchcock's editorial additions.

Ex. 5.23, Caccini, "Amarilli"

The *Third Booke* (c. 1618) opens with one of Campion's most moving
songs, "Oft have I sigh'd." Here, too, we find many of the expressive devices
discussed in connection with the previous song. Suspensions often "exasperate
the harmony," to use Morley's words.[47] At one point, Campion emphasizes
the "languishing" mentioned in the text with nearly Florentine skill
(Ex. 5.24).

Ex. 5.24, "Oh yet I languish"

[47]*A Plain and Easy Introduction*, 290.

Ex. 5.24, "Oh yet I languish" *(continued)*

The slide on the word "Oh," appearing off the beat and after a chord, and the other rapid notes sung off the beat all have antecedents in Italian monody. The chromatic descent from d″ to a′ – interrupted by "sighing" pauses – emphasizes the drooping languishment of the singer, and the repeated notes add a dramatic element to this already-monodic section of the piece.

Other examples of declamatory writing – from the speechlike passages in "O sweet delight" (3/21) to the exclaimed high notes on the words "Ile die" in "Leave prolonging" (4/1) – appear with modest regularity in the five books of Campion's ayres. Like the monodists, moreover, Campion focused on the outer voices of his songs and strove to make his text intelligible.[48] So in various ways, the characteristic features of Italian monody crop up in Campion's music. It is what we would expect from a confirmed neoclassicist who no doubt followed the activity of like-minded musicians and poets abroad. Already in his earliest published ayres, he revealed an interest in "quantitative" settings of naturalized neoclassical verse. But despite his evident interest in the experiments of the continental musical humanists, he mostly used other methods for setting texts, trying to find England's "proper Ayre." Native folk songs (and art songs) have shaped some of Campion's melodies. Yet the simplicity that often marks his ayres has deeper implications than one might at first suspect. With their chordal accompaniments and their straightforward vocal lines, the songs go against a tradition dedicated to complex polyphonic structures, a tradition best represented (in the lute-song

[48]In his treatise on composition, *A New Way of Making Fowre Parts in Counter-point* (c. 1613), Campion reduces some of his songs to mere trebles and basses; see *Works*, 345, 346, 352. A number of manuscripts from Campion's time exist in which lute-songs have been simplified as two-part pieces for voice and bass viol. Ulrich Olshausen discusses these (regarding them as arrangements made by unskilled amateurs) in "Das lautenbegleitete Sololied in England um 1600," diss., Johann Wolfgang Goethe-Universität, Frankfurt am Main, 1963, 24-26. He also suggests that such works are an important link between Elizabethan and Jacobean music and later works with continuo accompaniment (26).

repertoire) by John Daniel's songs to the lute. Campion publicly attacked word-painting, while using it himself from time to time, and found other ways to grace those words he considered "emphaticall." Again, Campion sides with the sterner neoclassicists, and again John Daniel emerges as the chief "offender" among Campion's contemporaries. So far, we have examined Campion's ayres with little reference to other Elizabethan and Jacobean lute-songs; this can give only a dim idea of his accomplishment. The perfect foil to illuminate Campion's aesthetic goals – as must be clear by now – presents itself in the songs of John Daniel.

Chapter 6

John Daniel's Songs

I n *Two Bookes of Ayres*, Campion included arrangements of his lute-songs for two, three, and four voices; he tells us, in the preface to that volume, about the origin behind these arrangements:

> These Ayres were for the most part framed at first for one voyce with the Lute, or Violl, but, upon occasion, they have since beene filled with more parts, which who so please may use, who like not may leave. Yet doe wee daily observe, that when any shall sing a Treble to an Instrument, the standers by will be offring at an inward part out of their owne nature; and, true or false, out it must, though to the perverting of the whole harmonie.[1]

The pieces were conceived as ayres to the lute or viol, not as part songs. The multi-voiced versions, as Campion's petulant note informs us, are given to forestall the clumsy improvisations of "standers by." So the part songs, in general, owe their very existence to the lute-songs.

For much of the sixteenth century, however, the process worked in reverse: lute-songs usually derived from earlier pieces for several voices. The first collections of lute-songs – Francesco Bossinensis' two collections of *frottole* (Venice, 1509 and 1511), Arnolt Schlick's *Lieder* (Mainz, 1512), Pierre Attaingnant's *chansons* (Paris, 1529), Adrian Willaert's arrangements of Verdelot's madrigals (Venice, 1536) – all contain pieces originally for voices or for a single voice and accompanying instruments. This does not mean that an arrangement for larger forces always provides the model for an early lute-song; important frottolists like Tromboncino and Pesenti played the lute and must have conceived some of their pieces originally as songs for lute and voice.[2] Luys Milan's *El maestro* (1536), moreover, contains vihuela-songs that are clearly not just literal arrangements of pre-existing works for several voices. But songs in which the lute part is an intabulation of vocal parts abound in the sixteenth century. The publisher Pierre Phalèse, in *Hortus musarum* (1553), included arrangements not only of contrapuntally dense *chansons* by composers like Crequillon and Clemens non Papa but also of motets and mass movements by Josquin and other masters of polyphony.

---

[1]*Works* (cited chap. 4, n. 4), 55.

[2]See, for example, the highly idiomatic lute part to the anonymous "Se mai per maraveglia," in Bossinensis, *Tenori e contrabassi . . . Libro secundo* (1511; Geneva: Minkoff, 1982), fols. V^v-VI.

England's first collection of lute-songs appeared only at the end of the sixteenth century. It was worth the wait. John Dowland's *First Booke of Songes or Ayres* (1597), graced with commendatory Latin verses by Thomas Campion, remains a stunning achievement to this day; it provided the model and set the standard for later collections of English lute-songs. A virtuoso lutenist, Dowland wrote accompaniments that, though complicated, are wholly idiomatic to the lute; he also provided vocal parts for alto, tenor, and bass so that most of the pieces could be performed either as lute-songs or as part songs. In his later books, he continued to provide alternative vocal settings, some of which are successful enough to make us wonder whether the lute-songs or the part songs came first.[3] Since the manner in which the accompaniments use the resources of the instrument shows consummate skill, the lute-song versions are more likely to represent the original forms of the works. That we even wonder whether some of the four-voice versions came first, however, reminds us that many of Dowland's songs are contrapuntally intricate, the separate lines played on the lute having considerable independence.

Also in 1597, Thomas Morley brought out his *Canzonets or Little Short Aers to Five and Sixe Voices*. For the first seventeen pieces, he included intabulations of the lower voices so that the "Aers" could be performed as songs to the lute. The popularity of the lute-song had grown substantially by 1600, when Morley, admitting that he was "no professor thereof, but like a blind man groping for [his] way,"[4] published his *First Booke of Ayres*. We learn, from the preface "To the Reader," that he has "happened upon a method" – not revealed – for composing ayres to the lute. The results at times prove frustrating; for while the songs are uniformly exquisite, the accompaniments (obviously not written by a lutenist) often make unreasonable demands on the player. Although Morley ingeniously uses the resources of the lute, as in the arpeggiated accompaniment at the conclusion of *"Thirsis and Milla"* (nos. 2 and 3), the ever-active polyphony suggests that in these songs, Morley's goal is more to write contrapuntal works in the abstract than to compose ayres specifically suited to the lute. Consort songs and works for mixed voices would no doubt have served as his models in some pieces; for example, the introduction to "Who is it that this darke night" (no. 7), with its imitative polyphony, recalls numerous similar openings to consort songs.

The consort song seems also to have influenced the ayres of Michael Cavendish and Thomas Greaves, who sometimes write introductory passages for the lute alone – we recall that Campion, in his preface of 1601, deemed such passages inappropriate for the lute-song: "to clogg a light song with a

---

[3]Diana Poulton, in *John Dowland: His Life and Works*, rev. ed. (Berkeley: University of California Press, 1982), rightly feels that in most cases, the lute-songs came first (212).

[4]*First Booke*, sig. A2v.

long Praeludium, is to corrupt the nature of it" (*Works*, 15). Their accompaniments, unlike Morley's, reveal the composers' thorough familiarity with the lute. Greaves included songs "for the Viols and Voice" in his *Songes of Sundrie Kindes* (1604) and, like Cavendish in his *14. Ayres in Tabletorie* (1598), appended some madrigals to his collection.

Of all the Elizabethan and Jacobean lute-songs, John Daniel's *Songs for the Lute Viol and Voice* (1606) are the most skillful in their use of complex, imitative polyphony. They assimilate elements of the ayre, the dance, the consort song, and – perhaps most significant for us – the madrigal. I say "most significant" because, as we have seen, the madrigal had come under fire from extreme classicists in the latter years of the sixteenth century; it allowed counterpoint to garble the text and employed word-painting to picture forth individual words and phrases. Neither technique had a classical precedent; both had dubious connections with "modern" (to us, medieval or early Renaissance) practices. The typical English song, however, used an approach quite different from that used in the madrigal, as Joseph Kerman succinctly explains: "the madrigal proper attempts to illustrate the meaning of words point by point, along certain conventional lines developed by the Italian composers. The English song on the contrary is an abstract composition that obeys purely musical rather than literary dictates, and looks stylistically either to an ancient native tradition of strophic song, or to the established idioms of English Church music, which are more Netherlandish than Italian in orientation."[5]

Daniel sets the first piece in his collection, "Coy *Daphne* fled" (with a text perhaps by John Daniel himself),[6] largely in the abstract way that Kerman outlines above; the music for the first stanza serves also for the second – a situation not conducive to word-painting, since the musical figures used to illustrate the ideas in the first stanza are not likely to be appropriate in succeeding stanzas. Yet even in this relatively simple song, one finds examples of word-painting. The first line in each stanza contains the phrase "*Phoebus hot pursuite*," which finds a musical parallel in the running figure played on the lute (Ex. 6.1).[7] Near the end of the song, Daniel assigns a four-note motive (a) to the words "she rests transform'd"; there ensues a section of

---

[5]*The Elizabethan Madrigal* (New York: American Musicological Society, 1962), 12.

[6]Edward Doughtie, in *Lyrics from English Airs 1596-1622* (Cambridge: Harvard University Press, 1970), noting a pun on the word *Greene* in line 13, suggests that either Anne Grene, the dedicatee, or John Daniel "may have written two parts of the poem" (549).

[7]The examples included in my text are transcribed from the originals as given in the Scolar Press facsimile edition, intro. David Greer (Menston, 1970). Here and throughout, I have given just the lute and voice parts; the viol usually doubles the bass line played on the lute. For commentary on all of Daniel's songs, see David Scott, "John Danyel: His Life and Songs," *Lute Society Journal* 13 (1971): 7-17. David Lindley also offers some enlightening observations on Daniel in "John Danyel's 'Eyes Looke No More,'" *Lute Society Journal* 16 (1974): 9-16.

imitative polyphony based on this motive (Ex. 6.2), which is "transform'd" in two ways: it appears on different steps of the scale, and the last note does not always reiterate the first (see asterisks). We can, I think, safely regard this passage as an example of Daniel's subtler word-painting. Note, incidentally, that in this passage Daniel employs stretto (that is, he makes the motives overlap), a device more common in works like the consort song, the instrumental fantasy, and the madrigal than in the lute-song. Thus already in the first song of the collection, he reveals an interest in contrapuntal intricacy and in a pictorial approach to the text.

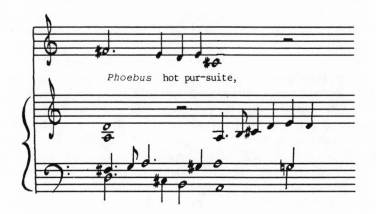

Ex. 6.1, "*Phoebus* hot pursuite"

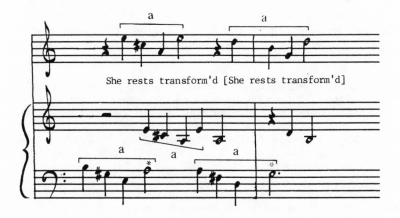

Ex. 6.2, "she rests transform'd"

The text of "Thou pretty Bird" (no. 2) is a translation of Guarini's "O come sei gentile," a poem later set by several madrigal composers, English and Italian.[8] Samuel Daniel, who met Guarini in Italy, might have translated the poem into English.[9] John Daniel's choice of text is apt, for in this piece, we have in effect a lute-song written as though it were a madrigal. Like most madrigals, this piece is through-composed. After a declamatory, homo-rhythmic opening, imitative polyphony (in varying degrees of complexity) pervades the piece; for example the words "Thou sing'st to her and so doe I addresse / My Musick to her eare that's mercilesse" play with a four-note motive (a) that passes from one voice to another in rapid succession (Ex. 6.3). Imitation, of course, appears in other lute-songs, especially in continental intabulations of vocal pieces. But such dense imitation – note again how often Daniel employs stretto – occurs in no other Elizabethan ayres. Near the end of the piece, Daniel employs an unmistakable madrigalism on the word *singing*. He repeats the word three times – repeated, the word calls attention to the singer's activity and naturally stresses the meaning of "singing" – in a lilting rhythm that plays with a similar motive in the accompaniment (Ex. 6.4). Playful syncopations like these run throughout the song. This short song, then, exhibits several madrigalian characteristics: Daniel uses imitation liberally, highlights the text with word-painting, and often shifts musical accents; these accentual shifts give his piece a rhythmic looseness characteristic of the madrigal.

Daniel's songs also imitate nonvocal models, such as those provided by dances and fantasies. And indeed in "He whose desires" (no. 3), with a text almost certainly by Samuel Daniel, the form is that of the galliard, a dance in ternary rhythm.[10] Though similar to other dance-songs, "He whose desires" differs from them in its occasional use of word-painting. In the last strain, for example, high notes in the voice and accompaniment parallel the words "high reaching," and David Scott rightly sees the sudden absence of the lute at the words "Rest alone" – leaving the voice on its own (and

---

[8]Orlando Gibbons set a translation of this text, "Dainty fine Bird" (no. 9), in his *First Set of Madrigals and Motets (1612)*, ed. Edmund Fellowes, rev. Thurston Dart (London: Stainer and Bell, 1964), 54-58; Thomas Vautor set a similar translation, "Dainty sweet bird" (no. 18), in his *Songs of Divers Airs and Natures (1619)*, ed. Edmund Fellowes, rev. Thurston Dart (London: Stainer and Bell, 1958) 154-65; and Claudio Monteverdi set the original Italian text in his *Settimo libro de madrigali* of 1619, in vol. 7 of *Tutte le opere*, ed. G. Francesco Malipiero, 16 vols. (1926-42; [Vienna]: Universal Edition, [1954]), 35-40.

[9]In the "Additional Notes" appended to David Scott's revision of Edmund Fellowes' edition of *John Danyel: Songs for the Lute, Viol and Voice (1606)* (London: Stainer and Bell, 1970), vi, Scott suggests Samuel Daniel as the possible author of this translation and of "Now the earth," the last text in the collection.

[10]See Appendix for the reasons behind my attributing the text of this to Samuel Daniel. For a perceptive discussion of Elizabethan dance songs, see Jorgens, *The Well-Tun'd Word* (cited chap. 5, n. 8), 127-69.

introducing musical rests) – as another instance of Daniel's pictorial approach to the text.[11] Unlike the dance-songs of Campion (some of which seem like galliards with the last strain lopped off), Daniel's song allows the lute to play without the voice for several beats in each strain. This reminds us again of the importance accorded to the accompaniments in Daniel's songs; the parts work together to form a contrapuntally intricate whole. For Campion, in contrast, the lute usually supplies chords to fill in the space between treble and bass. The different approaches, though partly a result of the two musicians' unequal compositional abilities, reveal a sharp contrast in artistic goals.

Ex. 6.3, "Thou sing'st to her"

Ex. 6.4, "Thou singing"

[11]Scott, "John Danyel," 12.

"Like as the Lute" (no. 4) has a text unquestionably by the composer's brother:

Like as the Lute delights or else dislikes,
As is his art that playes upon the same:
So sounds my Muse according as shee strikes
On my hart strings, high tun'd unto her fame.
Her touch doth cause the warble of the sound,
Which here I yeeld in lamentable wise:
A wayling descant on the sweetest ground,
Whose due reports gives honour to her eyes.
If any pleasing relish here I use,
Then Judge the world her beautie gives the same:
Else harsh my stile untunable my Muse,
Hoarse sounds the voice that praiseth not her name.
    For no ground else could make the Musicke such,
    Nor other hand could give so sweet a touch.

The poem first appeared as sonnet 47 in Samuel Daniel's Delia (1592); minor changes in the text suggest that John Daniel used a later version of the poem,[12] but he still may have written the song well before 1606. Indeed, the lyrics contain so many musical terms – "high tun'd," "warble," "ground," "relish" – that one wonders whether the poet originally wrote the song specifically for his brother to set; the vocabulary alone begs for accompanying music.[13] Perhaps the poem (not included in Newman's edition of Astrophel and Stella) was originally conceived as the text to a song rather than as a sonnet in a sequence. All this is, of course, conjecture. But the poem and its setting offer us something concrete.

First, "Like as the Lute" provides every phrase with new music, and this music parallels the meaning of the text with meticulous care. The opening words, "Like as the Lute delights or else dislikes," follow a short "Prae-ludium" (as Campion would have scornfully called it), which reminds us of Daniel's debt to the consort song.[14] The lute provides a melodic motive (a) that the voice will begin with and that the accompaniment will then repeat in the bass (Ex. 6.5).

[12]Ibid.

[13]Josef Guggenheim, in Quellenstudien zu Samuel Daniels Sonettencyklus "Delia" (Berlin, 1898), long ago found a precedent for "Like as the Lute" in a conceit developed by Tasso in the sestet of his sonnet "Allor, che ne' miei spirti intepidissi," Rime 93 (Guggenheim, 55); Tasso, however, uses fewer technical terms than Daniel.

[14]The beginning of Patrick Mando's consort song "Like as the Day" (in a manuscript that may postdate Daniel's collection) bears an interesting resemblance to the opening of "Like as the Lute"; see Philip Brett, ed., Consort Songs, Musica Britannica 22 (London: Stainer and Bell, 1967), 24.

Ex. 6.5, "Like as the Lute"

The words – commenting, as it were, on the instrumental solo that opens the piece – have a melody that is "like" what the lute played; the lute, in turn, plays the motive again, emphasizing the likeness between the vocal part and the accompaniment. The strategy here, to match the text with pictorial music, will persist throughout the song.

After the singer mentions the lutenist's "art," Daniel writes another brief solo for the instrument, demonstrating the player's skill. The words "So sounds my Muse," sung to a four-note motive (which promptly "sounds" again in the accompaniment), are repeated, for greater emphasis, at a higher pitch. The word "sounds" has surely governed the repetition here. A full chord at "strings" underscores the text ("she strikes / On my hart strings") by calling the listener's attention to the four resounding strings played at that moment; the next word, "high," jumps up an octave to e" – the highest note in the piece (Ex. 6.6). After a brief pause at the end of this phrase, the voice sings "Her touch" and, with the lute, becomes silent. The two isolated words, followed by silence, suggest a finger that touches and then pulls away; moreover, since Daniel has specifically indicated two rests in the accompaniment, he may have intended a tactile pun, for the lutenist must "touch"

the strings to cut short their sound (Ex. 6.7).[15] The repeated phrase "in
lamentable wise" finds a melodic companion in a scale descending a fifth;
downward scales, of course, often represent sorrow, dejection, falling tears,
and the like. The lute soon plays a hexachord of half-notes moving first
from e-flat to c′ and then from c′ back to e-flat – this being the "sweetest
ground" above which the "descant," with its accidentals and its angular
melody, "wails" (Ex. 6.8).

Ex. 6.6, "She strikes"

Ex. 6.7, "Her touch"

[15]Thomas Mace, in *Musick's Monument* (1676; Paris: CNRS, 1977), explains how to produce
the "tut" (an ornament) on the lute: strike the string "and immediately *clap on your next striking
Finger, upon the String which you struck*; in which doing, you suddenly *take away the Sound of the
Letter* [i.e., the tablature letter, the note originally played] . . ." (109, his italics). Mace's method
of "*tak*[*ing*] *away the Sound*" by clapping on a finger (thus *touching* the string), though in this
case intended to produce a small ornamental sound ("tut"), would no doubt have been familiar
to John Daniel.

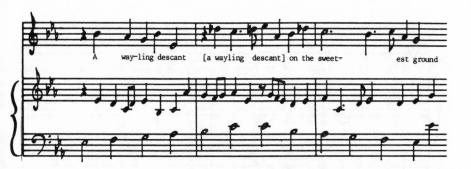

Ex. 6.8, "A wayling descant"

The next section, inspired by the words "whose due reports gives honour to her eyes," flaunts its "reporting" motive (b) sixteen times; and again Daniel makes extensive use of stretto, probably to convey the idea that the motive is being "reported" from one voice to another (Ex. 6.9).[16] At the words "If any pleasing relish here I use," a florid ornament (or "relish") appears exactly where the text would have it, on the word "here" (Ex. 6.10). The melody for the words "Else harsh my stile, untunable my Muse" revolves around g', moving either a half step below it or a whole step above – the singer seems to search for the right note here – and in the bass-line the two flats of the signature are canceled; the treatment of the outer voices thus emphasizes the "untunability" mentioned in the text (Ex. 6.11). Daniel places the next line, "hoarse sounds, The voice that prayseth not her name," in the singer's lower register, perhaps to strain the singer's voice.

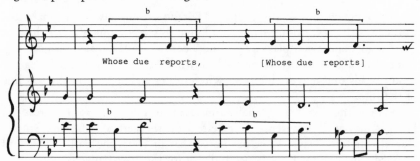

Ex. 6.9, "Whose due reports"

[16]The word *reports* was in fact used in the later seventeenth century as a musical term meaning "imitative motive" (see "Reports," *New Grove*); this meaning has not been traced back to the early 1600s, but John Daniel surely intended a musical pun on either the everyday or the musical sense of the word *reports*.

Ex. 6.10, "If any pleasing relish"

Ex. 6.11, "Else harsh my stile"

At the conclusion of the poem – "For no ground else could make the Musicke such / Nor other hand could give so sweet a touch" – the lute, as Scott points out, again plays a "ground," consisting of a scale first going up from c' to a' and then coming back down.[17] Less obvious than the earlier ground, this one moves chiefly in whole-notes and appears in the top line of the lute.

"Like as the Lute" is especially important to our study for two reasons. First, it may well represent a joint effort on the part of John and Samuel Daniel – indeed, David Price has noted that in 1603, the Earl of Hertford planned a masque for King James and sent for the "two danyells";[18] presumably this was not an isolated instance of collaboration between the brothers. Second, a careful analysis of this piece demonstrates how often John Daniel relies on word-painting to express the text. One could hardly find a better

[17]Scott, "John Danyel," 13.
[18]*Patrons and Musicians* (cited chap. 5, n. 41), 127.

example of the kind of song that Campion condemns in his 1601 preface
than "Like as the Lute." Beginning with a "long Praeludium," the piece
contains "Manie rests" in the voice part "for necessitie of the fuge"; it is
"long, intricate, bated with fuge, chaind with sincopation," and "the nature
of everie word is precisely exprest in the Note." It graces words that are not
"emphaticall"; in fact, it graces almost every element of the text with a
pictorial figure. Numerous phrases are repeated.[19]

But Campion also uses word-painting, and his song "When to her lute
Corinna sings" (BA/6) employs devices similar to those used in Daniel's
song; an octave leap, for example, occurs at the phrase "highest noates."
Campion, however, uses word-painting sparingly. For Daniel, it is an essential ingredient, sometimes determining the shape of the entire piece. And
there is another difference between Daniel's word-painting and Campion's.
Daniel often "translates" the text, as literally as he can, into music, whereas
Campion, in general, uses music merely to suggest a meaning. When Daniel
illustrates the words "Like as the Lute," he has the singer open with a motive
literally *like* the motive played on the *lute*; he uses an actual "relish" and an
actual "ground" to parallel the text. Campion, on the whole, avoids this
approach. He may use a relish to suggest sweetness, as in "All lookes be pale"
(1/21; Ex. 5.20), but not to represent a *relish*. And, as we have seen, when
Campion uses rapid notes to set the words "Haste you, sad noates," he later
changes the text, eliminating what must have seemed a "childish" trick.

"Time cruell Time," no. 8 in Daniel's collection, is the only song besides
"Like as the Lute" with a text indisputably by the composer's brother. The
text appeared first as a sonnet in Samuel Daniel's *Works* of 1601; in John
Daniel's song, the poem consists of four quatrains, the first two reproducing
almost exactly those in the earlier text. The opening line, however, contains
a significant change: originally a command ("Tyme, cruell tyme, come and
subdue that Brow"), it now poses a question ("Time cruell Time canst thou
subdue that Brow?"), as does the first line of the next quatrain, set to the
same music (Ex. 6.12). The melody, which remains on g′ for seven syllables,
lifts up for the final three, paralleling the rise in speech at the end of a
question. Whoever altered the text – John or Samuel – the reason was
probably to ensure a correspondence between the melody and the two inter-
rogative lines it carries.

[19]Campion does not overtly criticize the repetition of text, but many others did. The
musical humanist Nicola Vicentino, in *L'antica musica ridotta alla moderna prattica* (Rome, 1555),
condemns composers who utter a word twice, "for its repeat means nothing" ("*perche quella
replica non vuol dir niente*" [sig. Piiv]); text cited and translated in Don Harrán, *Word-Tone Relations
in Musical Thought: From Antiquity to the Seventeenth Century* (Neuhausen-Stuttgart: AIM, 1986),
458. The anonymous author (John Case?) of *The Praise of Musicke* (1586) mentions critics of
polyphonic church music who object to the "often repetition of the same things" (140).

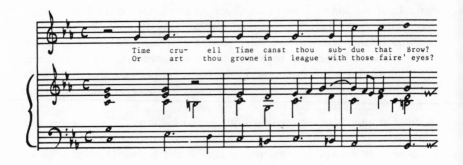

Ex. 6.12, "Time cruell Time"

The sestet of the original sonnet has undergone changes in form and content:

> And yet thou seest thy powre she disobaies,
> Cares not for thee, but lets thee waste in vaine,
> And prodigall of howers and yeares betraies
> Beautie and youth t'opinion and disdaine.
> Yet spare her Tyme, let her exempted bee,
> She may become more kinde to thee or mee. (1601)[20]

> Then doe so still although shee makes no steeme,
> Of dayes nor yeares, but lets them run in vaine:
> Hould still thy swift wing'd hours that wondring seeme
> To gase on her, even to turne back againe.
> And doe so still although she nothing cares,
> Doe as I doe, love her although unkinde,
> Hould still, yet O I feare at unawares,
> Thou wilt beguile her though thou seem'st so kinde. (1606)

Though not attributed to Samuel Daniel, the added quatrains could easily be his; except for the unfortunate rhyming of "kinde" and "unkinde" (which suggests desperation on the rhymer's part), the new lines are a marked improvement on the old. The couplet of the sonnet places the dull words "bee" and "mee" in the emphatic rhyming positions; "kinde," the one syllable in the final line that appeals to the imagination, is surrounded by prosaisms and thus loses its potential force; and the sentiment is simply too predictable. The song, however, starts the last two lines with a dramatic command, "Hould still," which condenses into two syllables an idea that the sonnet

[20]*Poems*, 177.

Ex. 6.13, "Then doe so still"

pleonastically stretches over ten ("Yet spare her Tyme, let her exempted bee"); the futility of this demand immediately makes itself felt: "yet O I feare at unawares, / Thou wilt beguile her though thou seem'st so kinde." Each verb or modifier generates its own strong connotations – "Hould still," "feare," "unawares," "beguile," "seem'st," "kinde" – and even the conjunctions "yet" and "though," both adversatives, carry a faint reminder of life's mutability. The rhyming word "kinde," directly related to the theme of the entire poem (and unprofitably buried in the sonnet), now concludes the song and modifies Time ("thou") rather than "her" (called "unkinde" two lines above). The simple exclamation "O," by unexpectedly following "yet," conveys surprise with all the more success.

In the music to the last two quatrains, several instances of word-painting occur (Ex. 6.13). After "Then doe so still," the lute "does" what the voice did by imitating its melody, and an imitative passage develops. The "dayes" and "yeeres" that "run in vaine" find their musical equivalent in running scales, and the long e' in the voice part forces the music to hold still at the command "Hould still." Samuel may have worked together with John on this part, for two phrases that inspire word-painting ("And doe so still," "Hould still") appear in parallel places in both of the last two quatrains, so as to fit the music on the repeat. At the words "wondring seeme" and, to the same music, "unawares," Daniel uses a remarkable cross relation (an a-flat in the accompaniment sounds against an a-natural in the voice) to express wonder and surprise. Of course, many English composers of the Renaissance favored the cross relation. Campion, for example, deftly places an e-flat after and e-natural in "Now let her change" (3/2) to underscore the text, as Lowbury, Salter, and Young have observed (Ex. 6.14).[21]

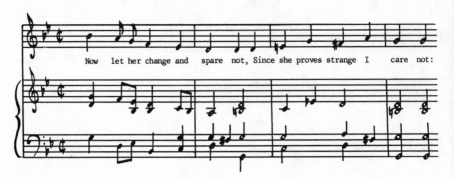

Ex. 6.14, "Now let her change"

[21]Lowbury et al., 154-55.

Campion's cross relation, however, causes merely a pleasing disturbance, while Daniel's sets the hair on end. The different effects have several causes. Campion's clashing notes sound not simultaneously but in succession, whereas Daniel's a-natural continues to sound above the lute's a-flat. More important, Campion's lute part consists largely of chords, so the song strikes the listener as a vocal line with a vertically conceived accompaniment, and the surprising e-flat leads quickly and inevitably to a comforting full cadence. Daniel's song, in contrast, calls attention to the harmonious interworking of the voices – sung and played – through constant motivic manipulation. The a-flat at first seems to arrive from nowhere and to have nowhere to go; a subversive element, it momentarily threatens to overthrow Daniel's carefully wrought structure. The significance of such a device in a song about Time's destructive effect on beauty is obvious. But the piece, I think, also represents the artist's triumph over Time. Samuel Daniel's sonnets, following a long tradition, often celebrate the poet's ability to preserve a woman's beauty in ageless verse. In a similar way, John Daniel has used music to create a beautiful order; chaos threatens to disturb that order but proves a false alarm as the composer leads the a-flat back to a little world framed in harmony.

If this today seems too romantic an interpretation of the dissonant a-flat, I doubt that it would have seemed so to Campion or the two Daniels. Renaissance literature repeatedly stresses the link between musical concord and cosmic harmony.[22] In his Epistle "To the Lady Margaret, Countesse of Cumberland,"[23] Samuel Daniel develops a conceit in which the "well-tun'd minde," stoically impassive while contemplating life's adversities, is a divinely created concord, resisting the assaults of "discords most unkinde":

This Concord (Madame) of a wel-tun'd minde
Hath beene so set by that all-working hand
Of heaven, that though the world hath done his worst,
To put it out, by discords most unkinde,
Yet doth it still in perfect union stand
With God and Man, nor ever will be forc't
From that most sweete accord, but still agree
Equall in Fortunes inequalitie. (116-23)

That Samuel Daniel chose the adjective "unkinde" to modify "discords" may have some incidental relevance to his brother's setting of "Time cruell Time,"

---

[22]Franciscus Niger, for example, defines harmony as the part of music "that arranges heaven and earth, and all things therein contained, in a certain order and, as it were, meter" ("quae caeli compagem et hunc terrarum orbem omniaque in eis contenta certa ratione: et quasi metro disponit"), in Grammatica (Venice, 1480), fol. [206v]. For a philological discussion of this general concept, see Leo Spitzer, "Classical and Christian Ideas of World Harmony: Prolegomena to an Interpretation of the Word 'Stimmung,'" Traditio 2 (1944): 409-64; 3 (1945): 307-64.

[23]Poems, 111-15.

which ends: "I feare at unawares / Thou wilt beguile her though thou seem'st so kinde." The woman will be taken "unawares" precisely because Time, for the moment, seems "kinde." In reality, of course, it shows mercy to none. Thus the most "unkinde" discord in the piece, the a-flat sounding at "unawares," admonishingly foreshadows the true nature of Time.

Dramatic, declamatory passages occur in Daniel's three-part lament, "Mrs. M. E. her Funerall teares for the death of her husband" (nos. 9-11). These passages, however, betray the influence not so much of Italian monody as of the elegiac English consort song.[24] Daniel's work opens with a pavanlike solo played on the lute; on entering, the voice sings "Griefe" four times, each "Griefe" being assigned a whole note, and all four separated from one another by whole rests. The introductory notes begin on d' and work slowly up to a'. Punctuated by "sighing" rests, this laborious ascent – which reflects the singer's mounting agony – has analogues in consort songs; the openings of Richard Farrant's "Ah, alas, you salt sea gods" and John Tomkins' "O thrice-blessed earthbed," for example, use similar devices (Ex. 6.15).[25]

Ex. 6.15, Daniel, "Griefe"; Farrant, "Ah, alas"; Tomkins, "O thrice-blessed"

Daniel also inserts some word-painting – witness his treatment of "Drop" and "trickle downe so fast" in the second part (Ex. 6.16) – and this too resembles the occasional pictorialism of consort songs like the anonymous "O death rock me asleep,"[26] in which the voice tintinnabulates at the words "Toll on the passing bell, / Ring out the doleful knell, / Let the sound my death tell" (Ex. 6.17).

[24]The first section of Philip Brett's edition of *Consort Songs* is devoted to "Elegies and Dramatic Laments" (1-33).

[25]Brett, *Consort Songs*, 15, 32.

[26]Ibid., 1.

Drop,   [drop,   drop,]   drop not,

nor   trickle,trickle,trickle downe so fast

Ex. 6.16, "Drop," and "trickle down"

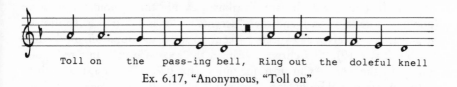

Toll on   the   pass-ing bell, Ring out   the doleful knell

Ex. 6.17, "Anonymous, "Toll on"

Daniel's musical teardrops may seem indecorously playful; but, unlike Campion, Daniel treated word-painting as a serious expressive device, acceptable in the gravest circumstances. Word play, analogously, could insinuate itself into profound tragedy; think of the quibble Laertes offers after hearing that his sister has drowned: "Too much of water hast thou, poor Ophelia, / And therefore I forbid my tears" (*Hamlet* 4.7.185-86).

Perhaps the best-known of John Daniel's works, songs 13-15, constitute another unified piece; the sequence frequently uses word-painting to bring out the meaning of its text, a classic piece of *poesia per musica*:

Can dolefull Notes to measur'd accents set,
Expresse unmeasur'd griefes that tyme forget?
No, let Chromatique Tunes harsh without ground,
Be sullayne Musique for a Tunelesse hart:
Chromatique Tunes most lyke my passions sound,
As if combynd to beare their falling part.

Uncertaine certaine turnes, of thoughts forecast,
Bring backe the same, then dye and dying last.

Samuel and John Daniel have both been put forward as possible authors of the text.[27] Since the words focus on musical rather than on poetic expression, John Daniel seems a likelier candidate than his brother. Certainly John, who authored the verses to Anne Grene prefacing his songbook, could have written the above poetry as easily as could the author of *Delia*; and of course the poetry may have come from someone outside the Daniel family.

Two aspects of this sequence immediately strike the listener: its complex, imitative polyphony and its delightfully wrenching use of chromaticism. (The difficult accompaniment resembles Dowland's expressive chromatic fantasies for solo lute, "Farewell" and "Forlorne Hope.")[28] Taking up four measures, the lengthy theme enters alone on the lute, passes to other registers of the accompaniment and then, after eight measures, appears in the voice. The themes frequently overlap, displaying Daniel's compositional virtuosity (Ex. 6.18).

Daniel's word-painting again reveals his creative method. The text allows for a "literal" depiction, in music, of the key words and phrases. Thus at "dolefull notes," we have a lugubrious melody; at "notes to measur'd accents set," the first four syllables are distributed evenly throughout the measure (one half note to a beat), and then "accents" – set as a dotted half followed by a quarter – receives its expected accent, in stress and duration, on the first syllable (Ex. 6.19). The chromaticism in the second part is inspired, quite simply, by the words "Chromatique tunes" (Ex. 6.20). While Daniel's chromaticism differs strikingly from Campion's, Hollander's comment that Campion "never . . . developed an insistent and personal chromaticism"[29] needs some qualification. True, Campion never uses chromaticism as extensively as Daniel does here, but the chromaticism in this piece springs directly from the text, imaging it in music. The melody for the words "Chromatique tunes" is a chromatic tune. We have observed the same approach to text-setting in "Like as the Lute." In Daniel's other songs, chromaticism appears with less frequency than in Campion's ayres. And Campion's chromaticism is, in a way, more personal than Daniel's. When Campion uses chromaticism, especially in his last four books, he introduces it at pathetic moments, much in the manner of the Italian monodists. But Daniel employs it as a constructive device; it turns the gears of his contrapuntal machine. Because Daniel was a first-rate craftsman, his songs are likely to seem more expressive and

[27]Scott, in "John Danyel," 14, suggests Samuel; Hollander, in *The Untuning of the Sky* (1961; New York: Norton, 1970), 189, suggests both Samuel and John.

[28]See *The Collected Lute Music of John Dowland*, ed. and transcr. Diana Poulton and Basil Lam (London: Faber, 1974), 13-19.

[29]*Vision and Resonance* (cited chap. 5, n. 32), 73.

"personal" than Campion's often amateurish efforts. The text to this
sequence, however, is important chiefly because it offers the composer new
musical motives to manipulate. If the song were arranged and performed as
a viol consort, I doubt that most listeners unfamiliar with the piece would
recognize the voice part as a voice part.

Ex. 6.18, "Can?"

Ex. 6.19, "Can dolefull notes"

Ex. 6.20, "No let Chromatique tunes"

The last two pieces in the collection differ from all the preceding in that they include four texted parts. "Now the earth, the skies, the Aire" (no. 20), which closes the book of ayres, has an unusual arrangement; for we have not only two sopranos, a tenor, and a bass but also two lutes (one a standard lute, the other a bass lute using an unusual tuning). The text presents us with a familiar *topos*: the spring comes, bringing joy to the natural world, but the speaker, alone, feels desolate:

Now the earth, the skies, the Aire,
All things faire,
Seemes new borne thoughts t'infuse,
Whil'st the returning spring,
Joyes each thing,
And blasted hopes renewes.
When onely I alone,
Left to mone,
Finde no times borne for mee,
No flowres, no Medow springs,
No Bird sings,
But notes of miserie.

The poem owes much to Petrarch's "Or ch'el ciel e la terra e'l vento tace" (sonnet 164) and "Zefiro torna" (sonnet 310)[30] – texts often set by madrigal

---

[30]Doughtie, *Lyrics from English Airs 1596-1622*, 553. My numbering of Petrarch's sonnets is based on that in Robert Durling's edition and translation of *Petrarch's Lyric Poems: The "Rime sparse" and Other Lyrics* (Cambridge: Harvard University Press, 1976).

composers. Again I am inclined to think Samuel Daniel the author, partly because of the high quality of the verse (one notes with pleasure the Keatsian penultimate line), partly because of verbal parallels between this poem and others definitely by Daniel.[31]

The music to this poem once more illustrates the text wherever possible. The opening lute duet, suggesting birdsong,[32] anticipates the celebration of spring in the first part of the poem. The words "Whil'st the returning spring" are repeated so as to make them "return," and the canto secundo, unaccompanied by lutes or voices, sings, "When onely I alone." The tricky rhythms occurring at the words "Finde no times" would perhaps have more significance to performers, trying to find their entrances, than to listeners. Throughout the piece, Daniel has mined the text for its ore of melodic motives; he is less concerned with making the words intelligible than with writing complex, varied polyphony. The voices and lutes weave in and out of the music with marvelous ease; a distinct text, however, does not emerge from the counterpoint – only repeated words and disjunct phrases.

Daniel, when composing for several voices as well as for one voice accompanied by the lute, consistently wrote complex polyphonic music. He wanted to create well-coordinated contrapuntal structures. In his ayres, though composed specifically for lute and voice, the music resembles those arrangements of motets, madrigals, and consort-songs in which the voice takes the upper part and the lute plays the rest. Daniel's approach to accompanied song represents an extreme opposite to, say, Caccini's. In the preface to his *Nuove musiche*, Caccini proudly relates how his monodies, with their simple, chordal accompaniments, moved skeptical listeners.[33] Daniel strives for an older ideal. For him, the music is not the "handmaid of the text"; on the contrary, the most important aspect of the text is that it serves as a source of musical inspiration. As we have repeatedly seen, words with any conceivable connection to sound give birth to – almost metamorphose into – their musical equivalents: the word "high" *is* high; the "descant" *does* wail upon a "ground." His is a madrigalian approach to word-painting – an approach that Campion scorned as "childish," "ridiculous."

Yet Daniel's songs always please; the same cannot be said about Campion's. Having mastered a style by no means easy to learn, Daniel provides his songs with infinite variety, glossing local beauties in the text with pictorial music. We are delighted by the brilliant dance of themes, one chasing another; by the playful transformation of word into motive; by the harmonious sum of

---

[31]See Appendix.

[32]Though impressionistic, comparing the lute duet to birdsong is not anachronistic; see "La Rosignoll," a lute duet imitating the nightingale's song, in *Jane Pickeringe's Lute Book* (facsimile of the tablature only), intro. Robert Spencer (Clarabricken: Boethius, 1985), fol. 8v.

[33]See Caccini, *Le nuove musiche* (cited chap. 5, n. 46), 45-46.

the melodic parts. By contrast, Campion's songs often seem amateurish, many growing stale when heard just a few times. The collection of his songs that most richly repays repeated listenings, *A Booke of Ayres*, has almost certainly profited from the hand of Philip Rosseter, a professional musician. But at his best – in a song like "Oft have I sigh'd." (3/1) – Campion on his own can focus our attention upon a melody that, combining the expressive power of Italian monody with elements of the native English ayre, couples words and notes together with moving results. He uses neoclassical devices to convey the text clearly, simply, and at times even passionately, while John Daniel entertains us with nonclassical word-painting, fascinates us with the intricacies of his counterpoint, and ravishes us with his inventive genius.

Part Three

Fin' amors and Eros

Chapter 7

From Provence to England

E nglish poets in the 1590s and early 1600s had at their disposal an enormously varied body of literature from which to draw inspiration: ancient (and indeed modern) texts in Greek and Latin, many available in translation; the Old and New Testaments; vernacular works produced on the continent; and, of course, English poetry by authors as diverse as Chaucer and Langland or Wyatt and Sidney. In much Elizabethan verse, we find contrary elements – the classical and the medieval, the pagan and the Christian – appearing side by side in harmony. This comes as no great surprise, for each era bequeaths to the next some part of itself: Sappho influences Catullus, works by Ovid and Virgil inspire countless medieval variations, and amatory conventions of the Middle Ages lurk behind a large number of Renaissance love lyrics. By the time we reach Elizabethan England, poets like Spenser and Shakespeare borrow without compunction from any source that provides them with a good plot, a stimulating conceit, a well-turned phrase.

Nevertheless, certain poets made a conscious effort to reject what they regarded as medieval barbarisms, while others relished the themes, the forms, and the very language of the Middle Ages. Spenser, for example, clearly took delight in medieval lore, *entrelacement*, verbal archaisms, and intricate rhyme-schemes – though even he experimented with quantitative verse in the vernacular. In general, we cannot simply separate Elizabethan poets into the categories "classical" and "medieval." But we can discern what *topoi* they favor and draw inferences about their poetic goals. In the case of Thomas Campion and Samuel Daniel, we are further assisted by the poets' polemical works. Campion, in the *Observations*, presents himself as an enemy of the Middle Ages ("those lack-learning times"), whereas Daniel, in the *Defence*, finds much to admire in medieval culture.

Yet Daniel often classicized, and Campion occasionally availed himself of Petrarchist imagery and language. The difference in temperament between the two poets shows most clearly in their lyric poetry, and even there one runs into difficulties of classification. In 1601, for example, Daniel published for the first time his poem "A Pastorall," which now closed his already-popular sonnet sequence *Delia*. The last three lines read thus:

Let's love, the sun doth set, and rise againe,
But when as our short light
Comes once to set, it makes eternall night.[1]

In the same year there appeared the following stanza, opening Campion's
first collection of lute-songs:

My sweetest Lesbia, let us live and love,
And, though the sager sort our deedes reprove,
Let us not way them: heav'ns great lampes doe dive
Into their west, and strait againe revive,
But, soone as once set is our little light,
Then must we sleepe one ever-during night.[2]

Both passages derive from the first six lines of Catullus' "Vivamus, mea
Lesbia." Campion, however, uses the original Latin poem as his starting point
and continues to classicize in the following stanza by paraphrasing some lines
of Propertius,[3] whereas Daniel is translating Catullus only through the inter-
mediary of Tasso, whose "O bella età de l'oro" (the famous chorus from
Aminta) is the original of Daniel's "Pastorall."[4] Daniel surely recognized the
Catullan allusion at the end of "O bella età"; but he meant to translate Tasso,
not Catullus. Campion, in contrast, went directly ad fontes.

Certain topoi so permeate Western literature that one simply cannot fix
them in one age or another. Campion's poem "The peacefull westerne
winde" (2/12) and Daniel's ode "Now each creature joyes the other" both
depict a speaker who, observing the beauty and fecundity of nature in spring-
time, laments being alone and unloved. Neither poem directly translates a
specific earlier lyric, though poems on the same theme abound. One thinks
immediately of Petrarch's "Zefiro torna" (Rime 310), perhaps the most
famous poem elaborating this topos.[5] But many others exist. An eleventh-
century Latin poem develops the same theme; here a woman utters the
lament:

---

[1]The text used is from the facsimile edition of the 1601 Delia at the end of Lars-Håkan
Svensson's Silent Art: Rhetorical and Thematic Patterns in Samuel Daniel's Delia (Lund: CWK
Gleerup, 1980), 30.

[2]The Works of Thomas Campion, ed. Walter R. Davis (1967; New York: Norton, 1970),
18; henceforth Works.

[3]See Davis' note to "My sweetest Lesbia" (Works, 18, n. 7).

[4]On Daniel's "plagiarism" of Tasso, see Sidney Lee, The French Renaissance in England
(1910; New York: Octagon Books, 1968), 236.

[5]Davis points out the similarity between Campion's poem and "Zefiro torna" – as well as
some other poems – in his note to "The peacefull westerne winde" (Works, 100, n. 27). All
references to Petrarch's poems are to the edition by Robert Durling, Petrarch's Lyric Poems: The
"Rime sparse" and Other Lyrics (Cambridge: Harvard University Press, 1976).

Levis exsurgit Zephirus
et Sol procedit tepidus:
iam Terra sinus aperit,
dulcore suo difluit.

. . . .

Cum mihi sola sedeo
et, hec revolvens, palleo,
si forte capud sublevo
nec audio nec video.

Zephyr arises gently and the warm Sun proceeds; Earth lays bare
her bosom, melting with her sweets.

. . . .

As I sit all alone, racked with thought and wan, if I should lift my
head, then I do not hear, I do not see.[6]

The theme crops up in classical times as well, as evidenced by Ovid's "Frigora
iam Zephyri minuunt" (*Tristia* 3.12), in which the poet complains about a
different kind of rejection – his exile from Rome:

iam violam puerique legunt hilaresque puellae,
rustica quae nullo nata serente venit;
prataque pubescunt variorum flore colorum,
indocilique loquax gutture vernat avis;

. . . .

ei mihi, iamne domus Scythico Nasonis in orbe est? (5-8, 51)

Now merry boys and girls are plucking the violets that spring up
unsown in the fields, the meadows are abloom with many- coloured
flowers, the chatty birds from unschooled throats utter a song of
spring. . . .

. . . .

Ah me! is Naso's home now in the Scythian world . . . ?[7]

---

[6]The text and translation are from Peter Dronke, *The Medieval Lyric*, 2d ed. (New York:
Cambridge University Press, 1977), 92-93.

[7]*Tristia* and *Ex ponto*, trans. Arthur Wheeler, Loeb Classical Library (Cambridge: Harvard
University Press, 1924), 146-51.

At times, then, assigning the labels "medieval" and "classical" is impossible. But many of Campion's lyrics translate or paraphrase works by the great Roman poets, and almost all the poems in Daniel's *Delia* contain passages closely translated from continental sonnets.[8] Scorned by Campion and others as a poetic Procrustean bed, the sonnet became the chief means of conveying to the lyric poets of Renaissance Europe those conventions often grouped, in modern times, under the heading "courtly love."[9] As they became increasingly aware of this debt to medieval conventions, confirmed classicists deliberately broke with the tradition that had gained momentum in vernacular languages with the lyric outpouring of the troubadours.

Peter Dronke has cogently argued that "the feelings and conceptions of *amour courtois* are universally possible, possible in any time or place and on any level of society."[10] Yet a substantial number of medieval lyrics elaborate on these "universally possible" feelings to a degree unmatched in antiquity. True, like the Greeks and Romans, the medievals will celebrate physical love – Guilhem IX does so with almost as much gusto as the ancient Augustans – and, in general, even the longest-suffering troubadours and trouvères pray for an eventual union of bodies. But in many poets – like Bernart de Ventadorn or Gace Brulé – we also find a deepened, devotional reverence for the courtly lady, and we encounter time after time the phrase *fin' amors* (or, in the north, *fine amour*). Though it did not have one fixed meaning, the term

---

[8]For Campion's sources, see the notes to each poem in Davis' edition, which draw on (and add to) remarks made in earlier editions of Campion's poetry; see also J. V. Cunningham, "Campion and Propertius," *Philological Quarterly* 31 (1952): 96; L. P. Wilkinson, "Propertius and Thomas Campion," *London Magazine*, n.s. 7 (April 1967): 56-65. The most thorough and important source study of *Delia* is Svensson's *Silent Art*, but the following are also of interest: Hermann Isaac, "Wie weit geht die Abhängigkeit Shakespeare's von Daniel als Lyriker?" *Jahrbuch der deutschen Shakespeare-Gesellschaft* 17 (1882): 165-200; Josef Guggenheim, *Quellenstudien zu Samuel Daniels Sonettencyklus "Delia"* (Berlin, 1898); L. E. Kastner, "The Italian Sources of Daniel's 'Delia,'" *Modern Language Review* 7 (1912): 153-56; George Brady, *Samuel Daniel: A Critical Study* (1923; Folcroft, Penn.: Folcroft Press, 1969); Janet Scott, *Les sonnets élisabéthains* (Paris: Librairie ancienne Honoré Champion, 1929), 115-28; Pierre Sept, *Samuel Daniel (1563-1619): Sa vie – son oeuvre* ([Paris]: Didier, 1968) 207-44; Claes Schaar, *An Elizabethan Sonnet Problem: Shakespeare's Sonnets, Daniel's Delia, and their Literary Background* (Lund: CWK Gleerup, 1960).

[9]The term "courtly love" is now fraught with controversy. See E. Talbot Donaldson's essay "The Myth of Courtly Love," *Speaking of Chaucer* (London: Athlone Press, 1970), 154-63. Francis Utley summarizes the attacks on the phrase "courtly love" in "Must We Abandon the Concept of Courtly Love?" *Medievalia et Humanistica*, n.s. 3 (1972): 299-324. The phrase *fin' amors*, which covers much of the same conceptual territory as "courtly love," has the advantage of being a term actually used by medieval poets.

[10]*Medieval Latin and the Rise of the European Love-Lyric*, 2d ed., 2 vols. (Oxford: Clarendon Press, 1968) 1:2 and *passim*.

is linked to certain recurring poetic themes.[11] Maurice Valency writes: "The adjective *fin, fis,* from Latin *fides,* had the sense of faithful, honest, sincere, true. The expression *fin amor,* frequently rendered as honest love, pure love, perfect love, or, after Gaston Paris, courtly love, is very well translated as true love. . . ."[12] Not mere lust (though lust may play a part in it), *fin' amors* is an ennobling desire. The "true lover" – remaining faithful to the beloved, even when faced with rebuffs, rumors, social and logistical impediments – seeks for "mercy" from a beautiful lady who can command him as she will.[13] The poets live in a world of emotional extremes. The lady's least kindness brings them giddy joy; her indifference or resistance makes them fear death. Her "cruelty," as recounted by the faithful lover, is not only the matter for a song but also "the measure of her worth and her power."[14]

During the thirteenth century, the love poetry of the troubadours began to exercise a direct influence on Italian poetry. In Sicily, Giacomo da Lentino imitated in his native language works of the Provençal poets, incorporating the ideas of the troubadours into the canzone and the sonnet, the latter a form he appears to have invented.[15] Like Giacomo, Dante learned from and admired the troubadours, composing sonnets and other short poems marked by passionate intensity and etherialized eroticism. Even for the humanist Petrarch (1304-74), the sonnet remains in large measure a vehicle for conveying medieval ideas on love; indeed, in the *Rime sparse,* Petrarch sometimes quotes and translates Provençal poetry.[16] (He resided in Provence for several years.) His great sonnet sequence, telling of his chaste love for Laura, spurred other poets on to write similar works, and the years between Petrarch's *Rime* and Samuel Daniel's *Delia* saw the production of countless sonnets – Petrarchan and anti-Petrarchan – in Western Europe.[17] Later theories of Christian-

---

[11]L. T. Topsfield, throughout *Troubadours and Love* (Cambridge: Cambridge University Press, 1975), shows that the term *fin' amors* means something a little different to each poet who uses it.

[12]*In Praise of Love* (1958; New York: Schocken Books, 1982), 142. The word *fin'* "develops the sense 'refined' which is related to Latin *finire* . . . ," as Bernard O'Donoghue notes in *The Courtly Love Tradition* (Manchester: Manchester University Press, 1982), 312.

[13]Valency, 145-46.

[14]Ibid., 169.

[15]Ibid., 198. See also Lisle C. John, *The Elizabethan Sonnet Sequences* (New York: Columbia University Press, 1938), 31, and J. W. Lever, *The Elizabethan Love Sonnet* (London: Methuen, 1956), 1-13.

[16]See, for example, *Rime sparse,* nos. 70 (which quotes a line in Provençal) and 239, line 36 of which imitates the envoi of Arnaut Daniel's "En cest sonet coind'e leri," as James Wilhelm points out in his edition of *The Poetry of Arnaut Daniel* (New York: Garland, 1981), 100, n. 44.

[17]Walter Mönch, in *Das Sonett* (Heidelberg: F. H. Kerle Verlag, 1955), 55-139, presents a good history of the sonnet from its inception to Elizabethan times. Mario Praz examines the more important developments in the history of the sonnet up to the Elizabethans in "Petrarch in England," *The Flaming Heart* (1958; New York: Norton, 1973), 264-86.

ized neo-Platonic love further rarefied the emotions voiced in the elevated amatory sonnet.

As James Hutton has shown, poets and critics midway through the sixteenth century often compared the sonnet with the epigram.[18] (This perhaps accounts for the "epigrammatic point" found in the couplet of the English sonnet.)[19] Yet, as we have seen, the sterner classicists of the sixteenth century condemned the sonnet; and Campion, who likened his ayres to epigrams, included no sonnets among them.

In the late 1500s, a number of poets could have traced the themes of the love sonnet to the lyric poetry of the troubadours. Parts of the troubadours' works appeared in France and Italy in 1575, when Jehan de Nostredame (brother of the famous astrologer) published his *Vies des plus celebres et anciens poëtes provensaux*. In the *Proesme au lecteur*, he proudly asserts that the Provençal poets wrote verse "long before the Tuscan poets in their mother tongue" ("*beaucoup avant les poëtes tuscans en leur langue maternelle*"); the Tuscan authors themselves – Dante, Petrarch, Boccaccio, Bembo, and others – have affirmed as much.[20] Citing Speroni, Nostredame reminds his readers of the debt that Tuscan poetry and oratory owe to the *Provensaux* (9). In France and Italy, then, there existed during the late sixteenth century a sense that the Petrarchan lyric tradition had roots in Provençal poetry. Some spoke of this link to the Middle Ages with pride, others with shame.

When we turn to the Elizabethans and try to understand their poetic goals, we receive some assistance from Thomas Watson, who (as though foreseeing his place of importance in the twentieth century) gave some pointers on how to interpret his poems. Watson's *Hekatompathia* (1582), a sequence of "Passions," includes before each poem a prose passage identifying the model on which the Passion is based and often explicating difficult or unusual concepts found therein. (He was perhaps following the lead of Ronsard and Spenser, both of whom had published lyrics accompanied by explanatory notes.) Watson drew from ancient Greek and Latin sources as well as from "modern" French and Italian ones. Discussing intertextuality in Renaissance lyric poetry, Thomas Greene describes one method of imitation as "eclectic" or "exploitative"; his description of the exploitative technique applies fairly well to Watson's type of imitation: "it essentially treats all traditions as stockpiles

---

[18]James Hutton, *Greek Anthology in France and in the Latin Writers of the Netherlands to the Year 1800* (Ithaca, N.Y.: Cornell University Press, 1946), 43; and *The Greek Anthology in Italy to the Year 1800* (Ithaca, N.Y.: Cornell University Press, 1935), 56.

[19]Praz also suggests a connection between the epigram and the the more pointed sonnets; see "The Flaming Heart: Crashaw and the Baroque," *The Flaming Heart*, 208-09. Hutton stresses, however, that "point" became less important than "conceit" as the Alexandrian epigram became more popular than the sharp epigrams of writers like Martial (*Greek Anthology in Italy*, 55).

[20]*Les vies des plus célèbres et anciens poètes provençaux*, ed. Camille Chabaneau (Paris: Librairie ancienne Honoré Champion, 1913), 7-8.

to be drawn upon ostensibly at random. . . . [W]hen it is employed with
artistic intelligence, the imitative poet commands a vocabulary of a second
and higher power, a second keyboard of richer harmonies. . . ."[21] Opinion
on Watson's poetic talent is divided; the introductions to his poems, however,
are valuable in that they give one a clear idea of the way some Elizabethans
went about imitating their foreign models.

Watson often borrows only selected passages from his continental sources;
in Passion 27, for example, he writes:

> In the first sixe verses of this Passion, the Author hath imitated
> perfectly sixe verses in an *Ode* of *Ronsard*, which beginneth thus:

> *Celui qui n'ayme est malheureux,*
> *Et malheureux est l'amoureux,*
>   *Mais la misere, &c?*

> And in the last staffe of this Passion also he commeth very neere to
> the sense, which *Ronsard* useth in an other place, where he writeth
> to his *Mistresse* in this manner:

> *En veus tu baiser Pluton*
> *La bas, apres che Caron*
> *T'aura mise en sa nacelle?*[22]

On rare occasions, he will translate an entire sonnet, padding it a bit to fill
out his eighteen-line form: "All this Passion (two verses only excepted) is
wholly translated out of *Petrarch* . . ." (Passion 5). More commonly, however, he takes only a few lines from his sources; the second "staffe" of Passion
39 is "borrowed from out the fifte Sonnet in *Petrarch part. I.*" Sometimes the
link between the English poem and its model is tenuous; the "invention" in
Passion 100 has only "some relation" to its model.

Although Campion and Daniel both borrow from their sources as Watson
does – a little from one poem, a little from another – their borrowing also
differs from his. Unlike Greene's "exploitative" poets, who indiscriminately
rifle through all earlier literature, Campion mostly avoids works in the
Petrarchan tradition, whereas Daniel continually resorts to them for inspiration. *Fin' amors* in its most spiritualized form pervades Daniel's *Delia*, while
Campion's lyrics often unequivocally express a wish for bodily gratification.
I do not mean to suggest that the sensuality in Campion's poems in itself

---

[21]*The Light in Troy: Imitation and Discovery in Renaissance Poetry* (New Haven: Yale University Press, 1982), 39.

[22]*The Hekatompathia or Passionate Centurie of Love (1582)*, intro. S. K. Heninger, Jr. (Gains-
ville, Fla.: Scholars' Facsimiles and Reprints, 1964), 27. All further references to Watson's
sequence are to this edition.

sets them apart from the Middle Ages; such a suggestion would be absurd. But frequent and explicit references to carnal acts are more common in the antique than in the medieval love-lyric. The anomalous "Pois En Raimons ni Truc Malecs," often attributed to Arnaut Daniel, satirizes some kind of noncoital sexual practice (metaphorically described as "blowing a horn").[23] That modern editors are not wholly in agreement about the act in question reminds us that medieval erotic poets often allegorized and mystified their descriptions of love-making. In contrast, the descriptions that classical poems give us of carnal desire and of sexual activity – coitus, fellatio, sodomy – leave no room for doubt.

Some Elizabethans themselves sensed the disparity between classical *eros* and more recent manifestations of desire (amorous customs inherited from the Middle Ages). For example, Thomas Nashe, in "A Choise of Valentines," tries consciously to write of love somewhat as Ovid did in his *Amores*; the prefatory sonnet reveals Nashe's purpose:

> Complaints and praises everie one can write,
> And passion-out their [pangs] in statelie rimes,
> But of loves pleasure's none did ever write
> That hath succeeded in theis latter times.[24]

So in Nashe's view – and Nashe wrote the preface to Newman's edition of *Astrophel and Stella*, the book that first made public the poetry of Daniel and Campion – most poets either bestow praise upon or complain about their ladies; they "passion-out their pangs" in the old medieval way. In these "latter times" (as opposed to classical antiquity), no one has succeeded in writing of "love's pleasure." The last phrase must mean "the sexual act," though the poem, which records several episodes of carnal frustration, could hardly be subtitled "The Joy of Sex." I suppose Nashe's point is that any kind of physical love, however inept, counts as "pleasure" when compared to the sufferings of the Petrarchan poets.

In his poem, Nashe amplifies an episode on impotence drawn from Ovid's *Amores* (3.7) – an episode Thomas Campion condenses into his short song "If any hath the heart to kill." Campion's sensual verse often has antecedents in classical poetry, and I suspect that Campion himself felt that his writing about "love's pleasure" represented a move in the direction of antiquity and away from the Middle Ages. But before examining Campion, we should turn to Daniel, a mainstream sonneteer who, in *Delia*, passioned out his many pangs in stately rhymes.

---

[23]See *The Poetry of Arnaut Daniel*, 74-77, 115-117.

[24]*Works*, ed. Ronald McKerrow, rev. F. P. Wilson, 5 vols. (Oxford: Basil Blackwell, 1958) 3:403. The poem is included among the "Doubtful Works" and has an odd manuscript history; see the notes on 397-402.

Chapter 8

Delia (1592)

S amuel Daniel traveled to France in 1586 and to Italy in 1591. Ronsard's funeral took place during Daniel's sojourn in Paris. While in Italy, Daniel met Guarini, whom he mentions as a personal acquaintance in a sonnet opening a translation of *Il pastor fido* into English.[1] Daniel's interest in continental poetry of the day reveals itself in his numerous translations and paraphrases of passages drawn from French and Italian lyrics. The lyric mode that most attracted him was not neoclassical – not Anacreontic verse, the Pindaric ode, or the Sapphic stanza. It was the Petrarchan sonnet. And Daniel seems to have known that Petrarch's lyric poetry belonged to an earlier medieval tradition: he asserts in the *Defence* that Petrarch "found whom to imitate," though he does not specify the troubadours, the trouvères, and their Italian followers.[2]

One cannot deny, however, that Daniel often classicized.[3] He wrote epistles espousing Stoic philosophy and plays that scrupulously obeyed the unities of time, plot, and place. And, like Spenser and Milton (who in true Virgilian style began their careers writing short pastoral and amatory poems and worked their way up to the epic), Daniel followed a classical masterplan when working out his poetic career. The epigraph to *Delia* (1592), used also in his later works, announces his intentions to the world: "*Aetas prima canat veneres postrema tumultus*" (Propertius, *Elegies* 2.10.7: "Let the young sing of love; the older, of war") – *Delia* today, *The Civil Wars* tomorrow. Yet despite the Latin epigraph, the lyrics in *Delia* belong not to a classical but to a medieval tradition, albeit filtered through the Italian and French Renaissance. Perhaps Daniel suffered a bout of neoclassical anxiety in 1599, for he left them out of his *Poeticall Essayes*, printed that year. But by 1601 he felt good

---

[1] Pierre Spriet, *Samuel Daniel* (cited chap. 7, n. 8), 45-85, esp. 46-47 (n. 16), 57-58, 79. The translation of *Il pastor fido* is anonymous, but Simon Waterson, the publisher, in his dedication mentions Edward Dymoke's "nearenesse of kinne to the deceased translator" (Spriet, 74, n. 153).

[2] *Poems and A Defence of Ryme*, ed. Arthur C. Sprague (1930; Chicago: University of Chicago Press, 1965), 140.

[3] Spriet points out Daniel's neoclassical tendencies throughout his study of Daniel.

enough about *Delia* – many of its sonnets now revised – to include it in his *Works*.[4]

The dramatic situation that Daniel presents in *Delia* comes principally from the Middle Ages. Unrequited love, the salient theme throughout the sequence, has inspired poetry in all countries and in all eras. But certain aspects of the relationship between the narrator and Delia smack strongly of similar relationships in medieval courtly poetry. Delia is the "cruel fair." She has a "hard heart," yet the poet continually hopes for "pity"[5] – and "pity" here differs from the "solace" described by Andreas Capellanus.[6] Not a euphemism for the sexual act, *pity* for Daniel means, quite simply, "pity." The word "disdain" appears far more often in Daniel's sonnets than in those of Sidney, Spenser, Drayton, or Shakespeare.[7] Whether based on a real woman or created out of Daniel's imagination, Delia strikes the reader as a being more removed than any of the women – to say nothing of Shakespeare's young man – addressed by the other great English sonneteers of the day.[8] One simply cannot imagine the narrator confronting Delia with the words "Since there's no help, come, let us kiss and part"; in fact, Daniel's narrator only once mentions kissing, and there (no. 38) he offers to kiss Delia's hand, not her lips; the mood is one of servility, not of eroticism. (For some, of course, servility and eroticism go hand in hand – but not, I think, for the narrator of *Delia*.) He will never torment himself over the "expense of spirit in a waste of shame." In sonnet 21, the dejected lover speaks of his "hungry thoughts," but his desire does not even whisper, much less cry, "Give me some food." An occasional kind look from Delia constitutes the most erotic

[4]Spriet, 115-20. *Delia* had gone through five printings – not including Newman's edition – by 1599, and already in 1594 Daniel had begun revising his sonnets with the end of reducing feminine rhymes.

[5]References to *Delia* are to the 1592 edition (Malone 276), published in facsimile as *Delia with The Complaint of Rosamund* (Menston: Scolar Press, 1969); Sprague's text, in *Poems and A Defence of Ryme*, is almost identical to this. The following sonnets in the 1592 edition use the words "hard hart" or a phrase to the same effect (sonnet numbers are followed by line numbers): 2.13; 13.14; 18.13; 29.14; 40.9. The following mention "pity" or "mercy": 4.12; 6.11; 16.8; 17.12; 19.2; 20.8; 27.10; 29.6.

[6]*The Art of Courtly Love*, trans. John J. Parry (1941; New York: Norton, 1969), 81-82 and *passim*.

[7]See Herbert Donow, *A Concordance to the Sonnet Sequences of Daniel, Drayton, Shakespeare, Sidney, and Spenser* (Carbondale, Ill.: Southern Illinois University Press, 1969), 148-49. In the sonnet sequences listed, Daniel uses the word *disdain* nineteen times (in Grosart's edition of *Delia*); Drayton uses it eight times (four times in one sonnet); Shakespeare, twice; Sidney, three times; Spenser, twice.

[8]The ladies addressed in continental sonnet sequences, however, can be quite forbidding; Du Bellay's Olive, for example, is every bit as cruel as Daniel's Delia, and Daniel often borrowed material from Du Bellay's sequence. In *French Poets and the English Renaissance* (New Haven: Yale University Press, 1978), Anne L. Prescott also notes Daniel's probable borrowings from Du Bellay's *Antiquités* and *Regrets* (59-60).

experience the poet enjoys – or, for that matter, openly desires – in the course of the sequence.

Daniel mentions Petrarch as a kind of *miglior fabbro* in sonnet 35 of *Delia* (1592):

> Thou canst not dye whilst any zeale abounde
> In feeling harts, that can conceive these lines:
> Though thou a *Laura* hast no *Petrarch* founde,
> In base attire, yet cleerely Beautie shines.
>
> . . . .
>
> But though that *Laura* better limned bee,
> Suffice, thou shalt be lov'd as well as shee.

As Svensson points out, moreover, Daniel's occasional mentioning of his "youth and error" represents an allusion to Petrarch's *"giovenile errore,"* a phrase used in the opening sonnet of the *Rime sparse*.[9] This phrase was picked up by several sonneteers who imitated Petrarch, and Daniel could well have found it in their works. In fact, Daniel drew most of his inspiration from Petrarchists rather than from Petrarch himself. But his models, whether from sixteenth-century France or fourteenth-century Italy, almost invariably owe a considerable debt to the Middle Ages. And, consequently, so does *Delia*.

Svensson persuasively contends that the 1601 edition of *Delia* follows a tripartite scheme – the first four sonnets constituting the *proemio*; the next forty-seven, the *narratio*; and the last six, the *uscita*.[10] Because the edition of 1592 is more accessible than that of 1601, I shall examine the earlier version, which, though shorter, follows the same general pattern of development as the later one. Of the four sonnets composing the *proemio*, the second best prepares the reader for the drift of the cycle as a whole and in fact served as the unnumbered introduction to the sonnets by Daniel printed in Newman's collection of 1591:

> Goe wailing verse, the infants of my love,
> Minerva-like, brought foorth without a Mother:
> Present the image of the cares I prove,
> Witnes your Fathers griefe exceeds all other.
> Sigh out a story of her cruell deedes,
> With interrupted accents of dispayre:
> A Monument that whosoever reedes,
> May justly praise, and blame my loveles Faire.

---

[9]Svensson, *Silent Art* (cited chap. 7, n. 1), 29, 61, 171-72.
[10]Ibid., 25-28.

Say her disdaine hath dryed up my blood,
And starved you, in succours still denying:
Presse to her eyes, importune me some good;
Waken her sleeping pittie with your crying.
Knock at that hard hart, beg till you have moov'd her;
And tell th'unkind, how deerely I have lov'd her.

Many of the themes that Daniel develops later in the sequence appear here
in germinal form. The "cruel fair" archetype enters in the second quatrain,
in which we read of the "cruell deedes" of the "loveles Faire." In this sonnet,
Daniel sets forth certain key words and phrases – "disdaine," "pittie," "hard
heart" – and reiterates other key words used in the first sonnet: "cares" (1.12;
2.3), "sigh" (1.7; 2.5), "eyes" (1.10; 2.11).[11] Comparing his work to a "monument," he prepares us for the sonnets that boast of making Delia immortal
(nos. 30, 34, 36, 46, 48). This *topos*, which recalls Horace's "exegi monumentum" (*Odes* 3.30.1-2), reminds us that Daniel, in his sonnets, borrowed
from antiquity from time to time. But Ovid's poetry was attractive to medieval poets as well as to Renaissance humanists, and in his lyric poetry, Daniel
makes no serious attempt to recreate or naturalize the spirit of Augustan
Rome.

The poem also illustrates the way Daniel derives material from continental
models. Commanding his book of poetry to go and sigh to the beloved
disdainful lady, Daniel recalls both Du Bellay's "Sus, chaulx soupirs, allez à
ce froid coeur" (*L'Olive* 67) and its model, Petrarch's "Ite, caldi sospiri, al
freddo core" (*Rime* 153).[12] Svensson discovers a number of parallels between
Daniel's sonnet and "Or sus, mes doux Enfans," the closing sonnet of Jacques
Grévin's sequence *L'Olimpe* (1560); there, too, the author, calling his verses
his children, tells them to go to his mistress. His children, however, are also
hers, since she inspired them, and in the final tercet Grévin plays with a
potentially indelicate conceit:

Allez . . . vous le pouvez bien faire,
Vous estes ses enfans, & elle est votre mere,
Car sans elle jamais vous n'eussiez esté faicts.[13]

Go . . . you can do it well; you are her children, and she is your
mother, for without her you never would have been made.

Svensson acutely remarks that "Grévin surprises the reader by insisting on a
full literal interpretation of the conceit, culminating in the playful sexual
innuendo contained in the last word," while "Daniel uses the myth of

[11]Ibid., 55. Svensson notes the reiteration of *cares, sigh,* and *eyes* (55).
[12]Ibid., 52.
[13]Reprinted in ibid., 54.

Minerva's miraculous birth from Zeus's head to suggest the absolute 'disdaine' showed by Delia and the complete loneliness and despair which, in his case, accompany the act of poetic creation" (54). The comparison of the French sonnet to its English analogue, while useful in illustrating Daniel's comparatively chaste desire, also reveals another facet of Daniel's poetics: his use of free association.[14] Grévin's sonnet sticks rather closely to the one central conceit, whereas Daniel's poem piles metaphor upon metaphor with dizzying speed. First the poems are likened to children, but, being without a mother (for Delia, who gives rise to their existence, is distant), they are immediately compared to Minerva (also motherless), whose reputation for chastity in turn reminds one of the unapproachable Delia herself. The "children" are now to present an "image" (a visual representation) of the poet's care, now to "sigh out a story" (a verbal representation) for the reader. Then the poems become a "monument" – linked, I suspect, to the previous ideas by a supposed inscription (not mentioned in the sonnet but understood by the reader) for passers-by to read.

The third quatrain begins with desiccation ("her disdaine hath dryed up my blood") and ends with moisture ("crying"). Daniel's conceit appears to work like this: Because of her disdain, my blood – associated with, and thus symbolizing, passion – is dried up; and my poems, which depend on and try to elicit her affection, are starved (for love). Gain her attention, my verse-children, by making her read (using her eyes), and waken her pity by crying (conveying my agony). Implicit in the last clause, I think, is the assumption that Delia, her pity awakened, will cry in sympathy (again using her eyes), watering and thus reviving Daniel's dried-up passion.

In the couplet, Delia's heart becomes a closed door upon which the verse-children ("starved," as we recall) are to pound like beggars. The begging metaphor no doubt inspired the pun on "deerely" (meaning both "affectionately" and "costing a great deal") in the last line.

So Daniel's poem, while lacking the unity of its continental models, gains a richness from its rapid succession of metaphors, most of them related loosely to one another. Although the central conceit – the comparison of the poems to needy children – never completely falls out of the picture, it often gives way for a short while to metaphors that come and go, one springing from another, as they catch the poet's fancy.

Like his choice of themes, his method of amplifying conceits – a method often employed in *Delia* – also marks Daniel as an author with poetic goals distinct from those of self-styled neoclassical writers like Jonson and Cam-

---

[14]Claes Schaar, in *An Elizabethan Sonnet Problem* (cited chap. 7, n. 8), curiously writes that he knows of "no single *Delia* sonnet that is strikingly reminiscent of Shakespeare's from the point of view of associative imagery" (95). Associative imagery, however, seems to me a decided point in common between the two poets.

pion. Plainer diction and more focused imagery characterize their poetry.[15] Indeed, according to Drummond, Jonson, who "wrott all his [verse] first in prose, for so his master Cambden had Learned him," maintained that "Verses stood by sense without either Colour's or accent, which yett other tymes he denied."[16] Jonson's sensible, prose-based language – which owes something to classical models[17] – and the spare, logical development of his ideas contrast sharply with the lush metaphors and free-associative style of *Delia*. In fact, in the 1616 version of *Every Man in His Humour* (dedicated to his old master, Camden), Jonson candidly mocks Daniel's style when Justice Clement reads aloud some verses discovered on Matthew, a poetaster given to plagiarism: "Unto the boundlesse Ocean of thy face, / Runnes this poore river charg'd with streames of eyes" (5.5.23-24).[18] Edward Kno'wel, evidently recognizing these as a corruption of the first two lines of *Delia* ("Unto the boundles Ocean of thy beautie / Runs this poore river, charg'd with streames of zeale"), cries out: "A *Parodie*! a *parodie*! with a kind of miraculous gift, to make it absurder then it was" (26-27).[19] Kno'wel's comment suggests that Jonson considered Daniel's original metaphors – "Ocean of thy beautie," "streames of zeale" – absurd in the first place. Having gone a step too far with Daniel's associative technique, Matthew has produced grotesque nonsense.

Though he did not publicly ridicule Daniel as Jonson did, Campion chose to write lyrics much closer in style to Jonson's than to Daniel's poems. When he compares his ayres to epigrams, Campion links his texts not only to the antique world but also (perhaps less consciously) to the plain style associated with the epigram.[20] For Daniel, in contrast, the preferred lyric vessel is the sonnet, with its cargo of dainty devices.

The *narratio* of *Delia* begins, according to Svensson (68), with the fifth sonnet, the first to employ the preterite tense. More unified than sonnet 2, it plays with the tale of Actaeon and Diana:

---

[15]For a discussion of the plain style in English Renaissance poetry, see Wesley Trimpi, *Ben Jonson's Poems: A Study of the Plain Style* (Stanford: Stanford University Press, 1962), esp. chaps. 5-7.

[16]*Ben Jonson*, ed. C. H. Herford, Percy Simpson, and Evelyn Simpson, 11 vols. (Oxford: Clarendon Press, 1925-52) 1:143.

[17]See Trimpi, chap. 3.

[18]*Ben Jonson*, 3:400.

[19]In the 1601 version of *Every Man in His Humour*, Jonson quotes the opening quatrain of Daniel's sonnet with almost no alteration of the original; the joke there revolves around the poetaster's plagiarism, and the glance at Daniel's style is not nearly so pronounced as in the later play, though Lorenzo Junior, in the 1601 version, delivers some harsh criticism of poetasters and appears to include Daniel among them (*Ben Jonson*, 3:285-86).

[20]Trimpi, 8, 16-19, and *passim*. See also Walter R. Davis, *Thomas Campion* (Boston: Twayne, 1987), 23-26.

Whilst youth and error led my wandring minde,
And set my thoughts in heedeles waies to range:
All unawares a Goddesse chaste I finde,
Diana-like, to worke my suddaine change.
For her no sooner had my view bewrayd,
But with disdaine to see me in that place:
With fairest hand, the sweete unkindest maide,
Castes water-cold disdaine upon my face.
Which turn'd my sport into a Harts dispaire,
Which still is chac'd, whilst I have any breath,
By mine owne thoughts: set on me by my faire,
My thoughts like houndes, pursue me to my death.
Those that I fostred of mine owne accord,
Are made by her to murther thus their Lord.

The content of the poem derives, of course, ultimately from Ovid's *Metamorphoses* (3.138-252);[21] but, as mentioned earlier, using Ovid does not in itself constitute neoclassicism. During the Middle Ages, Ovid's poetry inspired countless imitations and provoked countless allegorical readings having little to do with ancient Rome.[22] Daniel, in alluding to Ovid in sonnet 5, is trying not so much to revive the classical world as to use its mythology to keep alive medieval conventions. He was hardly the first to do so; numerous Renaissance sonneteers built conceits on the wondrous metamorphoses provided by Ovid. And Daniel himself pays tribute to the Petrarchan tradition by beginning with "youth and error," an allusion to Petrarch's *"giovenile errore."* He deifies Delia, calling her a "Goddesse" – but a chaste one, "Diana-like." Again, one of Delia's identifying features is disdain, and she once more plays the role of *la belle dame sans merci* ("the sweete unkindest maide," "my faire").

In the third quatrain, Daniel's conceit becomes quite involved. How are we to read the word *sport*? In the hunting metaphor, it makes perfect sense; but how does it fit into the love-story? It seems strangely frivolous for Daniel. One thinks of the exchange between Iago and Cassio when Othello is to consummate his marriage:

Iago: . . . He hath not yet made wanton the night with her; and she is sport for Jove.
Cassio: She's a most exquisite lady. (2.3.16-18)

---

[21]See Svensson, 70-71. Throughout the section on sonnet 5, Svensson adduces a large number of continental lyrics that might have influenced Daniel's phrasing and imagery.

[22]See Douglas Bush, *Mythology and the Renaissance Tradition in English Poetry* (1932; New York: Norton, 1963), 3-22, a chapter on "Classical Themes in the Middle Ages"; for a short survey of Ovid's influence on the Elizabethans, see 69-88.

Midway through the sixteenth century, *sport* had come to mean, among other things, "amorous dalliance or intercourse" (*OED* I.1.b); the meaning was common in Daniel's day. This does not mean that the word always carried with it sexual overtones. Thomas Watson begins his eighth Passion with an allusion to the Acteon myth and also uses the word *sport*:

> Actaeon lost in middle of his sport
> Both shape and life, for looking but a wry,
> Diana was afraid he would report
> What secretes he had seene in passing by:
>   To tell but trueth, the selfe same hurt have I
>   By viewing her, for whome I dayly die. . . .[23]

Because Watson uses *sport* in the first line, the word has little or no carnal nuance, whereas Daniel's *sport* is charged with the guilt of the erotic desire covertly expressed in the octave. I detect some self-criticism in Daniel's use of the word here, as though the narrator of the sequence felt that he somehow deserved Delia's disdain – a just punishment for regarding her, however briefly, as "sport." To be sure, unrequited love is chiefly responsible for unleashing the poet's houndlike thoughts; but guilt and shame – suggested by the words "error," "wandring," "heedeles," and perhaps "sport" – also contribute to his self-torment. Underlying the narrator's pained reaction to Delia's disdain is the assumption that he (like many medieval lovers) is not worthy of the beloved. And the pun on "sport" is promptly balanced out by a pun on "chac'd" (heard also as "chaste") in the next line: "Which turn'd my sport into a Harts dispaire, / Which still is chac'd. . . ." The second "Which" refers to "Hart" in its genitive form (a common construction in Elizabethan verse). The surface meaning is that the Hart is chased by thoughts; but the words also suggest that the "Heart" will remain ("still is") "chaste." The pun on "chac'd" – and I think one is intended – reminds us of the earlier reference to Delia as a "Goddesse chaste" and allows Daniel to write about erotic desire that is paradoxically not erotic. The paradox runs through much of Daniel's sequence. It is perhaps the natural consequence of writing in a tradition in which the beloved lady is often both desirable and untouchable.

In each quatrain of sonnet 8, Daniel addresses something close to himself – his heart, his eyes, his verse – and ends with an epigrammatically pointed couplet:

> Thou poore hart sacrifiz'd unto the fairest,
> Hast sent the incens of thy sighes to heaven:
> And still against her frownes fresh vowes repayrest,
> And made thy passions with her beautie even.

---

[23]*Hekatompathia* (cited chap. 7, n. 22), 22.

And you mine eyes the agents of my hart,
Told the dumbe message of my hidden griefe:
And oft with carefull turnes, with silent art,
Did treate the cruell Fayre to yeelde reliefe.
And you my verse, the Advocates of love,
Have followed hard the processe of my case:
And urg'd that title which dooth plainely prove,
My faith should win, if justice might have place.
Yet though I see, that nought we doe can move her,
Tis not disdaine must make me leave to love her.

The opening image may well owe something to a woodcut of a heart above a flaming censer, an emblem that appeared in Horapollo's collection of *Hieroglyphica* (first printed in 1505) with the text comparing the heart of a jealous man, which is "always on fire," to the heart of Egypt, which, "because of the heat, gives life in all things in itself and by itself."[24] (The narrator's heart is certainly heated, though not out of jealousy.) In any event, Daniel characteristically stresses the spiritual quality of the poet's love for Delia by using a conceit charged with religious imagery. In sonnet 5, Delia resembles the goddess Diana; in the opening quatrain of sonnet 8, she gains even more distance from her would-be lover and becomes "heaven." (His mistress, when she walks, floats on the clouds.) Although the sacrifice of a heart suggests pagan religious rites, the sacrifice of a hart – and the *heart-hart* pun occurs several times in *Delia* – is another matter. For Christ was often likened to a hart in the sixteenth century.[25] With this in mind, I suggest that the word "passions," with its etymological meaning of "sufferings" and its Christian overtones, may gently allude to another Passion, another sacrifice; and, in doing so, it may be calculated all the more effectively to elicit charity from Delia.

In the second quatrain, which addresses the narrator's eyes, Delia again assumes her role as the "cruell Fayre." The dominating conceit in these four lines is that the eyes are to act as "agents," stealthily bringing the poet's message (an entreaty for "reliefe") to Delia. Svensson points out classical precedents for the idea that the eyes can deliver silent messages, and he finds several examples of the "dumb eloquence" conceit in sonnets written by poets from Petrarch to Shakespeare (108-09). Two passages from Sidney's and Shakespeare's sonnets, mentioned by Svensson, deserve our attention:

---

[24]Svensson notes the similarity (105-6), reproducing the emblem and the Latin text. The English translation is that of George Boas, *The Hieroglyphics of Horapollo*, Bollingen Series 23 (New York: Pantheon, 1950), 72.

[25]See Anne L. Prescott, "The Thirsty Deer and the Lord of Life: Some Contexts for *Amoretti* 67-70," *Spenser Studies* 6 (1985): 33-76, which calls attention to several Renaissance sources that, following Patristic commentary, connect the hart with Christ.

Oft with true sighes, oft with uncalled tears,
Now with slow words, now with dumbe eloquence
I Stella's eyes assayll, invade her eares. (*Astrophel and Stella,N 61*)

O let my books be then the eloquence,
And domb presagers of my speaking brest,
Who pleade for love, and look for recompence,
More then that tonge that more hath more exprest. (Shakespeare,
sonnet 23)[26]

In Daniel's poem, the conceit lacks the aggression found in Sidney's
("assayll," "invade") and the directness in Shakespeare's ("speaking,"
"pleade"). Why is the atmosphere in Daniel's poem so quiet and secretive
("dumbe message," "hidden griefe," "carefull turnes," "silent art")? I suspect
that the ghost of a losengier – the court tattletale, a detested figure in medieval
literature – haunts this passage.[27] For in the poetic tradition to which *Delia*
ultimately belongs, even an ocular message from the lover to the beloved
must be delivered with due circumspection, lest the gossip-mongers should
begin to spread their troublesome rumors. Dante, in the fifth chapter of the
Vita nuova, tells us that for years he took care in public to gaze at Beatrice's
companion rather than at Beatrice herself – a ploy to keep his love secret.[28]
Thomas Campion was familiar with this tradition, for he mocks it in
"Though your strangenesse frets my hart" (2/16):

You perswade me, 'tis but Art,
That secret love must faine.
If another you affect,
'Tis but a shew t'avoid suspect.
Is this faire excusing? O no, all is abusing.

For Campion, the neoclassicist, the woman's reasoning is just abusive
trickery; his speaker roundly condemns it. Give him kind Amarillis; let him

---

[26]Cited in Svensson, 109; in the 1609 quarto of *Shake-speares Sonnets*, Svensson's "let my
looks" reads "let my books," a more probable reading, adopted above.

[27]Although the losengier makes few appearances in Elizabethan poetry, one still finds him
– somewhat altered – in characters like Iago and Marston's Malevole; C. S. Lewis regards
Adolesche, a character in Chapman's continuation of *Hero and Leander*, as a losengier, "love's
troubler all through the Middle Ages" (*English Literature in the Sixteenth Century Excluding Drama*
[Oxford: Clarendon Press, 1954], 515), and Valency notes that Spenser "still considered the
losengier the chief enemy of the courtier" (*In Praise of Love* [cited chap. 7, n. 12], 172).

[28]Dante Alighieri, *Dante's Vita nuova*, tr. Mark Musa (Bloomington: Indiana University
Press, 1973), 8.

sport with her in the shade. For Daniel, however, the secrecy and pleading and suffering form a necessary part of the game of love.[29]

Daniel addresses his verse in the last quatrain, and a legal conceit ensues. As Svensson notes, this legal *topos* was common in the Middle Ages: "several medieval French poems elaborate the idea of the Court of Love. . ." (111). The couplet reiterates the word "disdaine," yet the speaker, despite his ill treatment, will continue to love the cruel fair. Again, this last idea – that the man will remain faithful though he has no reason to expect mercy – is a commonplace in medieval love poetry. As Wyatt once put it: "Yea though my grief find no redress . . . Yet I profess it willingly / To serve and suffer patiently."[30]

Much has been written about Daniel's "If this be love, to draw a weary breath" (*Delia* 9), one of Daniel's better-known poems:[31]

If this be love, to drawe a weary breath,
Painte on flowdes, till the shore, crye to th'ayre:
With downward lookes, still reading on the earth;
The sad memorials of my loves despaire.
If this be love, to warre against my soule,
Lye downe to waile, rise up to sigh and grieve me:
The never-resting stone of care to roule,
Still to complaine my greifes, and none releive me.
If this be love, to cloath me with darke thoughts,
Haunting untroden pathes to waile apart;
My pleasures horror, Musique tragicke notes,
Teares in my eyes, and sorrowe at my hart.
If this be love, to live a living death;
O then love I, and drawe this weary breath.

Scholars have long viewed this sonnet as an imitation of Desportes's "Si c'est aimer que porter bas la veuë" (*Amours de Diane*, bk. 1, no. 29, itself modeled on Lelio Capilupi's "S'haver di, e notte gli occhi humidi, et bassi").[32] Like Desportes's sonnet, Daniel's repeats the opening subordinate clause in the

[29]See also Daniel's "Eyes hide my love," from *Hymens Triumph* (lines 1408-13), in *Complete Works in Verse and Prose*, ed. Alexander B. Grosart, 5 vols. (1885-96; New York: Russel and Russel, 1963) 3:381.

[30]Thomas Wyatt, *Collected Poems*, ed. Joost Daalder (London: Oxford University Press, 1975), 226.

[31]See Janet Scott, *Les sonnets* (cited chap. 7, n. 8), 119-20; Peter Ure, "Two Elizabethan Poets: Samuel Daniel and Sir Walter Ralegh," *The Age of Shakespeare*, ed. Boris Ford, (Harmondsworth: Penguin, 1955), 135-36; Svensson, 111-28.

[32]Janet Scott, in *Les sonnets*, was apparently the first to call attention to Daniel's debt to Desportes in this sonnet (119-20).

fifth and ninth lines;[33] the first two lines of Daniel's sonnet, moreover, derive
much of their substance from the fifth and sixth of the French model: "*Si
c'est aimer que de peindre en la nuë, / Semer sur l'eau, jetter ses cris au vant . . .*"[34]
("If to love is to paint on clouds, to sow on water, to cry to the wind . . .").
Svensson groups this poem with those – and there are many – in which the
lover's state is described as hellish; he remarks that this genre grew ultimately
out of the Provençal riddle-poem, the *devinahl*, though by the Renaissance
"the original riddle element [had] disappeared" (116). Of the poems by
Petrarch that fit into this category, "S'amor non è, che dunque è quel ch'io
sento?" (*Rime* 132) reached England already in the fourteenth century when
it appeared, paraphrased by Chaucer, in *Troylus and Criseyde* (1.400-20).
Thomas Watson, noting that Chaucer had already translated the poem into
English, included two translations of it in his *Hekatompathia* – one into
English, the other into Latin (Passions 5 and 6). The popular device of using
futile or morbid activities to characterize the downcast lover's hopeless desperation may, incidentally, have provoked this unsympathetic response from
Campion, in one of his devotional poems: "All earthly pompe or beauty to
expresse, / Is but to carve in snow, on waves to write" (1/7).

Daniel freely paraphrases Desportes's sonnet – adding lines, rearranging
ideas, eliminating phrases – as he sees fit. Using his technique of free association, however, Daniel manages in the second quatrain to write original
poetry in an essentially derivative poem. The phrase "to warre against my
soule" was meant, I think, to conjure up the image of an encounter in which
the speaker, engaged in battle, is cast down – an interpretation that the next
line suggests retroactively, for there he is initially prostrate (sleeping or trying
to sleep), wailing. (Daniel may have expected the reader to make a connection
between the wailing speaker of line 6 and the warring – perhaps wounded?
– speaker of line 5.) He then rises but remains miserable. The shift from a
recumbent to an upright position surely inspired the allusion to Sisyphus,
who, in a literal hell, continually descended and ascended while laboring
fruitlessly. Line 8 – "Still to complaine my greifes, and none releive me" –
describes the agony and desperation of a soul figuratively in hell and sums
up the entire quatrain. As in sonnet 2, Daniel has borrowed from a foreign
model and extended its conceits by allowing his imagination to go where it
will – unlike Campion, who, when imitating other poems (usually from
ancient Rome), tends to compress his borrowed material and to develop his
ideas sequaciously.

---

[33]Capilupi's sonnet repeats the word *Se* at the beginning of lines 1, 5, and 9; but the
anaphora extends no further than the conjunction.

[34]Desportes, *Les amours de Diane*, ed. Victor Graham, 2 vols. (Geneva: Droz, 1959) 1:69;
Graham notes that poems by Jamyn, Baïf, Tyard, and Ronsard also repeat the phrase "*Si c'est
aimer*" (1:69, n. 1), though these poems, some written after Desportes's, are not closely related
to Daniel's.

In the four sonnets thus far examined, one can find most of the themes dealt with in the first twenty-nine sonnets of *Delia*. Beginning at sonnet 30, however, a new theme enters. The narrator warns Delia that her beauty will fade and boasts that his poems alone will preserve it:

> I once may see when yeeres shall wrecke my wronge,
> When golden haires shall chaunge to silver wyer:
> And those bright rayes, that kindle all this fyer
> Shall faile in force, their working not so stronge.
> Then beautie, now the burthen of my song,
> Whose glorious blaze the world dooth so admire;
> Must yeelde up all to tyrant Times desire:
> Then fade those flowres which deckt her pride so long.
> When if she grieve to gaze her in her glas,
> Which then presents her winter-withered hew;
> Goe you my verse, goe tell her what she was;
> For what she was she best shall finde in you.
> Your firie heate lets not her glorie passe,
> But Phenix-like shall make her live anew.

Sonnet 30 differs in form and content from all the preceding poems. Like sonnet 33, it has an octave rhyming *abba abba*; but unlike every other sonnet in the sequence, it lacks a final couplet. This difference in form is coincidentally accompanied by a difference in content. The narrator now speaks with far greater confidence and authority than before. Daniel has once again borrowed from Desportes (*Cléonice* 62, "Je verray par les ans vangeurs de mon martyre").[35] Perhaps the most interesting change found in Daniel's reworking of Desportes's sonnet is the handling of the last lines. Desportes writes:

> Et peut estre qu'alors vous n'aurez deplaisir
> De revivre en mes vers chauds d'amoureux desir,
> Ainsi que le Phenix au feu se renouvelle.[36]

And perhaps then you will not be displeased to revive, in my verses, hot amorous desire, like the Phoenix, which renews itself in the fire.

---

[35]Svensson, 245-46. L. E. Kastner, in "The Italian Sources of Daniel's 'Delia,'" *Modern Language Review* 7 (1912), 153-56, points out that sonnet 30 "was not written without a knowledge of Desportes' adaptation (*Cléonice* 62) of Tasso's version" (156).

[36]Svensson, 246.

Daniel takes the same conceit and chastens it. Desportes calls his desire
"amoureux." When Daniel discusses his poems and the desires expressed in
them, he uses a different adjective:

Unhappy pen and ill accepted papers,
That intimate in vaine my chaste desiers,
My chaste desiers, the ever burning tapers,
Inkindled by her eyes celestiall fiers. (*Delia* 49.1-4)[37]

In order for the Phoenix conceit to work, the poetry must offer some kind
of heat corresponding to the flames and ashes from which the Arabian bird
arises. As the quatrain above proves, chastity and heat are by no means
mutually exclusive in *Delia*; and when Daniel writes of his verse's "firie
heate," he expects the reader to know that the heat comes not from carnal
desire, but from the "chastest flame that ever warmed hart" (*Delia* 36.4).

Sonnets 31 to 34 (perhaps even 35) form a sequence in which the last
line of one sonnet is repeated – either exactly or with a slight variation – as
the first line of the next.[38] Although sonnet 30 appeared in Newman's 1591
collection, sonnets 31 to 35 did not. This may be relevant. Many of the first
thirty sonnets of Delia had appeared in 1591; those that did not (nos. 1, 4,
5, 6, 7, 8, 12, 22) were, I believe, probably composed between the time that
Newman got hold of Daniel's sonnets in manuscript and the time that Daniel
submitted *Delia* for publication. Of the first thirty sonnets, those new to the
1592 edition generally present variations on themes already developed in the
1591 collection. Sonnet 1 acts as a more general introduction to the sequence
than sonnet 2, which, as we have seen, touches specifically on most of the
principal themes developed in *Delia*. Sonnets 4 through 8 were not included
in Newman's book; of these, sonnet 4 properly rounds off the *proemio* by
naming Delia for the first time, while the following four sonnets develop
the themes of feminine cruelty and disdain, which dominate the sequence
in any case. The last line of sonnet 9 also opens sonnet 10 (not included in
Newman). Because of the line they share, one might assume that the two
sonnets were written at the same time. But sonnet 9, with its echoes of
Desportes, differs substantially in content from sonnet 10 and lacks the

---

[37]No equivalent to the phrase "chaste desirers" appears in Desportes's "Cesse, ô maudite
main! cesse esprit incensé" (*Cléonice* 58), which seems, in Kastner's view, to have been Daniel's
"immediate model" ("Italian Sources," 155). Svensson also sees Daniel's rendering of Desportes's
tercet as "symptomatic of Daniel's general tendency to spiritualize his passion . . ." (247).

[38]Sonnet 35 repeats half of the last line of the preceding poem; 34 ends with "They will
remaine, and so thou canst not dye"; 35 begins with "Thou canst not dye whilst any zeale
abounde." Lacking the threatening overtones of the preceding four poems, however, sonnet 35
has a noticeably lighter mood. Svensson likens Daniel's method of joining sonnets here and
elsewhere in the sequence to the "*corona* technique" (129).

"intrinsic similarity" found in other groups of linked sonnets in Delia.[39]
Sonnet 12 emphasizes the spiritual quality of the poet's love by using religious
language ("spotles love," "temple," "imparadize"); and sonnet 22, on false
hope, apparently grew out of the couplet to sonnet 21 ("Thus she returnes
my hopes so fruitlesse ever, / Once let her love indeede, or eye me never").
Thus many of the sonnets included in Delia, but not in Newman's edition,
take as their starting point an idea or a phrase from the earlier printed works.
Sonnets 31 to 34, though related in content to sonnet 30, are, in theme and
form, without question more closely related to one another than to sonnet
30. All four sonnets liken Delia's youth and beauty to a flower (also mentioned in 30) and remind her that she too will wither and become undesirable.
   Classical authors employ the topos in which the poet compares a woman
to a flower and warns that when her beauty fades, men will no longer want
her.[40] Although the topos of the maiden as a flower crops up here and there
in Greek and Roman poetry, the two chief passages to make extended use
of the conceit are in Catullus (no. 62)[41] and an anomymous poem, "Ver erat
et blando mordenti a frigore sensu," long attributed to Ausonius.[42] In "Ver
erat," the poet advises virgins to gather roses before they fade, and draws the
inevitable parallel between the brief life of the flower and the relatively brief
period of the woman's beauty ("collige, virgo, rosas, dum flos novus et nova pubes,"
line 49).[43] This topos, though classical in origin, spread through European
literature in the fifteenth and sixteenth centuries. In the course of his essay
on the rose, John Addington Symonds cites the topos in vernacular poetry
written by such influential poets as Lorenzo de' Medici, Politian, Ariosto,
Tasso, Guarini, Ronsard, Spenser, and of course Daniel. Did the topos have
a classical aura about it for Daniel, or did it simply seem to belong to the
conventions – most of them medieval in origin – generally found in the
Renaissance love lyric? Thomas Greene has observed that if a "topos has
been everywhere, then it derives specifically from nowhere. The reader is
not expected to know its history but to recognize its conventionality, to

---

[39]Svensson points out that "there is no intrinsic similarity of the kind that exists between
[sonnets] VI and VII" (129).

[40]See John A. Symonds, "The Pathos of the Rose in Poetry," Essays Speculative and Suggestive,
New Edition (London: Chapman and Hall, 1893), 368-75.

[41]Catullus, Tibullus, and Pervigilium Veneris, trans. F. W. Cornish, J. P. Postgate, J. W.
Mackail; Loeb Classical Library, rev. ed. (Cambridge: Harvard University Press, 1962), 86-87.

[42]Symonds, 368-73. Throughout the essay, Symonds attributes "Ver erat" to Ausonius.
The poem is included in the "Appendix to Ausonius" in the Loeb Classical Library Ausonius,
trans. Hugh White, 2 vols. (Cambridge: Harvard University Press, 1919) 2:276-81. White
remarks that the poem cannot "be regarded as earlier than the fourth century A.D. . . . ."
(2:271). Svensson follows Symonds in ascribing the poem to Ausonius (251).

[43]Loeb Ausonius 2:280-81.

know it as a product of history."[44] His point is well taken, and the woman-as-rose *topos* has certainly "been everywhere" by the time it reaches Daniel. Perhaps, therefore, we should regard Daniel's sonnets on this theme as "conventional" rather than as specifically "classical."

Sonnet 31 thoroughly develops the *topos* discussed above:

Looke *Delia* how wee steeme the half-blowne Rose,
The image of thy blush and Summers honor:
Whilst in her tender greene she doth inclose
That pure sweete beautie, Time bestowes upon her.
No sooner spreades her glorie in the ayre,
But straight her ful-blowne pride is in declyning;
She then is scorn'd that late adorn'd the fayre:
So clowdes thy beautie, after fayrest shining.
No Aprill can revive thy withred flowers,
Whose blooming grace adornes thy glorie now:
Swift speedy Time, feathred with flying howers,
Dissolves the beautie of the fairest brow.
O let not then such riches waste in vaine;
But love whilst that thou maist be lov'd againe.

Most scholars regard two stanzas from Tasso's *Gerusalemme liberata* (16.14-15) as the source of Daniel's sonnet.[45] A close adaptation of Tasso's stanzas appeared in the second book of Spenser's *Faerie Queene* (12.74-75), and Daniel probably had both passages in mind when writing his sonnet. Tasso's "*dal verde suo*"[46] ("from its green") – not translated in Spenser's stanzas – becomes "in her tender greene" in Daniel's poem. (Tasso's "*modesta*," near the word "*verde*" though not modifying it, may have inspired Daniel's "tender.") The last line of the poem, however, has perhaps more in common with Spenser's translation than with Tasso's original:

But love whilst that thou maist be lov'd againe (Daniel).

Gather the Rose of love, whilest yet is time,
Whilest loving thou mayst loved be with equall crime (Spenser, 2.12.75.8-9).[47]

[44]*The Light in Troy* (cited chap. 7, n. 21), 50.

[45]Spriet questions this (*Samuel Daniel*, 213-14), but Svensson argues persuasively for Tasso (251).

[46]*Gerusalemme liberata*, ed. Anna Maria Carini (Milan: Feltrinelli, 1961), 357.

[47]Edmund Spenser, *Poetical Works*, ed. J. C. Smith and E. de Selincourt (1912; London: Oxford University Press, 1970), 138.

cogliam d'amor la rosa: amiamo or quando
esser si puote riamato amando (Tasso, 16.51.7-8).

Let us gather the rose of love; let us love now while, loving, it is
possible to be loved in return.

In any case, Daniel's immediate sources were not the Latin poems mentioned
by Symonds, but passages from chivalric narratives of the sixteenth century.[48]
Spenser's *Faerie Queene* represents as conscious an attempt to medievalize
contemporary poetry as Milton's *Paradise Lost* does to classicize it.

But Daniel has not simply combined Tasso's and Spenser's stanzas, con-
densing them into a sonnet. Even in this poem, essentially a working out of
the *carpe diem* theme, he has slipped in some of his earlier themes. The beauty
of the rose, the symbol for Delia, is "pure" and "sweete." Like the disdainful
Delia, the rose flaunts its "ful-blowne pride." The line "She then is scorn'd
that late adorn'd the fayre" significantly alters Tasso's idea – "[the rose] does
not adorn which was once desired by a thousand ladies and a thousand lovers"
("*quella non par che desiata inanti / fu da mille donzelle e mille amanti*") – for in
the Italian, the ladies and lovers seem indifferent to, rather than scornful of,
the faded rose. Yet Delia herself epitomizes the scornful lady; and in pointing
out how the rose, once faded, is scorned, the poet reminds Delia that she
herself may receive the same harsh treatment that she makes him endure. At
the end, he is pleading, I think, not for sexual gratification (Spenser's "equall
crime") but for pity in the form of *amor purus*.

Daniel, in any event, makes it hard for us to accept this argument as a
genuine attempt at seduction. For in *The Complaint of Rosamund*, presented
as a companion poem to *Delia* in the 1592 edition, a "seeming Matrone, yet
a sinfull monster" (sig. [I4]; line 216) urges Rosamund to take advantage of
the king's romantic interest in her, using an all-too-familiar stratagem:

> Thou must not thinke thy flowre can always florish,
> And that thy beautie will be still admired:
> But that those rayes which all these flames doe nourish,
> Canceld with Time, will have their date expyred,
> And men will scorne what now is so desired:
>   Our frailtyes doome is written in the flowers,
>   Which florish now and fade ere many howers. ([I4v]; 239-45)

---

[48]A thorough account of the neoclassical controversy surrounding the epics of Ariosto and
Tasso is in Bernard Weinberg, *History of Literary Criticism in the Italian Renaissance* (Chicago:
University of Chicago Press, 1961), chaps. 19, 20

The narrator's contempt for the monstrous matron and her glozing words is as palpable as Milton's contempt for Comus. If the passage from *Rosamund* does not wholly cancel out the effectiveness of the reasoning in sonnet 31, it certainly forces us to reconsider Daniel's intentions.

The following sonnet develops the same theme; sonnets 33 and 34, also in the *carpe diem* vein, add the idea that the sequence will outlive Delia and the poet:

> This may remaine thy lasting monument,
> Which happily posteritie may cherish:
> These collours with thy fading are not spent;
> These may remaine, when thou and I shall perish.
> If they remaine, then thou shalt live thereby;
> They will remaine, and so thou canst not dye. (34.9-14)

If the idea that the poem is a monument has its roots in classical sources like Horace's "Exegi monumentum" (*Odes* 3.30) and Ovid's "Iamque opus exegi" (*Metamorphoses* 15.871-72), Daniel nonetheless only touches on the theme, not developing it as he does the medieval themes.[49]

The remaining sonnets continue to develop *topoi* popular among continental sonneteers. On one rare occasion, the poet boldly asks not only for a kind look but also for an outstretched hand; and, though it has given him "woundes," he will "give it kisses" (38.12). Here Daniel seems unusually close to Delia, but he never oversteps his amatory bounds by offering to kiss her lips. The characters involved in the drama presented in Daniel's sequence remain distant from each other throughout.

If Delia is really Mary Sidney, as Spriet suggests,[50] then one can understand why Daniel would so carefully keep the poet-lover at a distance from his loved one. But Cecil Seronsy observes – justly, I believe – that the identification of Delia "with the Countess of Pembroke or anybody else is tenuous, if not wholly unacceptable."[51] The story of *Delia*, insofar as one exists, derives mainly from countless love lyrics in which lovers "seem to be always weeping and always on their knees before ladies of inflexible cruelty."[52] A marked contrast to the Delia of Tibullus' racy elegies (another woman subjected to

---

[49]Francis Meres, in *Palladis Tamia* (1598; New York: Scholar's Facsimiles and Reprints, 1938), 282-83, cites the passages from Horace and Ovid and boasts that he can say the same about several of his contemporaries, among them Daniel and Shakespeare.

[50]Spriet, *Samuel Daniel*, 90-91. John Pitcher, in "Samuel Daniel, The Hertfords, and a Question of Love," *The Review of English Studies*, n.s. 35 (1984): 449-62, presents evidence linking Delia with Frances Seymour, though he hastens to add that the "connection between Delia and Lady Frances is . . . strictly a fictional one" (454).

[51]Cecil Seronsy, *Samuel Daniel* (New York: Twayne, 1967), 25.

[52]C. S. Lewis, *The Allegory of Love* (London: Oxford University Press, 1936), 1.

the grievances of a discontented lover), Daniel's mistress is what her anagrammatic name implies: a poetic "ideal."[53]

[53]One thinks also of Maurice Scève's *Délie*, an anagram of *l'idée* (cf. Drayton's *Idea*), and Richard Linche's *Diella* (1596), another anagram of "ideall." John Pitcher, in "Samuel Daniel, The Hertfords," points out that "Delia," also an anagram for "ladie," can yield "ideal ladie" (454).

Chapter 9

Campion's Lyric Poetry

Near the beginning of Anthony Burgess' novel *Earthly Powers*, Kenneth Toomey, the central character, has occasion to discuss Thomas Campion. Living in Malta, Toomey finds it difficult to get hold of many books because of government censorship. The General Post Office, however, allows a book of Campion's poems to slip by, mistaking Thomas Campion for the "great English martyr." With a perverse delight, Toomey recounts the story before a visiting archbishop and adds: "The great English martyr was Edmund, not Thomas. Thomas Campion wrote some rather dirty little songs. Clean songs too, of course, but some quite erotic."[1]

Campion himself acknowledged that his verses were at times *risqué*; in the preface "To the Reader" from his fourth *Booke of Ayres* (c. 1618), he writes that "if any squeamish stomackes shall checke at two or three vaine Ditties in the end of this Booke, let them powre off the clearest, and leave those as dregs in the bottome. Howsoever, if they be but conferred with the *Canterbury Tales* of that venerable Poet *Chaucer*, they will then appear toothsome enough."[2] But despite the ribald element in a number of his songs, Campion generally keeps his emotional distance from his subject matter. "His poetry is as nearly passionless," writes C. S. Lewis, "as great poetry can be."[3]

A. H. Bullen, the first to publish Campion's collected poetry, assumed that Campion had written the poetry to Rosseter's songs.[4] Yet a number of later scholars questioned Campion's authorship of the lyrics in Rosseter's book. Kastendieck found them unworthy of Campion.[5] In 1943, Ralph Berringer argued persuasively that the lyrics in Rosseter's book differed substantially in content and quality from Campion's usual work, that they moved "not a jot beyond the Petrarchan languishing already growing stale

---

[1]Anthony Burgess, *Earthly Powers* (London: Hutchinson, 1980), 16.

[2]*Works* (cited chap. 7, n. 2), 168.

[3]*English Literature in the Sixteenth Century* (cited chap. 8, n. 27), 556.

[4]*The Works of Dr. Thomas Campion*, ed. A. H. Bullen (London, 1889), xiv.

[5]*England's Musical Poet: Thomas Campion* (New York: Oxford University Press, 1938), 68-69. See also the introduction to Percival Vivian's edition of *Campion's Works* (1909; Oxford: Clarendon Press, 1966), lii-liii.

in the middle nineties."[6] While noticing a difference between the mood of
poems like "It fell upon a sommers day," by Campion, and "If I urge my
kinde desires," from Rosseter's collection, Berringer did not overtly state that
the difference is in large part that between the frank expression of physical
desire found in much classical amatory verse and the more spiritual yearning
for love in the tradition of *fin' amors*.[7]

In his study of Campion's works, Christopher R. Wilson emphasizes the
importance of Campion's Latin poetry and its role in "fashioning his English
poetry."[8] Indeed, some of Campion's poems appear both in English and in
his own Latin versions, as Vivian and others have pointed out.[9] The medieval
poet whom Campion most admired, it seems, was Chaucer; in the elegy
opening his *Elegiarum liber* of 1595, Campion alludes with praise to the
"Knight's Tale," *Troylus and Criseyde*, the "Plowman's Tale" (now considered
apocryphal), and the "Miller's Prologue and Tale."[10] And, as we have seen,
Campion in the preface to his fourth *Booke of Ayres* refers approvingly to
Chaucer. One can well imagine the delight that Campion must have taken
while reading the "Miller's Tale," a story in which "hende Nicolas" is as
openly sensual when approaching Alisoun as Campion's Jamy is when
approaching Bessie (BA/8, discussed later). We might wonder, however,
what drew Campion, a self-proclaimed enemy of the Middle Ages, to works
like the "Knight's Tale" and *Troylus* – works that rank high on the list of
medieval masterpieces in English. In a way, of course, this is not a problem
at all, since the Elizabethans in general revered Chaucer, regarding him
almost as one of the ancients. But perhaps Campion also found in Chaucer's
works an attitude toward antiquity comfortingly like his own. A. C. Spearing
has recently stressed Chaucer's desire to return to the classics, his marked
preference for realism over the fantastic; in the "Knight's Tale," the
"Franklin's Tale," and *Troylus*, as Spearing sees it, Chaucer tried to re-create
"a past world with its own customs, its own view of life, and, most important
of all, its own pagan religion."[11] This view of Chaucer may help us to
understand why Campion, instead of scorning Chaucer's work as "vulgar

[6]"Thomas Campion's Share in *A Booke of Ayres*," *Publications of the Modern Language Association* 58 (1943): 940.

[7]Berringer, 943. He does mention Catullus' influence on Campion but says nothing about Horace, Ovid, Propertius, and Martial, whose works also had a marked influence on Campion's English and Latin poetry.

[8]"Words and Notes Coupled Lovingly Together" (Ph.D. diss., Oxford University, 1981), 25.

[9]In the notes to his edition of Campion's *Works*, Percival Vivian points out correspondences between the English and the Latin poems.

[10]Walter Davis lists the Chaucerian allusions (*Works*, 405, n. 4).

[11]*Medieval to Renaissance in English Poetry* (Cambridge: Cambridge University Press, 1985), 40.

and easie" (adjectives used in the *Observations* to describe medieval rhymed poetry), praised it, no doubt recognizing the older master as a kindred spirit, another poet who tried to understand the classical world on its own terms. Campion apparently worked on his Latin poems to the end of his life, and these he presented to the public as literature to be read.[12] *Thomae Campiani poemata* (1595) included lengthy poems in dactyllic hexameters, elegies realling Propertius and Ovid, and a large number of epigrams in the style of Martial and Catullus. But Campion's English poetry (with the exception of a few dedicatory verses, lyrics in masques, examples from the *Observations*, and occasional poems) appeared as lyrics to lute-songs: as words to be sung and heard, not to be read silently. Campion speaks slightingly of his English poems ("eare-pleasing rimes without Arte") but reminds us that he regards ayres as musical equivalents of epigrams. Often, in his rhymed lyrics, Campion tries at once to classicize the native English love lyric and to naturalize the *topoi* found most commonly in antique poetry.

Yet some of Campion's poems seem pretty well entrenched in the Petrarchan tradition, and indeed certain earmarks of the Petrarchan school proved inseparable from standard English love lyrics of the sixteenth century. The following lines do not easily fit into the category of neoclassicism:

> Her rosie cheekes, her ever smiling eyes,
> Are Spheares and beds where Love in triumph lies:
> Her rubine lips, when they their pearle unlocke,
> Make them seeme as they did rise
> All out of one smooth Currall Rocke. (2/20)

The comparison of cheeks to roses reaches back to classical antiquity;[13] but the rubies, pearls, and coral – all these belong more to the Petrarchan tradition. Shakespeare himself mocks such conventional comparisons in "My mistress' eyes are nothing like the sun." So why does Campion – of all people – use them? Part of the answer surely lies in the rest of the stanza, especially in the last two lines:

> Oh, that of other Creatures store I knew
> More worthy, and more rare:
> For these are old, and shee so new,
> That her to them none should compare.

[12]Campion's Latin poems appeared in 1595 and in 1619, a year before his death. For a discussion of these works, see J. W. Binns, "The Latin Poetry of Thomas Campion," in J. W. Binns, ed., *The Latin Poetry of English Poets* (London: Routledge and Kegan Paul, 1974), 1-25.

[13]See M. B. Ogle, "The Classical Origin and Tradition of Literary Conceits," *American Journal of Philology* 34 (1913): 147-49. Ogle cites Campion's poem "There is a Garden in her face" (4/7) as an example of the conceit in English Renaissance poetry (147).

The comparisons, however elegantly phrased, are brought forward chiefly to be mocked as "old," hackneyed, unworthy of the woman being praised. So Campion here uses courtly language and then repudiates it.

One finds a similar impulse to reject traditional romantic themes and sentiments in a number of songs that Campion presented in two versions. We have already seen how "the place of *Cupids* fire" shifts from the eyes in "Mistris, since you so much desire" (BA/16) to the genitals in "Beauty, since you so much desire" (4/22), an instance in which a later text in effect cancels out the original. Campion uses this method elsewhere. The songs "Followe thy faire sunne" (BA/4) and "Seeke the Lord" (1/18), for example, share the same melodies and basses, so the texts invite comparison. As Walter R. Davis has suggested, "the fact that this song ['Seeke'] is set to the music created for the Petrarchan love lament 'Follow thy faire sunne' . . . may introduce a touch of sacred parody, a song about joyful giving up the world set to the music used before for a very worldly song of despair."[14] Davis exercises admirable caution in suggesting only a possible "touch of sacred parody," but verbal parallels between the two texts make it likely indeed that the later text comments on the earlier one. The dominating conceit in "Followe" presents the disdainful lady as a "sunne" and the speaker as her servile shadow. Light and dark imagery pervades the poem. Not surprisingly, "Seeke" also uses light and dark imagery, and once more the new images cancel out the old. In "Followe," the woman of solar beauty is "made of *light*"; the "shaddowe" is to "Follow her whose *light* thy *light* depriveth . . . whose *light* the world reviveth" (my italics). In the third stanza of "Seeke," however, a new attitude toward earthly delights presents itself:

> Farewell, World, thou masse of meere confusion,
>   False light with many shadowes dimm'd,
>   Old Witch with new foyles trimm'd,
> Thou deadly sleepe of soule, and charm'd illusion.

In the secular text, the woman's "light" revives the "world"; here, the very "World" itself is renounced as a "false light with many shadowes dimm'd." The words "World," "light," and "shadowes" surely refer back to the earlier poem and, in each case, comment on their earlier use with disapproval. The characterization of the "World" as an "Old Witch," moreover, strengthens the connection between the "False light" and the sun-woman. The third stanza of the earlier poem focuses on the woman's "pure beames," her "kind beames." The later poem, picking up the key word, tells us that in heaven, the soul shall see "such sights . . . / That worldly thoughts shall by their beames be drowned." The supposed purity of the woman's earthly "beames"

[14]*Thomas Campion* (cited chap. 8, n. 20), 53.

becomes doubtful when one compares them to the celestial beams that drown
all "worldly thoughts." The speaker in the devotional poem concludes:

I the King will seeke of Kings adored,
   Spring of light, tree of grace and blisse,
   Whose fruit so sov'raigne is
That all who taste it are from death restored.

The speaker in "Followe" – who, deprived of the woman's light, feels
"digrac't" – gives place to a speaker who seeks "light" and "grace" from a
more reliable source.

Another set of companion pieces, "Follow your Saint" (BA/10) and "Love
me or not" (4/10), further illustrates Campion's tendency to deromanticize
his poems. The settings, almost identical for the first half of both songs,
again constitute the link between the texts. The earlier poem contains, for
Campion, an unusually large number of phrases and ideas associated with
medieval love-conventions. Like a troubadour in an *envoi*, the poet addresses
his song and (canonizing the beloved in the first line) tells it to follow his
"Saint":

Follow your Saint, follow with accents sweet,
Haste you, sad noates, fall at her flying feete;
There, wrapt in cloud of sorrowe, pitie move,
And tell the ravisher of my soule I perish for her love.
But if she scorns my never-ceasing paine,
Then burst with sighing in her sight, and nere returne againe.

The self-abasement implied in the command to the notes to "fall at her flying
feete"; the desire to move pity from a venerated lady, feared for her potential
scorn; the continual agony of the speaker – all this derives from *fin' amors*.
The poem's final words – "Then let my Noates pursue her scornefull flight:
/ It shall suffice that they were breath'd, and dyed, for her delight" – depict
a speaker satisfied with his lady's disdain, as long as his efforts have in some
measure pleased her. This does not sound like the usual speaker in Campion's
lyrics, and the later text opens in a different vein:

Love me or not, love her I must or dye;
Leave me or not, follow her needs must I.
O, that her grace would my wisht comforts give:
How rich in her, how happy should I live!

All my desire, all my delight should be
Her to enjoy, her to unite to mee:
Envy should cease, her would I love alone:
Who loves by lookes, is seldome true to one.

The woman – stripped of her sainthood, no longer "the ravisher of my soule" – is referred to throughout simply as "her," never even rising from the accusative to the nominative case, from a passive object to an active subject. But she is still desirable: "All my desire, all my delight should be / Her to enjoy, her to unite to mee." With such desires, the speaker could hardly regard her as hopelessly inaccessible, and he craves far more than to have his song "breath'd . . . for her delight." Both poems refer to music in the final stanzas; in "Follow your Saint," it has no power to charm the woman:

> All that I soong still to her praise did tend,
> Still she was first, still she my songs did end.
> Yet she my love and Musicke both doeth flie,
> The Musicke that her Eccho is, and beauties simpathie;
> Then let my Noates pursue her scornefull flight:
> It shall suffice that they were breath'd, and dyed, for her delight.

Despite the unswerving loyalty of the speaker, whose music echoes the woman's beauty, she remains unsympathetic, flying from both him and his songs of praise. The conclusion of the later poem perhaps alludes ironically to these lines:

> Could I enchant, and that it lawfull were,
> Her would I charme softly that none should heare.
> But love enforc'd rarely yeelds firme content;
> So would I love that neyther should repent.

Although the speaker uses conditionals to describe what he might do with magical charms – and every poet with any learning knew that to *enchant* and to *charm* involved singing – he is patently confident that such incantations would prove effective. The woman would not "flie" *his* "love and Musicke." But the speaker hopes for "firme content" (as in Arnaut Daniel's "Lo ferm voler," the word "firme" appears to have literal as well as figurative significance), and he would "love that neyther should repent" – both by avoiding forbidden, coercive magic and, presumably, by gratifying both his and her bodily desires.

In "Followe thy faire sunne" and "Follow thy Saint," Campion presents situations rarely found in his other writings; placed on a pedestal, the woman is admired and pursued by a speaker who hopes, without much confidence, to receive her pity. That Campion revised these poems, making the speakers less wretched and servile, comes as no surprise. In general he seems to have little patience with himself after giving vent to dejection and despair. Thus "The Sypres curten of the night" (BA/9) – the one poem expressing pure *Weltschmerz*, pain not specifically arising from frustrated love – also finds a corrective in "Lift up to heav'n, sad wretch, thy heavy spright" (1/12), which uses most of the same music for the outer voices. As in Dowland's lugubrious songs "Come heavy sleep," "Flow my teares" and "In darknesse let mee dwell,"[15] the speaker in Campion's ayre agonizes for no stated reason:

The Sypres curten of the night is spread,
And over all a silent dewe is cast.
The weaker cares by sleepe are conquered;
But I alone, with hidious griefe agast,
In spite of Morpheus charmes a watch doe keepe
Over mine eies, to banish carelesse sleepe.

. . . .

Griefe, ceaze my soule, for that will still endure
When my cras'd bodie is consum'd and gone;
Beare it to thy blacke denne, there keepe it sure,
Where thou ten thousand soules doest tyre upon:
Yet all doe not affoord such foode to thee
As this poore one, the worser part of mee.

The symptoms resemble those of wretched lovers, tossing in bed, entreating sleep to relieve their misery;[16] but the cause, no doubt intentionally, has been withheld. This morose lamenting elicits a comforting response in "Lift up to heav'n":

Lift up to heav'n, sad wretch, thy heavy spright,
What though thy sinnes thy due destruction threat?
The Lord exceedes in mercy as in might;
His ruth is greater, though thy crimes be great.
Repentance needes not feare the heav'ns just rod,
It stayes ev'n thunder in the hand of God.

The language of *fin' amors*, of course, often borrows from the language of devotion: a *fin amador* speaks of his mistress with great reverence and prays for "mercy," "pity," "grace," and "ruth." Campion himself, as we have seen in "Follow thy Saint," uses these term in an amatory context. And perhaps he bore this in mind when writing, in a devotional reply to secular despair, "The Lord exceedes in *mercy*," "His *ruth* is greater, though thy crimes be great," and, in the second stanza, "With chearefull voyce to him then cry for *grace*" (my italics). Here, as elsewhere, Campion offers an alternative to the self-pity of the ever-complaining courtly lover.

---

[15]See Edward Doughtie, ed., *Lyrics from English Airs* (Cambridge: Harvard University Press, 1970), 82, 101, 351-52.

[16]The *topos* in which the lover begs Sleep for mercy is a commonplace in sonnets; see, for example, Sidney's "Come, sleep, O sleep" (*Astrophel and Stella* 39) and Daniel's "Care-charmer sleepe" (*Delia* 45).

"There is a Garden in her face" (4/7) again employs language associated
with Petrarchan sonneteers:

There is a Garden in her face,
Where Roses and white Lillies grow;
A heav'nly paradice is that place,
Wherein all pleasant fruits doe flow.
There Cherries grow, which none may buy
Till Cherry ripe themselves doe cry.

Cherry lips are surely more appetizing than rubine ones – we might expect
the latter in a woman *"Plus dure que un dyamant,"* as Machaut once put it –
and the woman does not put off her suitors as summarily as does, say, Daniel's
Delia. Campion's horticultural beauty may be related to another garden
mistress, who appears in Rosseter's half of *A Booke of Ayres* (no. 2):

And would you see my Mistris face?
it is a flowrie garden place,
Where knots of beauties have such grace
that all is worke and nowhere space.

Campion's text – which in its opening lines also uses the words *garden, face*,
and *place* (the last two as rhymes) – seems in part a response to the poem his
friend set. Along with praise, Rosseter's lyrics include some cautionary jesting
in the penultimate stanza:

It is a face of death that smiles,
pleasing, though it killes the whiles,
Where death and love in pretie wiles
each other mutuallie beguiles.

This may have inspired Campion's final sixain, in which the woman stands
ready to smite with her arsenal of pulchritude:

Her Eyes like Angels watch them still;
Her Browes like bended bowes doe stand,
Threatning with piercing frownes to kill
All that attempt with eye or hand
Those sacred Cherries to come nigh,
Till Cherry ripe themselves doe cry.

But throughout Campion's poem, we have the feeling (encouraged by the
line concluding every stanza) that those delectable cherry lips will declare
themselves ripe before long. In this regard, Campion's text differs radically
from his friend's. The speaker in Rosseter's poem idealizes the woman ("th'
Idaea of her sexe"); one feels that he admires her from afar, though his
"soule" will continue to pursue her. Campion's women – especially in the

later books, where they sometimes deliver the text – are, as a rule, by no means untouchable goddesses or saints; those who reject suitors rightly suspect the men's motives.

Campion seems especially comfortable when Anglicizing and modernizing ancient Roman poetry. He took his own Latin poetry seriously, even if many of his neo-Latin works were mere *nugae*. Several times he wrote English and Latin poems on the same theme. "It fell on a sommers day" (BA/8), for example, exists in two Latin versions by Campion himself.[17] The poem reveals much about Campion's classicizing technique:

> It fell on a sommers day,
> While sweete Bessie sleeping laie
> In her bowre, on her bed,
> Light with curtaines shadowed;
> Jamy came, shee him spies,
> Opning halfe her heavie eies.
>
> Jamy stole in through the dore,
> She lay slumbring as before;
> Softly to her he drew neere,
> She heard him, yet would not heare;
> Bessie vow'd not to speake,
> He resolv'd that dumpe to breake.
>
> First a soft kisse he doth take,
> She lay still, and would not wake;
> Then his hands learn'd to woo,
> She dreamp't not what he would doo,
> But still slept, while he smild
> To see love by sleepe beguild.
>
> Jamy then began to play,
> Bessie as one buried lay,
> Gladly still through this sleight
> Deceiv'd in her own deceit;
> And, since this traunce begoon,
> She sleepes ev'rie afternoone.

The characters' names, Bessie and Jamy, and the language in general ("He resolv'd that dumpe to breake") give the narrative such a thoroughly English feeling that one would not ordinarily suspect a classical origin. Yet Campion's central *topos* derives from poems by Propertius (*Elegies* 1.3, 2.29A ["Mane

[17]*Works*, 31, n. 20.

erat"]) and Ovid.[18] Indeed, "It fell on a sommers day" is, on the whole, a "compression" of Ovid's elegy "Aestus erat" (*Amores* 1.5).[19]

In Ovid's poem, the male narrator lies down in his room on a hot afternoon, his partly open window letting in some light. In walks Corinna, whom the narrator seizes and with whom he briefly struggles. Having torn off her tunic, he admires her naked body for a while; the reader must guess the rest. The poem ends with a wish: "May my lot bring many a midday like to this!" (*"proveniant medii sic mihi saepe dies!"*).[20] Campion's poem, like the two by Propertius, makes the woman the sleeper and the man the intruder. Still, much of Ovid's poem shows through its Anglicized version. Instead of Ovid's direct statement, "*Aestus erat*" ("It was hot"), Campion gives us an introduction that suggests English folksong: "It fell on a sommers day." The line is manifestly related to formulaic openings like "It was intill a pleasant time, / Upon a simmer's day" and "But it fell ance upon a day."[21] The language of Campion's poem is thoroughly English; the *topos*, Roman.

Unlike Ovid's narrator (who is awake, though lying down), Bessie lies sleeping. Ovid places the action in the afternoon ("and the day had passed its mid hour" – *"mediamque dies exegerat horam"*), the same time that Bessie, by the end of the poem, chooses for her daily nap. Her room, like that in Ovid's poem, is dimly lit. Several details in the first stanza, then, recall the Latin elegy.

Happily, the second and third stanzas introduce some changes. Without a struggle, Jamy steals into Bessie's bed and gives her a "soft kisse" – whether "soft" because he fears waking her or because he is gentler than Ovid's male, we cannot say. But the whole scene lacks the violence that forms an integral part of the erotic experience in Ovid's poem. We are not appalled that Jamy, incubus-like, preys upon Bessie; for Jamy is playing a game, and Bessie herself enjoys the game enough to repeat it daily. (In Ovid's poem, the narrator can only hope for more such afternoons, and we learn nothing of Corinna's feelings.) Brute desire in the Latin elegy becomes mutually enjoyed wantonness in the English ayre.

What does Campion want to do in this song? Some answers suggest themselves when we examine his epigram "In Lycium et Clytham," which deals with the same subject:

[18]See L. P. Wilkinson, "Propertius and Thomas Campion," *London Magazine*, n.s. 7 (April 1967): 56-65.

[19]David Lindley, *Lyric* (London: Methuen, 1985), 11. In *Thomas Campion* (Leiden: E. J. Brill: 1986), Lindley specifically identifies "Aestus erat" as the model for Campion's poem (40).

[20]*Heroides and Amores*, trans. Grant Showerman, rev. G. P. Goold, 2nd ed., Loeb Classical Library (Cambridge: Harvard University Press, 1977), 332-35.

[21]From "The Earl of Mar's Daughter" and "The Twa Knights," in Francis Child, ed., *The English and Scottish Popular Ballads*, 5 vols. (1882-98; New York: Dover, 1965) 5:25, 40

Somno compositam iacere Clytham
Advertens Lycius puer puellam,
Hanc furtim petit, et genas prehendens
Molli basiolum dedit labello.
Immotam ut videt, altera imprimebat
Sensim suavia, moxque duriora;
Istaec conticuit velut sepulta.
Subrisit puer, ultimumque tentat
Solamen, nec adhuc movetur illa
Sed cunctos patitur dolos dolosa.
Quis tandem stupor hic? cui nec anser
Olim, par nec erat vigil Sibilla;
Nunc correpta eadem novo veterno,
Ad notos redit indies sopores.

The youth Lycius, noticing the maid Clytha lying stretched out
asleep, stealthily approached her, and, taking her cheeks, placed a
little kiss on her sweet little lips. As he saw her motionless, he gently
planted a second round of sweet kisses, and soon more forceful ones;
she was still as the tomb. The youth smirked and tested his utmost
pleasure, and still she was not moved but treacherously suffered all
his treacheries. What trance was this, I pray? she had neither goose
nor wakeful sybil; now this same maid, overcome with a strange
lethargy, returns every day to her familiar slumbers.[22]

The Latin poem, while paralleling its English counterpart in content,
differs from it markedly in mood, achieving a poetic distance missing in the
English version. Naturally, the difference between English and Latin (especially for an Anglophone audience) accounts for much of the distance. But
that is not the whole story. Campion's English epigrams – those presented
in the *Observations* – also seem oddly distant. "Somno compositam" is a *poiema*,
a "made thing," while the English version is a *carmen*, a "song." The clever
syntax of the Latin poem contrasts noticeably with the simple parataxis of
the English work. The juxtaposition of *"puer"* ("boy") and *"puellam"* ("girl"),
or of *"dolos"* ("deceptions") and *"dolosa"* ("deceitful"), strikes one as more
artificial – in the Renaissance sense of the word – than the comparable
wordplay in "Deceiv'd in her own deceit"; and the parallel construction of
"sensim suavia, moxque duriora" ("first sweet [kisses], then harder [ones]") is

---

[22]*Works*, 428-31. Campion presents this theme also in "Assidue ridet Lycius" (430-31) and
Umbra, lines 57-84 (380-83); and see "Sweet, exclude mee not" (2/11): "Women are most apt
to be surprised / Sleeping, or sleepe wisely fayning." The "goose" (*"anser"*) of line 11 alludes,
as Davis notes, to the "warning of a goose sacred to Juno [that] saved the Roman Capitol in
the Gallic war" (*Works*, 431, n. 9).

more subtle than the compound sentence "First a soft kisse he doth take, /
She lay still, and would not wake." The differences in syntax underscore the
differences in the male characters' personalities, for the simple parataxis in
the English poem suggests naïveté while the tricky constructions in the Latin
suggest cunning: Jamy is playful; Lycius, sly.

Campion defended his native ayres in the preface to *Two Bookes of Ayres*
(c. 1613): "some there are who admit onely *French* or *Italian* Ayres, as if
every Country had not his proper Ayre, which the people thereof naturally
usurpe in their Musicke."[23] In many of his English poems, Campion seems
to have a similar idea in mind. He knows that the genius of the language
will not admit certain constructions in English. (If this seems obvious to us,
it was not always so to Renaissance classicists: think of Stanyhurst's *Aeneid*
translations.) "It fell on a sommers day" represents a virtuosic reworking of
Latin poems and themes in a thoroughly English form – so English that the
reader, while sensing that such poetry differs from the standard Petrarchan
fare of Campion's contemporaries, does not suspect its origins in classical
antiquity. And such disguised classicism runs through many of Campion's
rhymed lyrics.

Of course, Campion did not always conceal his classicism. The poems in
the *Observations* (1602) are overtly classical – with their unrhymed, pseudo-
quantitative verse forms – though Campion has again tried to naturalize
them. Thus we get the English names – Harry, Barnzy, Kate – and some
topical themes (Puritan churlishness, Elizabeth's divinity, and so on). Yet
the poems almost invariably sound like translations from the Latin. The fifth
epigram, for example, has a disturbing ring to it:

> Thou telst me, *Barnzy, Dawson* hath a wife:
> Thine he hath, I graunt; *Dawson* hath a wife.[24]

The diminutive "Barnzy," obviously meant to make the poem sound all the
more natural, in fact sounds strained; one feels that Campion had to work
hard to make his poem read like something other than Martial Englished.
Martial, one of Campion's favorite poets, certainly gives us poems on similar
themes:

> Quare non habeat, Fabulle, quaeris
> uxorem Themison? habet sororem. (12.20)

> Do you ask, Fabullus, why Themison has not got a wife? He has a
> sister.[25]

---

[23]Ibid., 55.

[24]Ibid., 308.

[25]*Epigrams*, trans. Walter Ker, rev. ed., Loeb Classical Library, 2 vols. (Cambridge: Harvard
University Press, 1968), 2:332-33. Ker notes that "sister" may also mean "mistress"

In both epigrams, the poet poses a question concerning a man's having or not having a wife; a vocative interrupts the first line of each poem; a pointed answer ends the couplet. Campion's "point," however, is hardly as scandalous as Martial's. Campion freely writes about adultery and genitalia, but his classicism does not take him into the world of incest.

"When the God of merrie love" (BA/15), which generally slips by without much notice in discussions of Campion's poetry, presents a patchwork of classical themes:

> When the God of merrie love
> As yet in his cradle lay,
> Thus his wither'd nurse did say:
> Thou a wanton boy wilt prove
> To deceive the powers above;
> For by thy continuall smiling
> I see thy power of beguiling.
>
> Therewith she the babe did kisse,
> When a sodaine fire out came
> From those burning lips of his,
> That did her with love enflame;
> But none would regard the same,
> So that, to her daie of dying,
> The old wretch liv'd ever crying.

Campion may have derived some of his ideas, again, from Ovid's *Amores*. In "Esse quid hoc dicam" (1.2), the poet imagines Cupid in a victorious triumph, wounding victims as he passes by.[26] From this description, Campion could have derived his predictions that the "God of merrie love" would grow up to inflict pain on others; Cupid's inflammatory qualities are also present. But Campion's poem seems more Grecian than Roman. The Cupid of the *Anacreontea* and the *Greek Anthology*, like Campion's Cupid, often seems an insufferable brat. For example, in an Anacreontic poem especially popular during the Renaissance, the narrator, late one night, discovers Cupid, wet from the rain. Taking pity on the child, the narrator harbors him from the elements. Cupid, in return for this kindness, tests his bow and wounds his host, who will suffer the pangs of love.[27] In Campion's poem, the nurse

---

(333, n. 2); but the poem has a sharper epigrammatic point if we take "*sororem*" simply to mean "sister" or "a close female relation."

[26]*Heroides and Amores*, 322-25, lines 23-46.

[27]*Elegy and Iambus with the Anacreontea*, trans. J. M. Edmunds, Loeb Classical Library, 2 vols. (Cambridge: Harvard University Press, 1931) 2:63. For a discussion of the Ovidian and Anacreontic representations of Cupid in the Renaissance, see Lisle C. John, *The Elizabethan Sonnet Sequences* (cited chap. 7, n. 15), 39-76.

kisses Cupid with no intention of becoming sexually aroused; but "those burning lips of *his*" cause her to fall hopelessly in love. Like the kind, unsuspecting host in the Greek poem, she has a future of pain awaiting her.

An immensely popular Alexandrian poem on Cupid is Moschus' "Fugitive Love" (*Greek Anthology* 9.440).[28] Here, Aphrodite has lost her child and offers a description of him – as well as a warning to flee from his poisonous kisses. Like Campion's deceitful "wanton boy," Moschus' Cupid is "Lying, and false," "A craftie lad" with "cruell pastimes."[29] Aphrodite admits that her son's arrows wound even her – an idea roughly corresponding to the nurse's falling in love with Cupid. Both Aphrodite and the nurse remark upon Cupid's dangerously beguiling smile. Aphrodite *knows* that Cupid's kiss is poisonous, whereas the nurse finds out the hard way.

In Spenser's *Anacreontics* (ending the *Amoretti*), Campion may also have found some inspiration for his own poem. Among the Greek *Anacreontea* is a poem in which Cupid is stung by a bee. Like the other two poems we have examined, this one enjoyed considerable popularity during the Renaissance. In Spenser's version, Venus tends her son's wounds with scandalous affection:

> She drest his wound and it embaulmed wel
>   with salve of soveraigne might:
> And then she bath'd him in a dainty well
>   the well of deare delight.
> Who would not oft be stung as this,
> to be so bath'd in Venus blis?[30]

Campion's nurse does not go so far as to bathe Cupid in her "well of deare delight," but the erotic kiss between the old nurse and the young Cupid (still in his cradle) suggests a tabooed act similar to, if milder than, Venus' incestuous assuaging of her son in Spenser's poem. In any event, Campion's poem clearly derives a great deal from ancient poems (or imitations of them) in which Cupid appears as a deceiving troublemaker.

In general, Campion modernizes and naturalizes classical poetry by taking a few lines from one poem, a few from another; and, of course, he freely

---

[28]James Hutton, in his two books on the *Greek Anthology* in France and in Italy (cited chap. 7, n. 18), lists many Latin versions of Moschus' *Amor fugitivus*. See also his "*Amor Fugitivus*: The First Idyl of Moschus in Imitations to the Year 1800," *Essays on Renaissance Poetry*, ed. Rita Guerlac (Ithaca, N.Y.: Cornell University Press, 1980), 74-105.

[29]From the 1593 translation by Barnabe Barnes (whom Campion knew), in *Parthenophil and Parthenophe*, ed. Victor A. Doyno (Carbondale: Southern Illinois University Press, 1971), xxxiii. For the original with a prose translation, see *The Greek Anthology*, trans. W. R. Paton, Loeb Classical Library, 5 vols. (Cambridge: Harvard University Press, 1916) 3:245-47.

[30]Spenser, *Poetical Works* (cited chap. 8, n. 47), 578, lines 45-50. See also Hutton's essay "Cupid and the Bee," *Essays on Renaissance Poetry*, 106-31.

inserts his own material as well. In "The man of life upright,"[31] an imitation
of Horace's "Integer vitae" (Odes 1.22), Campion follows his model somewhat loosely for four stanzas – longer than usual – and then goes off on his
own:

> The man of life upright,
>   Whose guiltlesse hart is free
> From all dishonest deedes,
>   Or thought of vanitie,
>
> The man whose silent dayes
>   In harmeles joyes are spent,
> Whome hopes cannot delude,
>   Nor sorrow discontent,
>
> That man needes neither towers
>   Nor armour for defence,
> Nor secret vautes to flie
>   From thunders violence.
>
> Hee onely can behold
>   With unafrighted eyes
> The horrours of the deepe,
>   And terrours of the Skies.
>
> Thus, scorning all the cares
>   That fate, or fortune brings,
> He makes the heav'n his booke,
>   His wisedome heev'nly things,
>
> Good thoughts his onely friendes,
>   His wealth a well-spent age,
> The earth his sober Inne,
>   And quiet Pilgrimage.

He set the poem twice (BA/18, 1/2). In the later version, he made some
significant changes in the opening stanza; a comparison of Horace's first
stanza with Campion's two renditions of it brings out some of Campion's
naturalizing devices:

> Integer vitae scelerisque purus
> non eget Mauris iaculis necque arcu

---

[31]As Davis notes (Works, 43, n. 38), some manuscripts attribute this poem to Francis Bacon.

nec venenatis gravida sagittis,
   Fusce, pharetra. . . .

He who is upright in his way of life and unstained by guilt, needs
not Moorish darts nor bow nor qii ver loaded with poisoned arrows,
Fuscus.[32]

The man of life upright
   Whose guiltlesse hart is free
From all dishonest deedes,
   Or thought of vanitie. . . . (BA/18, 1601)

The man of life upright
   Whose chearfull minde is free
From waight of impious deedes,
   And yoake of vanitee. . . . (1/2, c. 1613)

Horace, like many of his contemporaries, uses tautology for its rhetorical
force. The meaning of *integer* (here meaning "someone *not* blemished") is
reinforced by *scelerisque purus* ("untainted by guilt"). Campion's first version
retains the effect of the Roman pleonasms – "upright," "guiltlesse," "free /
From all dishonest deedes." Like Horace, Campion stresses what the upright
man lacks: his heart is guilt*less*, *free* of *dis*honest deeds. The later translation
moves further away from its pagan model and begins to sound more like a
Christian hymn. Campion replaces "guiltlesse heart" with "cheerfull minde,"
and his new upright man seems related to the Jacke and Jone who "thinke
no ill, / But loving live, and merry still; / Doe their weeke dayes worke,
and pray / Devotely on the holy day" (1/20). Phrases like "waight of impious
deedes" and "yoake of vanitee" continue to transform Campion's ayre into
a "divine and morall" song; indeed, Lowbury, Salter, and Young rightly call
attention to the similarity between "The man of life upright" and the first
Psalm.[33] Campion has consistently rejected Horace's specific images for a
more general paraphrase. Where Horace writes of menacing clouds and a
malignant Jupiter (19-20), Campion gives us simply the "terrours of the
Skies." Jupiter, of course, would not fit in with the implied Christian message
of the poem. And no one in Campion's poem corresponds to the sweetly
laughing, sweetly speaking Lalage, who supplies the love interest in Horace's
ode. This aspect of the poem would naturally be out of place in a devotional
song, though it could easily appeal to a sonneteer. Petrarch, in fact, found

---

[32]Horace, *The Odes and Epodes*, trans. C. E. Bennett, Loeb Classical Library (Cambridge:
Harvard University Press, 1927), 64-65.

[33]Edward Lowbury, Timothy Salter, and Alison Young, *Thomas Campion: Poet, Composer,
Physician* (New York: Barnes and Noble, 1970), 113.

inspiration for at least two sonnets in "Integer vitae."[34] When writing sonnets, Petrarch is for the most part in his medieval mode, and a look at his
method of amplifying a classical source will throw Campion's neoclassicism
into sharper relief. In sonnet 145 ("Ponmi ove'l sole"), Petrarch takes as his
starting point the last two stanzas of Horace's ode:

> pone me pigris ubi nulla campis
> arbor aestiva recreatur aura,
> quod latus mundi nebulae malusque
>   Iuppiter urget;
>
> pone sub curru nimium propinqui
> solis in terra domibus negata:
> dulce ridentem Lalagen amabo,
>   dulce loquentem. (17-24)

Place me on the lifeless plains where no tree revives under the
summer breeze, a region of the world oppressed by clouds and a
malignant Jupiter; place me beneath the chariot of the sun where it
draws too near the earth, in a land unfit for dwellings. I will love
my sweetly laughing, sweetly speaking Lalage.[35]

Surrey translated Petrarch's poem, adding to it (a common practice when
one turns Italian polysyllables into English monosyllables) but nonetheless
following his model with reasonable accuracy:

> Set me wheras the sunne doth parche the grene,
> Or where his beames do not dissolve the yse:
> In temperate heate where he is felt and sene:
> In presence prest of people madde or wise.
> Set me in hye, or yet in lowe degree:
> In longest night, or in the shortest daye:
> In clearest skye, or where clowdes thickest be:
> In lusty youth, or when my heeres are graye.
> Set me in heaven, in earth, or els in hell,
> In hyll, or dale, or in the fomyng flood:
> Thrall, or at large, alive where so I dwell:
> Sicke, or in health: in evyll fame, or good.

---

[34]Sonnets 145 and 176; perhaps also 159. In his edition of the *Petrarch's Lyric Poems* (cited
chap. 7, n. 5), Robert Durling mentions the Horatian echoes in sonnets 145 and 159.

[35]*Odes and Epodes*, 64-65. I have altered Bennet's translation in places to make it more
literal.

Hers will I be, and onely with this thought
Content my selfe, although my chaunce be nought.[36]

One sees immediately that Petrarch (with help from Surrey) and Campion have imitated Horace in entirely different ways. The reason is not simply that one poem praises moral behavior while the other professes profane love. It is deeper than that. Petrarch has explored possibilities for expanding the Latin text, adding numerous illustrative examples to the few presented in the ode, and his goal is *amplificatio*.[37] Indeed, Puttenham, in his *Arte of English Poesie* (1589), cites Surrey's translation (wrongly attributed to Wyatt) as an especially apt example of the "Distributer," a rhetorical figure occurring "when we may conveniently utter a matter in one entier speach or proposition and will rather do it peecemeale and by distribution of every part for amplification sake . . . "; he admires the Tuscan poet for stretching into fourteen lines an idea that "might have bene said in these two verses. *Set me wheresoever ye will, / I am and wilbe yours still.*"[38] Campion moves in the opposite direction. Stripping away as many particulars as possible, he strives for compression and clarity – the plain style. Petrarch adds to Horace's purple patches; Campion tries to paint them out of the picture. In Horace's secular poem, Campion has found the stuff of a moral text; removing any traces of excess in his classical model, he uses spare language along with the idioms and formal elements found in English hymns and psalm translations to naturalize "Integer vitae."

The pagan world once again overlaps with the Judeo-Christian in Campion's "Come, let us sound with melody the praises" (BA/21), which in places recalls Psalm 19. Since Campion has written the poem in Sapphic stanzas, one might reasonably assume that he, like many other humanist poets, believed that the psalms had originally been written in quantitative verse. Nevertheless, his later paraphrases of the psalms (1/4, 1/14, 1/15) use rhyme and accent. If the divine and moral songs that fill Campion's *First Booke of Ayres* (c. 1613) seem out of character in that they lack the classical touch ("The man of life upright" excepted), the songs also lack – naturally enough – any trace of romantic love. The psalms themselves, long antedating the poems of Augustan Rome, belonged to the antique world that Campion so admired, the world as yet unpolluted by the barbaric culture – as he saw it – of the Middle Ages. Campion, I suspect, felt that his moral texts belonged

---

[36]In *Songs and Sonnets: Tottel's Miscellany*, a facsimile edition of Richard Tottel's collection *Songes and Sonettes* (1557; Menston: Scolar Press, 1970), sig. Bii.

[37]For medieval interpretations of the classical rhetorical term *amplificatio*, see William W. Ryding, *Structure in Medieval Narrative* (The Hague: Mouton, 1971), 66-82. The discussion centers on longer narrative works but has some bearing on notions of amplification in general.

[38]*The Arte of English Poesie*, ed. Edward Arber (1906; Kent, Ohio: Kent State University Press, 1970), 230-31.

not so much to the tradition of medieval (or even Protestant) hymnody as to a tradition older than that of even the ancient Romans – that of Old Testament lyric poetry.

In his *Fourth Booke of Ayres* (c. 1618), Campion includes some texts that he himself regards as ribald – nothing as lubricious as what, say, Catullus often describes, but a far cry from anything in Daniel. In a poem on impotence (4/21), Campion once again borrows material from antiquity:

> If any hath the heart to kill,
>   Come rid me of this wofull paine.
> For while I live I suffer still
>   This cruell torment all in vaine:
>   Yet none alive but one can guesse
>   What is the cause of my distresse.
>
> Thanks be to heav'n, no grievous smart,
>   No maladies my limbes annoy;
> I beare a sound and sprightfull heart,
>   Yet live I quite depriv'd of joy:
>   Since what I had, in vaine I crave,
>   And what I had not, now I have.
>
> A Love I had, so fayre, so sweet,
>   As ever wanton eye did see.
> Once by appointment wee did meete;
>   Shee would, but ah, it would not be:
>   She gave her heart, her hand shee gave;
>   All did I give, shee nought could have.
>
> What Hagge did then my powers forespeake,
>   That never yet such taint did feele?
> Now shee rejects me as one weake,
>   Yet am I all compos'd of steele.
>   Ah, this is it my heart doth grieve:
>   Now though shee sees, shee'le not believe!

Formal elements – iambic tetrameter, the *ababcc* rhyme-scheme – already do much to disguise the classical origin of the poem. The theme of impotence is, of course, by no means the exclusive property of antiquity. In the famous song "I have bene a foster" (c. 1515), we read the following:

> Every bowe for me ys to bygge;
>   Myne arow ny worne ys;
> The glew ys slypt frome the nyk;

When I shuld shoote I myse;
Yet have [I bene a foster.]

Lady Venus hath commaundyd me
    Owt of her courte to go;
Ryght playnly she shewith me
    That beawtye ys my foo;
Yet have I b[ene a foster.][39]

Delivering its message with metaphors drawn from archery, the earlier poem is in a way more explicit (certainly less subtle) than Campion's. Yet the persistent allegorizing makes even as sharp an image as the poet's "arow" less vivid than the implied object to which Campion's fair "Love" gives her hand. Like Nashe in "A Choise of Valentines" (lines 121-42), Campion has borrowed this idea from Ovid's *Amores* (3.7): "Moreover my girl did not refrain from applying her hand and gently coaxing it" (*"Hanc etiam non est mea dedignata puella / molliter admota sollicitare manu . . ."*).[40] And indeed much of Campion's poem derives from this Roman elegy on impotence.[41] Once again, Campion disguises his classicism by beginning his poem in a vein different from that of the original. The opening lines, in which the poet bewails his agonized state, lead the reader to expect a poem on unrequited or forbidden or postponed love. But Campion soon leads his reader down an unexpected path. In the second stanza, the poet stresses his physical well-being; although the speaker in Ovid's poem does not emphasize his health, he makes sure to mention his youth and recent – indeed, staggering – virility, which allowed him to make love nine times in one night with no apparent difficulty (lines 17-26). In the third stanza, Campion borrows heavily from Ovid; the woman was "fayre," and her looks provoked a "wanton eye"; both parties sought sexual union, and both were disappointed. The opening of Ovid's elegy covers the same territory.[42] In the fourth stanza, the poet questions whether some "Hagge" has magically brought about his impotence. The idea comes once again from Ovid's elegy, though there the woman, not the poet, suggests that a sorceress may have been at work on him (79-80). At the end of Campion's poem, the narrator regains his potency, but now he lacks a fair companion; Ovid's poem complains of the same predicament (67-68). As in "It fell on a sommers day," Campion has con-

[39]From Henry VIII's MS., reprinted in John Stevens' *Music and Poetry in the Early Tudor Court* (1961; Cambridge: Cambridge University Press, 1979), 409.

[40]*Heroides and Amores*, 478-79, lines 73-74.

[41]In *Thomas Campion*, 35-37, David Lindley also notes Campion's debt to Ovid in this poem.

[42]*Heroides and Amores*, 474-75.

densed a substantial piece of Roman poetry into a few stanzas of English verse, using diction and idioms native to English song.

In his lyrics, we find Campion continually rejecting those love conventions that, having become codified in the Middle Ages, carried into most amatory verse of the Renaissance. True, Campion sometimes borrowed from the Petrarchan tradition, especially in his earliest published poetry in English. But he seems to have had second thoughts about the poems most indebted to *fin' amors*, criticizing them through religious or bawdy parodies. His principal source of inspiration was ancient Rome. One method to emulate the ancients – a method tried on the continent throughout the sixteenth century – involved rejecting rhyme and adopting quantitative verse. Like other neoclassicists, Campion tried his hand at this; unlike them, he wrote a poem in this mode that has enjoyed lasting popularity, "Rose-cheekt *Lawra*." Such experiments in ancient (or pseudo-ancient) meters, however, often sound forced or peculiar in English, and Campion's fine ear no doubt detected this. His most successful classicizing, then, comes in those songs in which the spirit of ancient Rome hides behind an Elizabethan mask. Indeed, much of Campion's art lies in its self-concealment: for in naturalizing his ancient themes, Campion disguises the very classicism that he deftly incorporates into his songs.

Postlude

The foregoing chapters have focused mainly on poetic and musical elements that could be identified – and, in the Renaissance, often *were* identified – as either classical or medieval (or "modern," or simply nonclassical). Sixteenth-century writers themselves tended to oversimplify issues, and I am aware that my own argument might seem facile and reductive. It may therefore be prudent to restate certain points, clarifying those most vulnerable to misinterpretation.

First, a number of sixteenth-century authors, artists, and musicians felt the need to purge their culture of what they regarded as the barbarous inheritance of the Middle Ages. They wanted a return to classical ideals. The classicizing movement, however, did not have a uniform program for reform. For authors, a radical solution was to write not only in Latin but in Latin aping Cicero's style down to the finest detail. And what of the vernacular – say, Italian? To some, it was a mere corruption of Latin, to be avoided in serious verse and prose. But, then again, it *was* the language people actually spoke. So attempts to classicize the vernacular began. In verse, they might involve just the elimination of rhyme or might extend to the constitution of individual feet in a poetic line. The spectrum of experimentation was quite wide. In music, meanwhile, the primary enemy was intricate polyphony; the best way to counter this enemy was to write either homorhythmic counterpoint or monody, both giving the words an importance they had allegedly been denied in elaborate settings.

Along with the efforts to reject the medieval came the equally strong efforts both to adopt classical verse forms, idioms, and themes, and to attempt recreations of antique song. Yet the music and poetry of the Renaissance had roots in the Middle Ages, and there was no way around that reality. For some, of course, it was not a problem. Sidney, for example, could write sonnets and sestinas, Sapphics and asclepiades; all was fair game. Others, like Du Bellay, might write elegies in Latin and sonnets in the vernacular, satisfying the need to flaunt their learning and to express themselves in the mother tongue. In the field of music, while some critics condemned polyphony, others hailed the Renaissance masters of counterpoint as modern Arions and Orpheuses.

Extreme classicists wanted (or said they wanted) to extirpate all traces of Gothic pollution from contemporary art, music, and poetry. Campion sided with this group, whose goals were unattainable in a culture still steeped in medieval traditions. Yet we see the rhymer Campion, at his most polemical, rejecting rhyme and standard accentual verse in favor of classical or pseudo-classical models. He appears, moreover, to have deliberately revised those portions of his songs indebted to what the troubadours called *fin' amors*, preferring to model his amatory verse on that of the Augustan masters. In his songs, he increasingly rejects the nonclassical word-painting associated with the madrigal and adopts methods of text-setting developed by continental composers seeking to recreate the effect of antique song.

John Daniel, in contrast, madrigalized the lute-song. He did not, of course, deliberately choose to flout the neoclassicists. He simply enjoyed what the madrigalists did with words; he admired how the contrapuntists manipulated their musical motives, and with great skill he composed works that combined the playfulness of the madrigal, the polyphonic seriousness of the motet, and the verbal clarity of the lute-song.

His brother, Samuel Daniel, wrote works in many different genres: the sonnet, the verse epistle, the classical tragedy, the epic, the prose history, the polemical tract. He found inspiration in classical, medieval, and contemporary literature. (Montaigne's essays deeply impressed him.) His *Cleopatra* – written partly to please the Countess of Pembroke – is as manifestly neoclassical as the plays by Garnier and Jodelle that served as his models. But his neoclassicism did not prevent him from writing *The Queenes Arcadia* or *Hymens Triumph*, both patterned after Guarini's *Il pastor fido*, a play whose questionable genre – the pastoral tragicomedy – provoked rough criticism from Aristotelian purists. Daniel's epic, *The Civil Wars* (which bears some similarity to medieval verse chronicles), certainly owes a debt to Lucan, and Daniel expects us to draw parallels between his work and the *Bellum civile*. Yet even here we find in Daniel a poet whose epic style differs from that of his more classically inclined contemporaries, for *The Civil Wars* is written in the *ottava rima* stanzas associated with chivalric narratives like *Orlando furioso* and *Gerusalemme liberata*. The ideas are compartmentalized, each placed in a "room" (Daniel himself puns on this meaning of *stanza* in 1.5.8). Here is Daniel imitating Lucan:

> What furie, ô what madnes held thee so,
> Deare *England* (too too prodigall of blood),
> To waste so much, and warre without a foe,
> Whilst *France*, to see thy spoyles, at pleasure stood! (1.2.1-4)[1]

The model is unmistakably Lucan (*Bellum civile* 1.8-12), granted. But the neatly proportioned verses, the rhymes, the end-stopped lines – these are not Lucan Englished. This is Marlowe's translation of the passage Daniel chose to imitate:

---

[1] *The Civil Wars*, ed. Laurence Michel (New Haven: Yale University Press, 1958), 71.

Romans, what madnes, what huge lust of warre
Hath made *Barbarians* drunke with *Latin* bloud?
Now *Babilon*, (proud through our spoile) should stoop,
While slaughtered *Crassus* ghost walks unreveng'd,
Will ye wadge war, for which you shall not triumph? (8-12)[2]

Marlowe's passage – through the rough vigor of the lines, the absence of rhyme, the more involved syntax, and the greater use of enjambment – transmits properties of the Latin that are absent in Daniel's version. For the most part, Daniel took tools ready to hand to build his poetic structures, not rejecting rhyme in general or *ottava rima* in particular,[3] not scorning the sonnet as a Procrustean bed, not casting aside the conventions of *fin' amors* – whether or not he thought of them as such.

It is revealing that Campion's "epic," *De pulverea coniuratione*, is in Latin. Its topic – the gunpowder plot – is thoroughly English. Yet it seems that, for Campion, English verse (even unrhymed) does not have enough power to raise the narrative to epic heights; instead, he uses the language of Virgil, whose *Aeneid* is echoed several times in *De pulverea coniuratione*.[4] Virgil, however, wrote in his native tongue; Campion rejects his. Again, linguistic and historical realities intrude upon Campion the neoclassicist.

In *Musophilus* (1599), Samuel Daniel has this to say about fault-finding readers:

Why should civill learning seeke to wound
And mangle her own members with despight?
Prodigious wits that study to confound
The life of wit, to seeme to know aright,
As if themselves had fortunately found
Some stand from of the earth beyond our sight,
Whence overlooking all as from above,
Their grace is not to worke, but to reprove. (207-14)[5]

It is Daniel in his didactic, Horatian mode (he is about to translate some of the *Ars poetica*) – a mode as natural to him as his Petrarchan and Guarinian modes. A poet who writes so ardently about verse and learning, and so

---

[2]*The Complete Works of Christopher Marlowe*, ed. Fredson Bowers, 2d ed., 2 vols. (Cambridge: Cambridge University Press, 1981) 2:280.

[3]In the *Defence*, Daniel proudly states that Tolomei's experiments in vernacular quantitative verse could "never induce *Tasso* the wonder of *Italy*, to write that admirable Poem of *Jerusalem*, comparable to the best of the ancients, in any other forme then the accustomed verse" (*Poems and A Defence of Ryme* [cited chap. 8, n. 2], 141).

[4]See Sowerby's introductory notes to *De puluerea coniuratione (On the Gunpowder Plot)*, ed. David Lindley, trans. Robin Sowerby (Leeds: Leeds Studies in English, 1987), 23-27.

[5]*Poems and A Defence of Ryme*, 75.

scornfully about carping critics, is not likely to accept accusations of barbarism from anyone, certainly not from Campion, a man "whose commendable Rymes, albeit now himselfe an enemy to ryme, have given heretofore to the world the best notice of his worth" (*Defence*, 130). The contradictions inherent in Campion's invective against rhyme made Daniel's counterargument a relatively easy matter. Daniel sought out the best in all works of the past, not binding himself to the "authoritie of Antiquitie," and he understood the limitations of art and of language:

> They are the smallest peeces of the minde
> That passe this narrow organ of the voyce.
> The great remaine behinde in that vast orbe
> Of th'apprehension, and are never borne.[6]

In not rejecting the Middle Ages, in admitting that medieval culture had as much wisdom to offer as any other, Daniel breaks with years of humanist prejudice and relies on his own judgment and experience to determine what is good and what is bad. "It is not bookes," he writes in the *Defence*, "but onely that great booke of the world, and the all-overspreading grace of heaven that makes men truely judiciall. Nor can it be but a touch of arrogant ignorance, to hold this or that nation Barbarous, these or those times grosse, considering how this manifold creature man . . . hath always some disposition of worth . . . (139-40). The statements could scarcely be simpler – or more profound.

---

[6]*Hymens Triumph* (lines 1287-90), in *Complete Works* (cited chap. 8, n. 29) 3:377.

Appendix

Two Anonymous Texts
Probably by Samuel Daniel

"He whose desires"

No one, to my knowledge, has called attention to the parallels between the text to John Daniel's "He whose desires" and Samuel Daniel's writings. The song lyrics run as follows:

> He whose desires are still abroad I see,
> Hath never any peace at home the while:
> And therefore now come back my hart to mee,
> It is but for superfluous things we toile.
> Rest alone with thy selfe be all within,
> For what without thou get'st thou dost not win.
> Honour, wealth, glory, fame, are no such things,
> But that which from Imagination springs.
> High reaching power that seemes to over grow,
> Doth creepe but on the earth, lies base and low.

Daniel's Epistle "To the Lady Margaret, Countesse of Cumberland" (in *Poems and A Defence of Ryme* [cited chap. 8, n. 2], 111-15) contains the largest number of obvious parallels. Like the song, the epistle generalizes by beginning with the word *He* followed by a relative pronoun. As in the seventh line of the song, the epistle regards "honor, power, renowne" as "onely gay afflictions" (lines 15-16). The song urges the listener to "Rest alone with thyself be all within," and the epistle speaks approvingly of Lady Margaret for remaining "in the region of [her] selfe" (77). Four stanzas from the end of the epistle, Daniel writes:

> how turmoyld they are that levell lie
> With earth, and cannot lift themselves from thence,
> That never are at peace with their desires. . . . (100-102)

The sentiment expressed and the use of several key words found also in the song – *earth, never, peace, desires, lie(s)* – already make Samuel Daniel a good candidate for authorship. In addition, we find the following passage in the chorus concluding the second act of Daniel's *Philotas* (ed. Laurence Michel [New Haven: Yale University Press, 1949], 122):

> How dost thou weare, and weary out thy dayes,
> Restlesse ambition never at an end!
> Whose travels no Herculean pillar stayes,

But still beyond thy rest thy labours tend,
Above good fortune thou thy hopes dost raise,
Still climing, and yet never canst ascend:
    For when thou hast attaind unto the top
    Of thy desires, thou hast not yet got up. (712-19)

As in the song, rest is unattainable for the ambitious, and the final couplet warns that
the high desires of the power-seeker will ironically keep him low. The various
thematic and verbal correspondences among these poems strongly suggest that Samuel
Daniel composed the text for "He whose desires."

"Now the earth, the skies, the Aire"

The text in John Daniel's song (given in chapter 6) bears a distinct resemblance to
the ode immediately following *Delia* (*Poems and A Defence of Ryme*, 36):

Nowe each creature joyes the other,
    Passing happy daies and howers:
One byrd reports unto another,
    In the fall of silver showers,
Whilst the earth our common mother,
    Hath her bosome deckt with flowers.

            . . . .

Whilst that she O cruell Maide,
    Doth me, and my true love dispise:
My lives florish is decayde
    That depended on her eyes:
But her will must be obaide,
    And well he'ends for love who dies.

Further parallels occur in "The Complaint of Rosamund" (*Poems and a Defence of
Ryme*, 43):

        nature decks her [a woman] with her proper fayre,
    Which cheeres the worlde, joyes each sight, sweetens th'ayre. (132-33)

Along with the obvious correspondences (similar themes and vocabulary), the presence of "joys" in all three poems as a transitive verb apparently meaning "brings joy
to" – not a widespread usage – suggests Daniel's hand in the anonymous text.

Bibliography

Abbreviations

AIM	American Institute of Musicology.
CMM	Corpus Mensurabilis Musicae.
CNRS	Centre National de la Recherche Scientifique.
DTÖ	Denkmäler der Tonkunst in Österreich.
ELS	English Lute Songs (Scolar Press Facsimiles).
LSW	The English School of Lutenist Song Writers (edited and transcribed by Edmund Fellowes).
VfMW	*Vierteljahrsschrift für Musikwissenschaft.*
Warburg	*Journal of the Warburg and Courtauld Institutes.*

Musical Editions Used

Alison, Richard. *The Psalmes of David in Meter.* ELS 1. 1599. Reprint. Menston: Scolar Press, 1968.

Antico, Andrea, pub. *Canzoni sonetti strambotti et frottole, libro tertio (1517).* Edited by Alfred Einstein. Northampton, Mass.: Smith College, 1941.

Arcadelt, Jacobus. *Opera omnia 9.* Edited by Albert Seay. CMM 31. N.p.: AIM, 1968.

Bataille, Gabrielle, pub. *Airs de differents autheurs, mis en tablature de luth. Cinquiesme livre.* 1614. Reprint. Geneva: Minkoff, 1980.

————, pub. *Airs de differents autheurs, mis en tablature de luth. Troisiesme livre.* 1611. Reprint. Geneva: Minkoff, 1980.

Bossinensis, Franciscus, ed. *Tenori e contrabassi intabulati col sopran in canto figurato per cantar e sonar col lauto Libro primo.* 1509. Reprint. Geneva: Minkoff, 1977.

————, ed. *Tenori e contrabassi intabulati in canto figurato per cantar e sonar col lauto Libro secundo.* 1511. Reprint. Geneva: Minkoff, 1982.

Brett, Philip, ed. *Consort Songs.* Musica Britannica 22. London: Stainer and Bell, 1967.

Byrd, William. *Psalms, Sonnets and Songs (1588).* Edited by Edmund Fellowes, revised by Philip Brett. London: Stainer and Bell, 1965.

Caccini, Giulio. *Le nuove musiche.* Edited and translated by H. Wiley Hitchcock. Madison, Wis.: A-R Editions, 1970.

————. *Le nuove musiche.* Introduction by Francesco Vatielli. 1601. Rome: Reale accademia d'Italia, 1934.

Campion (also Campian), Thomas. *First Book of Airs circa 1613.* LSW Series 2: 1. London: Stainer and Bell, 1925.

————. *Second Book of Airs circa 1613.* LSW Series 2: 2. London: Stainer and Bell, 1925.

_____. *The Songs from Rosseter's Book of Airs (1601)*. LSW Series 1: 4 and 13. Revised by Thurston Dart. London: Stainer and Bell, 1969.

_____. *The Third and Fourth Booke of Ayres*. ELS 5. c. 1618. Reprint. Menston: Scolar Press, 1969.

_____. *Third* and *Fourth Booke of Ayres circa 1617*. LSW Series 2: 10 and 11. London: Stainer and Bell, 1926.

_____. *Two Bookes of Ayres. The First Containing Divine and Morall Songs: The Second, Light Conceits of Lovers*. ELS 4. c. 1613. Reprint. Menston: Scolar Press, 1967.

Daniel (also Danyel), John. *Songs for the Lute, Viol and Voice (1606)*. Edited by Edmund H. Fellowes, revised by David Scott. The English Lute-Songs, Second Series 8. London: Stainer and Bell, 1970.

_____. *Songs for the Lute Viol and Voice*. Introduction by David Greer. ELS 13. 1606. Reprint. Menston: Scolar Press, 1970.

Dowland, John. *The Collected Lute Music of John Dowland*. Edited and transcribed by Diana Poulton and Basil Lam. London: Faber, 1974.

Dowland, Robert, ed. *A Musicall Banquet*. ELS 19. 1610. Reprint. Menston: Scolar Press, 1969.

Este (East), Thomas, pub. *The Whole Book of Psalms*. Edited by Edward Rimbault. London, 1844.

Gibbons, Orlando. *First Set of Madrigals and Motets (1612)*. Edited by Edmund Fellowes and revised by Thurston Dart. London: Stainer and Bell, 1964.

Göpel's deutsches Lieder- und Commers-Buch. Stuttgart, [1847].

Goudimel, Claude. *Oeuvres complètes*. Edited by Pierre Pidoux. 14 vols. New York: Institute of Mediaeval Music, 1967-83.

Handford, George. *Ayres to be Sunge to the Lute*. Introduction by David Greer. Menston: Scolar Press, 1970.

Harrán, Don, ed. Vol. 1^2 of *The Anthologies of Black-Note Madrigals*. 5 vols. in 6. CMM 73. Neuhausen-Stuttgart: AIM, 1978-81.

Isaac, Heinrich. *Weltliche Werke I*. Edited by Johannes Wolf. DTÖ 28. 1907. Reprint. Graz: Akademische Druck- und Verlagsanstalt, 1959.

Jane Pickeringe's Lute Book. Introduction by Robert Spencer. Clarabricken: Boethius, 1985.

Josquin des Pres. *Werken van Josquin des Pres*. Edited by A. Smijers. 5 vols. and a Supplement. Amsterdam:Vereniging voor nederlandse Musiekgeschiedenis, 1922-69.

Judenkünig, Hans. *Utilis & compendiaria introductio*. In *Österreichische Lautenmusik im XVI. Jahrhundert*. Edited by Adolf Koczirz. DTÖ 37. 1911. Reprint. Graz: Akademische Druck- und Verlagsanstalt, 1959.

La Fage, Adrien de. *Essais de diphthèrographie musicale*. 1864. Reprint. 2 vols. in 1. Amsterdam: Frits A. M. Knuf, 1964.

Lesure, François, et al., eds. *Anthologie de la chanson parisienne au XVIe siècle*. Monaco: L'Oiseau Lyre, 1953.

Monteverdi, Claudio. *Settimo libro de Madrigali*. Vol. 7 of *Tutte le opere di Claudio Monteverdi*. Edited by G. Francesco Malipiero. 16 vols. 1926-42. Reprint. [Vienna]: Universal Edition, [1954].

Morley, Thomas. *The First Booke of Ayres.* ELS 33. 1600. Reprint. Menston: Scolar Press, 1970.

Mudarra, Alonoso. *Tres libros de música en cifra para vihuela.* Edited and transcribed by Emilio Pujol. Monumentos de la Música Espagñol 7. Barcelona: Instituto espagñol de musicología, 1949.

Osthoff, Wolfgang. *Theatergesang und darstellende Musik in der italienischen Renaissance (15. und 16. Jahrhundert).* 2 vols. Tutzing: Hans Schneider, 1969.

Peri, Jacopo. *Le Musiche sopra l'Euridice.* 1600. Reprint. New York: Broude Brothers, 1973.

Rosseter, Philip, and Thomas Campion. *A Booke of Ayres, Set foorth to be song to the Lute, Orpherian, and Base Violl.* ELS 36. 1601. Reprint. Menston: Scolar Press, 1970.

Schwartz, Rudolf, ed. *Ottaviano Petrucci Frottole, Buch I und IV.* 1935. Reprint. Hildesheim: Georg Olms, 1967.

Senfl, Ludwig. *Sämtliche Werke.* Edited by Arnold Geering and Wilhelm Altwegg. 11 vols. Wolfenbüttel: Möseler Verlag, 1961.

Souris, André, ed. *Poèmes de Donne, Herbert et Crashaw mis en musique par leurs contemporains.* Paris: CNRS, 1961.

Vautor, Thomas. *Songs of Divers Airs and Natures (1619).* Edited by Edmund Fellowes, revised by Thurston Dart. London: Stainer and Bell, 1958.

Verchaly, André, ed. *Airs de cour pour voix et luth (1603-1643).* Paris: Société française de musicologie, 1961.

Whythorne, Thomas. "It Doth Me Good When Zeph'rus Reigns." Edited by Peter Warlock. *The Oxford Choral Songs from the Old Masters,* no. 360. London: Oxford University Press, 1927.

_____. "Though Choler Cleapt the Heart About." Edited by Peter Warlock. *The Oxford Choral Songs from the Old Masters,* no. 354. London: Oxford University Press, 1927.

Works Cited

Alighieri, Dante. *Dante's Vita nuova: A Translation and an Essay.* Translated by Mark Musa. Bloomington: Indiana University Press, 1973.

Ammann, Peter. "The Musical Theory and Philosophy of Robert Fludd." *Warburg* 30 (1967): 198-227.

Andreas Capellanus. *The Art of Courtly Love.* Translated by John J. Parry. 1941. Reprint. New York: Norton, 1969.

Ascham, Roger. *English Works.* Edited by William Aldis Wright. Cambridge: Cambridge University Press, 1904.

Atkins, J. W. H. *English Literary Criticism: The Renascence.* 2d ed. London: Methuen, 1951.

Attridge, Derek. *Well-Weighed Syllables: Elizabethan Verse in Classical Metres.* Cambridge: Cambridge University Press, 1974.

Aubigné, Théodore Agrippa d'. *Oeuvres complètes de Théodore Agrippa d'Aubigné.* Edited by Réaume and de Caussade. 6 vols. Paris, 1873-92.

Augé-Chiquet, Mathieu. *La vie, les idées et l'oeuvre de Jean Antoine de Baïf.* 1909. Geneva: Slatkine Reprints, 1969.

Augustine. *On Music, Books 1-6.* Translated by R. Catesby Taliaferro. Annapolis: The St. John's Bookstore, 1939.

Ausonius, Decimus Magnus. *Ausonius.* Translated by Hugh White. Loeb Classical Library. 2 vols. Cambridge: Harvard University Press, 1919.

Barnes, Barnabe. *Parthenophil and Parthenophe: A Critical Edition.* Edited by Victor A. Doyno. Carbondale: Southern Illinois University Press, 1971.

Barnett, Howard. "John Case–An Elizabethan Music Scholar." *Music and Letters* 50 (1969): 252-66.

Baron, Hans. *The Crisis of the Early Italian Renaissance.* Revised editon. Princeton: Princeton University Press, 1966.

Baroway, Israel. "The Hebrew Hexameter: A Study in Renaissance Sources and Interpretation." *English Literary History* 2 (1935): 66-91.

Beaujoyeulx, Baltasar de. *Le balet comique de la royne 1581.* Translated by Carol and Lander MacClintock. N.p.: AIM, 1971.

Bennett, Walter. *German Verse in Classical Metres.* The Hague: Mouton, 1963.

Bergmans, Paul. "Deux amis de Roland de Lassus: les humanistes Charles Utenhove et Paul Melissus Schede." *Académie royale de Belgique, Bulletin de la classe des beaux-arts* 15 (1933): 101-12.

Berringer, Ralph. "Thomas Campion's Share in *A Booke of Ayres.*" *Publications of the Modern Language Association* 58 (1943): 938-48.

Binet, Claude. *La vie de P. de Ronsard (1586).* Edited by Paul Laumonier. Paris: Librairie Hachette, 1909.

Binns, J. W. "John Case and 'The Praise of Musicke.'" *Music and Letters* 55 (1974): 444-53.

————. "The Latin Poetry of Thomas Campion." In J. W. Binns, ed., *The Latin Poetry of English Poets,* 1-25. London: Routledge and Kegan Paul, 1974.

Boethius, Anicius Manlius Severinus. *Fundamentals of Music.* Translation and introduction by Calvin Bower. Edited by Claude Palisca. New Haven: Yale University Press, 1989.

Bower, Calvin. "Boethius' *The Principles of Music,* an Introduction, Translation, and Commentary." Ph.D. diss. George Peabody College for Teachers, 1967.

Boyd, Morrison Comegys. *Elizabethan Music and Musical Criticism.* 2d ed. Philadelphia: University of Pennsylvania Press, 1967.

Brady, George. *Samuel Daniel: A Critical Study.* 1923. Reprinted Folcroft, Penn.: Folcroft Press, 1969.

Burgess, Anthony. *Earthly Powers.* London: Hutchinson, 1980.

Bush, Douglas. *Mythology and the Renaissance Tradition in English Poetry.* 1932. New revised edition. New York: Norton, 1963.

Buxton, John. *Sir Philip Sidney and the English Renaissance.* London: Macmillan, 1954.

Campion, Thomas. *Campion's Works.* Edited by Percival Vivian. 1909. Reprint. Oxford: Clarendon Press, 1966.

————. *De puluerea coniuratione (On the Gunpowder Plot).* Edited by David Lindley, translated by Robin Sowerby. Leeds Texts and Monographs, n.s. 10. Leeds: Leeds Studies in English, 1987.

————. *The Works of Dr. Thomas Campion.* Edited by A. H. Bullen. London, 1889.

————. *The Works of Thomas Campion.* Edited by Walter R. Davis. 1967. Reprint. New York: Norton, 1970.

Capellanus. See Andreas Capellanus.

D. D. Carnicelli, ed. *Lord Morley's Tryumphes of Fraunces Petrarcke.* Cambridge: Harvard University Press, 1971.

Carpenter, Nan Cooke. *Music in the Medieval and Renaissance Universities.* 1958. Reprint. New York: Da Capo, 1972.

Case, John. *Apologia musices tam vocalis quam instrumentalis et mixtae.* Oxford, 1588.

Case, John (?). *The Praise of Musicke.* Oxford, 1586.

Castiglione, Baldassare. *The Book of the Courtier.* Translated by Thomas Hoby. London: Dent, 1928.

Catullus, Gaius Valerius, et al. *Catullus, Tibullus, and Pervigilium Veneris.* Translated by F. W. Cornish, J. P. Postgate, J. W. Mackail. Revised edition. Loeb Classical Library. Cambridge: Harvard University Press, 1962.

Chamard, Henri. *Histoire de la Pléiade.* 4 vols. Paris: Henri Didier, 1939-40.

Chaucer, Geoffrey. *The Complete Poetry and Prose of Geoffrey Chaucer.* Edited by John H. Fisher. New York: Holt, Rinehart and Winston, 1977.

Child, Francis, ed. *The English and Scottish Popular Ballads.* 5 vols. 1882-98. Reprint. New York: Dover, 1965.

Cleland, James. *Hērōpaideia, or the Institution of a Young Noble Man.* Oxford, 1607.

Cochlaeus, Johannes. *Grammatica.* N.p., 1515.

————. *Tetrachordum musices.* Nuremberg, 1514.

————. *Tetrachordum musices.* Translated and edited by Clement A. Miller. N.p.: AIM, 1970.

Cochrane, Kirsty. "Orpheus Applied: Some Instances of His Importance in the Humanist View of Language." *Review of English Studies,* n.s. 19 (1968): 1-13.

Cunningham, J. V. "Campion and Propertius." *Philological Quarterly* 31 (1952): 96.

Daniel, Arnaut. *The Poetry of Arnaut Daniel.* Edited by James Wilhelm. New York: Garland, 1981.

Daniel, Samuel. *The Civil Wars.* Edited by Laurence Michel. New Haven: Yale University Press, 1958.

————. *The Complete Works in Verse and Prose of Samuel Daniel.* Edited by Alexander B. Grosart. 5 vols. 1885-96. Reprint. New York: Russel and Russel, 1963.

————. *Delia with The Complaint of Rosamund.* 1592. Reprint. Menston: Scolar Press, 1969.

————. *Poems and A Defence of Ryme.* Edited by Arthur Colby Sprague. 1930. Reprint. Chicago: University of Chicago Press, 1965.

————. *The Tragedy of Philotas by Samuel Daniel.* Edited by Laurence Michel. New Haven: Yale University Press, 1949.

Dante. See Alighieri.

Dart, Thurston. "Lord Herbert of Cherbury's Lute-Book." *Music and Letters* 38 (1957): 136-48.

Davis, Walter R. *Thomas Campion.* Twayne's English Authors Series 450. Boston: Twayne, 1987.

Desportes, Philippe. *Les amours de Diane.* Edited by Victor Graham. 2 vols. Geneva: Droz, 1959.

Disertori, Benvenuto. *La frottola nella storia della musica.* Cremona: Athenaeum Cremonese, 1954.

Donaldson, E. Talbot. "The Myth of Courtly Love." In *Speaking of Chaucer,* 154-63. London: Athlone Press, 1970.

Donow, Herbert. *A Concordance to the Sonnet Sequences of Daniel, Drayton, Shakespeare, Sidney, and Spenser.* Carbondale, Ill.: Southern Illinois University Press, 1969.

Dorsten, J. A. van. *Poets, Patrons, and Professors: Sir Philip Sidney, Daniel Rogers, and the Leiden Humanists.* Leiden: Sir Thomas Browne Institute at the University Press, 1962.

Doughtie, Edward. *English Renaissance Song.* Twayne's English Authors Series 424. Boston: Twayne, 1986.

————, ed. *Lyrics from English Airs 1596-1622.* Cambridge: Harvard University Press, 1970.

Dronke, Peter. *Medieval Latin and the Rise of the European Love-Lyric.* 2d ed. 2 vols. Oxford: Clarendon Press, 1968.

————. *The Medieval Lyric.* 1968. 2d. ed. New York: Cambridge University Press, 1977.

Du Bellay, Joachim. *Oeuvres françoises de Joachim Du Bellay.* Edited by Ch. Marty-Laveaux. 2 vols. Paris, 1866-67.

Einstein, Alfred. *The Italian Madrigal.* Translated by Alexander Krappe, Roger Sessions, and Oliver Strunk. 3 vols. 1949. Reprint. Princeton: Princeton University Press, 1971.

Elegy and Iambus with the Anacreontea. Translated by J. M. Edmonds. Loeb Classical Library. 2 vols. Cambridge: Harvard University Press, 1931.

Emslie, McDonald. "Nicholas Lanier's Innovations in English Song." *Music and Letters* 41 (1960): 13-27.

Faber Stapulensis. *Musica libris demonstrata quattuor.* [Paris], 1496.

Feldman, Martha. "In Defense of Campion: A New Look at His Ayres and *Observations.*" *Journal of Musicology* 5 (1987): 226-56.

Ficino, Marsilio. *Commentaire sur le Banquet de Platon.* Translated by Raymond Marcel. Paris: Société d'Édition "Les Belles Lettres," 1956.

————. *Opera omnia.* Introduction by Paul O. Kristeller. 2 vols. 1576. Reprint. Torino: Bottega d'Erasmo, 1959.

————. *Three Books on Life.* Translated and edited by Carol V. Kaske and John R. Clark. Binghamton, N.Y.: Center for Medieval and Early Renaissance Studies, State University of New York at Binghamton, 1989.

Finney, Gretchen Ludke. *Musical Backgrounds for English Literature: 1580-1650.* New Brunswick: Rutgers University Press, 1962.

Finney, Oliver John. "Thomas Campion, Music and Metrics." Ph.D. diss. University of Kansas, 1975.

Fortune, Nigel. "Solo Song and Cantata." In Gerald Abraham, ed., *The Age of Humanism, 1540-1630,* 125-217. The New Oxford History of Music 4. London: Oxford University Press, 1968.

French, Peter J. *John Dee: The World of an Elizabethan Magus.* London: Routledge and Kegan Paul, 1972.

Friedman, John Block. *Orpheus in the Middle Ages.* Cambridge: Harvard University Press, 1970.

Gaffurius, Franchinus. *De harmonia musicorum instrumentorum opus.* Translated and edited by Clement Miller. N.p.: AIM, 1977.

————. *Practica musicae.* Translated and edited by Clement Miller. N.p.: AIM, 1968.

Galilei, Vincenzo. *Dialogo della musica antica, et della moderna.* 1581. Reprint. New York: Broude Brothers, 1967.

Gil, Alexander. *Logonomia Anglica.* 2d ed. 1621. Reprint. Menston: Scolar Press, 1968.

Glareanus (Glarean), Henricus. *Dodecachordon.* 1547. Reprint. New York: Broude Brothers, 1967.

————. *Dodecachordon.* Translated and edited by Clement Miller. 2 vols. N.p.: AIM, 1965.

The Greek Anthology. Translated by W. R. Paton. Loeb Classical Library. 5 vols. Cambridge: Harvard University Press, 1916.

Greene, Thomas. *The Light in Troy: Imitation and Discovery in Renaissance Poetry.* New Haven: Yale University Press, 1982.

Greer, David. "Campion the Musician." *Lute Society Journal* 9 (1967): 7-16.

Greg, W. W., ed. *Gesta Grayorum.* n.p.: Oxford University Press, 1914.

Guazzo, Stefano. *Dialoghi piacevoli del Sig. Stefano Guazzo.* Venice, 1586.

Guggenheim, Josef. *Quellenstudien zu Samuel Daniels Sonettencyklus "Delia".* Berlin, 1898.

Hall, Kathleen. *Pontus de Tyard and his "Discours Philosophiques".* London: Oxford University Press, 1963.

Hankins, James. "Cosimo de' Medici and the 'Platonic Academy.'" *Warburg* 53 (1990): 144-62.

Hanning, Barbara Russano. *Of Poetry and Music's Power: Humanism and the Creation of Opera.* Ann Arbor: UMI Research Press, 1980.

Hardison, O. B., Jr. *Prosody and Purpose in the English Renaissance.* Baltimore: Johns Hopkins University Press, 1989.

Harrán, Don. *Word-Tone Relations in Musical Thought: From Antiquity to the Seventeenth Century.* Neuhausen-Stuttgart: AIM, 1986.

Hartmann, Karl-Günther. *Die humanistische Odenkomposition in Deutschland: Vorgeschichte und Voraussetzungen.* Erlanger Studien 15. Erlangen: Palm und Enke, 1976.

Harvey, Gabriel. *The Works of Gabriel Harvey, D.C.L.* Edited by Alexander Grosart. 3 vols. London, 1884-85.

Herbert of Cherbury, Edward. *The Autobiography of Edward Lord Herbert of Cherbury.* Edited by C. H. Herford. N.p.: The Gregynog Press, 1928.

Hollander, John. *The Untuning of the Sky.* 1961. New York: Norton, 1970.

————. *Vision and Resonance: Two Senses of Poetic Form.* New York: Oxford University Press, 1975.

Hooker, Richard. *Of the Laws of Ecclesiastical Polity.* Edited by W. Speed Hill. 3 vols. The Folger Library Edition of the Works of Richard Hooker. Cambridge: Belknap Press of Harvard University Press, 1977-81.

Hoppin, Richard. *Medieval Music.* New York: Norton, 1978.

Horace (Quintus Horatius Flaccus). *Odes and Epodes.* Translated by C. E. Bennett. Loeb Classical Library. Cambridge: Harvard University Press, 1927.

_____. *Satires, Epistles, and Ars Poetica.* Translated by H.R. Fairclough. Loeb Classical Library. Cambridge: Harvard University Press, 1929.

Horapollo. *The Hieroglyphics of Horapollo.* Translated by George Boas. Bollingen Series 23. New York: Pantheon, 1950.

Hutton, James. *"Amor Fugitivus:* The First Idyl of Moschus in Imitations to the Year 1800." In *Essays on Renaissance Poetry,* ed. Rita Guerlac, 74-105. Ithaca, N.Y.: Cornell University Press, 1980.

_____. "Cupid and the Bee." In *Essays on Renaissance Poetry,* 106-31.

_____. *The Greek Anthology in France and in the Latin Writers of the Netherlands to the Year 1800.* Cornell Studies in Classical Philology 28. Ithaca, N.Y.: Cornell University Press, 1946.

_____. *The Greek Anthology in Italy to the Year 1800.* Cornell Studies in English 23. Ithaca, N.Y.: Cornell University Press, 1935.

Isaac, Hermann. "Wie weit geht die Abhängigkeit Shakespeare's von Daniel als Lyriker?" *Jahrbuch der deutschen Shakespeare-Gesellschaft* 17 (1882): 165-200.

Jacquot, Jean, ed. *Musique et poésie au XVIe siècle.* Paris: CNRS, 1954.

Jeffery, Brian. "The Idea of Music in Ronsard's Poetry." In Terence Cave, ed., *Ronsard the Poet,* 209-39. London: Methuen, 1973.

John, Lisle Cecil. *The Elizabethan Sonnet Sequences: Studies in Conventional Conceits.* New York: Columbia University Press, 1938.

Jonson, Ben. *Ben Jonson.* Edited by C. H. Herford, Percy Simpson, and Evelyn Simpson. 11 vols. Oxford: Clarendon Press, 1925-52.

Jorgens, Elise Bickford. *The Well-Tun'd Word: Musical Interpretations of English Poetry 1597-1651.* Minneapolis: University of Minnesota Press, 1982.

Judd, Percy. "The Songs of John Danyel." *Music and Letters* 17 (1936): 118-23.

Kastendieck, Miles Merwin. *England's Musical Poet: Thomas Campion.* New York: Oxford University Press, 1938.

Kastner, L. E. "The Italian Sources of Daniel's 'Delia.'" *Modern Language Review* 7 (1912): 153-56.

Kerman, Joseph. *The Elizabethan Madrigal: A Comparative Study.* New York: American Musicological Society, 1962.

Kinkeldey, Otto. "Franchino Gafori and Marsilio Ficino." *Harvard Library Bulletin* 1 (1947): 379-82.

Knight, Ellen. *"The Praise of Musicke:* John Case, Thomas Watson, and William Byrd." *Current Musicology* 30 (1980): 37-51.

Kristeller, Paul Oskar. *The Philosophy of Marsilio Ficino.* Translated by Virginia Conant. Gloucester, Mass.: Peter Smith, 1964.

Lebègue, Raymond. "Ronsard et la musique." In Jacquot, ed., *Musique et poésie,* 105-19.

Lee, Sidney. *The French Renaissance in England: An Account of the Literary Relations of England and France in the Sixteenth Century.* 1910. Reprint. New York: Octagon Books, 1968.

_____. "Ben Jonson on the Sonnet." *Athenaeum* 4002 (9 July 1904): 49.

Lefèvre d'Étaples, Jacques. See Faber Stapulensis.

Le Huray, Peter. *Music and the Reformation in England 1549-1660.* 1967. Corrected reprint. Cambridge: Cambridge University Press, 1978.

Le Jeune, Claude. *Le printemps.* Edited by Henry Expert. *Les Maîtres Musiciens de la Renaissance Française* 12-14. Paris: Alphonse Laduc, 1900-1.

Lever, J. W. *The Elizabethan Love Sonnet.* London: Methuen, 1956.

Lewis, C. S. *The Allegory of Love: A Study in Medieval Tradition.* London: Oxford University Press, 1936.

_____. *English Literature in the Sixteenth Century Excluding Drama.* Oxford: Clarendon Press, 1954.

Levy, Kenneth Jay. "Vaudeville, vers mesurés et airs de cour." In Jacquot, ed., *Musique et poésie*, 185-201.

Lievsay, John. *Stefano Guazzo and the English Renaissance 1575-1675.* Chapel Hill: University of North Carolina Press, 1961.

Liliencron, Rochus von. "Die Chorgesänge des lateinisch-deutschen Schuldramas im XVI. Jahrhundert." *VfMW* 6 (1890): 309-87.

_____. "Die Horazischen Metren in deutschen Kompositionen des 16. Jahrhunderts." *VfMW* 3 (1887): 26-91.

Lindley, David. "John Danyel's 'Eyes Looke No More.'" *Lute Society Journal* 16 (1974): 9-16.

_____. *Lyric.* The Critical Idiom 44. London: Methuen, 1985.

_____. *Thomas Campion.* Medieval and Renaissance Authors Series 7. Leiden: E. J. Brill, 1986.

Lindley, Mark. *Lutes, Viols and Temperaments.* Cambridge: Cambridge University Press, 1984.

Lowbury, Edward, Timothy Salter, and Alison Young. *Thomas Campion: Poet, Composer, Physician.* New York: Barnes and Noble, 1970.

Lowinsky, Edward. "Humanism in the Music of the Renaissance." In vol. 1 of Lowinsky, *Music in the Culture of the Renaissance.* Edited by Bonnie Blackburn, 154-218. 2 vols. Chicago: University of Chicago Press, 1989.

_____. "Music in the Culture of the Renaissance." *Journal of the History of Ideas* 15 (1954): 509-53. Also in *Music in the Culture of the Renaissance* 1:19-39.

_____. Revision of *Der musikalische Humanismus im 16. und fruehen 17. Jahrhundert*, by D. P. Walker. *Musical Quarterly* 37 (1951): 285-89.

Luisi, Francesco. *La musica vocale nel Rinascimento: Studi sulla musica vocale profana in Italia nei secoli XV e XVI.* Torino: Rai Radiotelevisione Italiana, 1977.

Mace, Thomas. *Musick's Monument.* 1676. Reprint. Paris: CNRS, 1977.

McFarlane, Ian D. *Buchanan.* London: Gerald Duckworth, 1981.

McGrady, Richard. "Campion and the Lute." *Music Review* 47 (1986/87): 1-15.

Marius, Richard. *Thomas More.* New York: Knopf, 1984.

Marlowe, Christopher. *The Complete Works of Christopher Marlowe.* Edited by Fredson Bowers. 2d. ed. 2 vols. Cambridge: Cambridge University Press, 1981.

Martial (M. Valerius Martialis). *Epigrams.* Translated by Walter C. Ker. Rev. ed. Loeb Classical Library. 2 vols. Cambridge: Harvard University Press, 1968.

Masson, Paul-Marie. "L'humanisme musical en Allemagne au XVIe siècle: Introduction à l'étude des oeuvres françaises de musique 'mesurée à l'antique.'" *Mercure musical* 2 (Dec. 1906): 394-403.

————. "L'humanisme musical en France au XVIe siècle: Essai sur la musique 'mesurée à l'antique.'" *Mercure musical* 3 (April and July 1907): 333-66, 677-718.

Maylender, Michele. *Storia delle accademie d'Italia.* 5 vols. Bologna: Licinio Cappelli, 1926-30.

Maynard, Winifred. *Elizabethan Lyric Poetry and Its Music.* Oxford: Clarendon Press, 1986.

Mei, Girolamo. *Letters on Ancient and Modern Music to Vincenzo Galilei and Giovanni Bardi.* Edited by Claude Palisca. N.p.: AIM, 1960.

Meres, Francis. *Palladis Tamia (1598).* Introduction by Don Cameron Allen. New York: Scholars' Facsimiles and Reprints, 1938.

Milton, John. *Complete Poems and Major Prose.* Edited by Merritt Y. Hughes. Indianapolis: Odyssey Press, 1957.

Minturno, Antonio Sebastiano. *L'arte poetica.* 1564. Reprint. Munich: Wilhelm Fink Verlag, 1971.

Mönch, Walter. *Das Sonett: Gestalt und Geschichte.* Heidelberg: F. H. Kerle Verlag, 1955.

More, Thomas. *Utopia with the 'Dialogue of Comfort' of Sir Thomas More.* Translated (*Utopia* only) by Raphe Robinson. London: Dent, [1910].

————. *L'Utopie de Thomas More.* Edited and translated by André Prévost. Paris: Mame, 1978.

Morley, Thomas. *A Plain and Easy Introduction to Practical Music.* Edited by R. Alec Harman. 2d ed. New York: Norton, 1963.

Moser, Hans Joachim. *Paul Hofhaimer: ein Lied- und Orgelmeister des deutschen Humanismus.* Stuttgart: J. G. Cotta'sche Buchhandlung Nachfolger, 1929.

Mulcaster, Richard. *The First Part of the Elementary, 1582.* Reprinted. Menston: Scolar Press, 1970.

Myers, Joan. "Caccini-Dowland: Monody Realized." *Journal of the Lute Society of America* 3 (1970): 22-34.

Nashe, Thomas. *The Works of Thomas Nashe.* Edited by Ronald McKerrow, revised by F. P. Wilson. 5 vols. Oxford: Basil Blackwell, 1958.

Niemöller, Klaus Wolfgang. *Untersuchungen zu Musikpflege und Musikunterricht an den deutschen Lateinschulen.* Regensburg: Gustav Bosse Verlag, 1969.

————. "Zum Einfluss des Humanismus auf Position und Konzeption von Musik im deutschen Bildungssystem der ersten Hälfte des 16. Jahrhunderts." In Rüegg and Schmitt, eds., *Musik in Humanismus,* 77-97.

Niger, Pescennius Franciscus. [*Grammatica.* Venice, 1480.]

————. *Grammatica.* Basel, 1500.

Nolhac, Pierre de. *Un poète rhénan ami de la Pléiade: Paul Melissus.* Paris: Librairie ancienne Honoré Champion, 1923.

Nostredame, Jehan de. *Les vies des plus cèlèbres et anciens poètes provençaux.* Edited by Camille Chabaneau; introduction and commentary by Joseph Anglade. Paris: Librairie ancienne Honoré Champion, 1913.

O'Donoghue, Bernard, ed. *The Courtly Love Tradition.* Manchester: Manchester University Press, 1982.

Ogle, M. B. "The Classical Origin and Tradition of Literary Conceits." *American Journal of Philology* 34 (1913): 125-52.

Olshausen, Ulrich. "Das lautenbegleitete Sololied in England um 1600." Diss. Johann Wolfgang Goethe-Universität, Frankfurt am Main, 1963.

Orgel, Stephen, and Roy Strong. *Inigo Jones: The Theatre of the Stuart Court.* 2 vols. Berkeley: University of California Press, 1973.

Orgel, Stephen. *The Jonsonian Masque.* Cambridge: Harvard University Press, 1967.

Ornithoparchus (Andreas Vogelsang). *Musicae activae micrologus.* Translated by John Dowland. In Ornithoparchus/Dowland, *A Compendium of Musical Practice.* Introduction by Gustave Reese and Stephen Ledbetter. New York: Dover, 1973.

Ovid (Publius Ovidius Naso). *Heroides and Amores.* Translated by Grant Showerman, revised by G. P. Goold. 2d. ed. Loeb Classical Library. Cambridge: Harvard University Press, 1977.

————. *Tristia* and *Ex ponto.* Translated by Arthur Wheeler. Loeb Classical Library. Cambridge: Harvard University Press, 1924.

Pace, Richard. *De fructu qui ex doctrina percipitur (The Benefit of a Liberal Education).* Edited and translated by Frank Manley and Richard Sylvester. New York: Frederick Ungar, 1967.

Palisca, Claude V. *Baroque Music.* Englewood Cliffs, N.J.: Prentice Hall, 1968.

————. "The Beginnings of Baroque Music; Its Roots in Sixteenth Century Theory and Polemics." Ph.D. diss. Harvard, 1953.

————. "The 'Camerata fiorentina': A Reappraisal." *Studi Musicali* 1 (1972): 203-36.

————. ed. and trans. *The Florentine Camerata: Documentary Studies and Translations.* New Haven: Yale University Press, 1989.

————. *Humanism in Italian Renaissance Musical Thought.* New Haven: Yale University Press, 1985.

Panofsky, Erwin. *Renaissance and Renascences in Western Art.* 1969. New York: Harper and Row, 1972.

Pattison, Bruce. *Music and Poetry of the English Renaissance.* 1948. Reprint. Folcroft, Penn.: Folcroft Press, 1969.

Pearsall, Derek. *John Lydgate.* London: Routledge and Kegan Paul, 1970.

Petrarch (Francesco Petrarca). *Petrarch's Lyric Poems: The "Rime sparse" and Other Lyrics.* Edited and translated by Robert Durling. Cambridge: Harvard University Press, 1976.

Phillips, James E. "Daniel Rogers: A Neo-Latin Link between the Pléiade and Sidney's 'Areopagus.'" In *Neo-Latin Poetry of the Sixteenth and Seventeenth Centuries,* 5-28. Los Angeles: University of California, 1965.

————. "George Buchanan and the Sidney Circle." *Huntington Library Quarterly* 12 (1948-49): 23-55.

Pinvert, Lucien. *Lazare de Baïf.* Paris: Ancienne librairie Thorin et fils, 1900.

Pirrotta, Nino. "Music and Cultural Tendencies in 15th-Century Italy." *Journal of the American Musicological Society* 19 (1966): 127-61.

————. "Temperaments and Tendencies in the Florentine Camerata." *Musical Quarterly* 40 (1954): 169-89.

Pitcher, John. "Samuel Daniel, the Hertfords, and a Question of Love." *The Review of English Studies,* n.s. 35 (1984): 449-62.

Poulton, Diana. *John Dowland: His Life and Works*. Revised edition. Berkeley: University of California Press, 1982.

Pratt, Waldo Selden. *The Music of the French Psalter of 1562*. New York: Columbia University Press, 1939.

Praz, Mario. *The Flaming Heart: Essays on Crashaw, Machiavelli, and Other Studies in the Relations between Italian and English Literature from Chaucer to T. S. Eliot*. 1958. Reprint. New York: Norton, 1973.

Prescott, Anne Lake. *French Poets and the English Renaissance*. New Haven: Yale University Press, 1978.

_____. "The Thirsty Deer and the Lord of Life: Some Contexts for *Amoretti* 67-70." *Spenser Studies* 6 (1985): 33-76.

Price, David. *Patrons and Musicians of the English Renaissance*. Cambridge: Cambridge University Press, 1981.

Puttenham, George. *The Arte of English Poesie*. Edited by Edward Arber. 1906. Reprint. Introduction by Baxter Hathaway. Kent, Ohio: Kent State University Press, 1970.

Ratcliffe, Stephen. *Campion: On Song*. Boston: Routledge and Kegan Paul, 1981.

Rees, Joan. *Samuel Daniel*. Liverpool: Liverpool University Press, 1964.

Reese, Gustave. *Music in the Middle Ages*. New York: Norton, 1940.

Ronsard, Pierre de. *Oeuvres complètes de P. de Ronsard*. Edited by Paul Laumonier. 8 vols. Paris: Librairie Alphonse Lemerre, 1914-19.

Rüegg, Walter, and Annegrit Schmitt, eds. *Musik in Humanismus und Renaissance*. Weinheim: Acta Humaniora, 1983.

Ryding, Erik S. "Collaboration between Campion and Rosseter?" *Journal of the Lute Society of America* 19 (1986): 13-28.

Ryding, William W. *Structure in Medieval Narrative*. The Hague: Mouton, 1971.

Sadie, Stanley, ed. *The New Grove Dictionary of Music and Musicians*. 20 vols. London: Macmillan, 1980.

Sbaragli, Luigi. *Claudio Tolomei: Umanista senese del cinquecento*. Siena: Accademia per le arti e per le lettere, 1939.

Schaar, Claes. *An Elizabethan Sonnet Problem: Shakespeare's Sonnets, Daniel's Delia, and Their Literary Background*. Lund Studies in English 28. Lund: CWK Gleerup, 1960.

Schrade, Leo. "L' 'Edipo tiranno' d'Andrea Gabrieli et la renaissance de la tragédie grecque." In Jacquot, ed., *Musique et poésie*, 275-83.

_____. *La représentation d' "Edipo" tiranno au Teatro Olimpico*. Paris: CNRS, 1960.

Scott, David. "John Danyel: His Life and Songs." *Lute Society Journal* 13 (1971): 7-17.

Scott, Janet. *Les sonnets élisabéthains: Les sources et l'apport personnel*. Paris: Librairie ancienne Honoré Champion, 1929.

Sebillet, Thomas. *Art poetique Françoys*. 1555. Reprint. Geneva: Slatkine Reprints, 1972.

Seronsy, Cecil. *Samuel Daniel*. Twayne's English Authors Series 49. New York: Twayne, 1967.

Shakespeare, William. *The Riverside Shakespeare*. Edited by G. Blakemore Evans et al. Boston: Houghton Mifflin, 1974.

_____. *Pericles.* Edited by F. D. Hoeniger. London: Methuen, 1963.

Sidney, Philip. *Syr P. S. His Astrophel and Stella.* London, 1591.

_____. *The Countess of Pembroke's Arcadia (The Old Arcadia).* Edited by Jean Robertson. Oxford: Clarendon Press, 1973.

_____. *The Poems of Sir Philip Sidney.* Edited by William A. Ringler, Jr. Oxford: Clarendon Press, 1962.

_____. *Prose Works.* Edited by Albert Feuillerat. 4 vols. 1912. Reprint. Cambridge: Cambridge University Press, 1962.

Sir Orfeo. Edited by A. J. Bliss. London: Oxford University Press, 1954.

Smith, G. Gregory, ed. *Elizabethan Critical Essays.* 2 vols. Oxford: Clarendon Press, 1904.

Solerti, Angelo. *Le origini del melodramma.* Torino: Fratelli Bocca, 1903.

Spearing, A. C. *Medieval to Renaissance in English Poetry.* Cambridge: Cambridge University Press, 1985.

Spechtshart von Reutlingen, Hugo. *Flores musicae (1332/42).* Edited by Karl-Werner Gümpel. Wiesbaden: Akademie der Wissenschaften und der Literatur in Mainz, 1958.

Spencer, Terence, and Stanley Wells, eds. *A Book of Masques in Honour of Allardyce Nicoll.* 1967. Reprint. Cambridge: Cambridge University Press, 1970.

Spenser, Edmund. *Poetical Works.* Edited by J. C. Smith and E. de Selincourt. 1912. Reprint. London: Oxford University Press, 1970.

Speroni, Sperone. *Dialogo delle lingue.* In Villey, *Les sources italiennes.*

Spitz, Lewis. *Conrad Celtis: The German Arch-Humanist.* Cambridge: Harvard University Press, 1957.

Spitzer, Leo. "Classical and Christian Ideas of World Harmony: Prolegomena to an Interpretation of the Word 'Stimmung.'" *Traditio* 2 (1944): 409-64; 3 (1945): 307-64.

Spriet, Pierre. *Samuel Daniel (1563-1619): Sa vie – son oeuvre.* [Paris]: Didier, 1968.

Stevens, John. *Music and Poetry in the Early Tudor Court.* 1961. Reprint. Cambridge: Cambridge University Press, 1979.

_____. *Words and Music in the Middle Ages: Song, Narrative, Dance and Drama, 1050-1350.* Cambridge: Cambridge University Press, 1986.

Strong, Roy. *Henry, Prince of Wales and England's Lost Renaissance.* New York: Thames and Hudson, 1986.

Strunk, Oliver, ed. *Source Readings in Music History.* New York: Norton, 1950.

Svensson, Lars-Håkan. *Silent Art: Rhetorical and Thematic Patterns in Samuel Daniel's "Delia".* Lund Studies in English 57. Lund: CWK Gleerup, 1980.

Symonds, John Addington. "The Pathos of the Rose in Poetry." In *Essays Speculative and Suggestive,* 368-87. New Edition. London: Chapman and Hall, 1893.

Taille, Jacques de la. *La manière.* Edited by Pierre Han. University of North Carolina Studies in the Romance Languages and Literatures 93. Chapel Hill: University of North Carolina Press, 1970.

Tasso, Torquato. *Gerusalemme liberata.* Edited by Anna Maria Carini. Milan: Feltrinelli, 1961.

Thomas, Henry. "Musical Settings of Horace's Lyric Poems." *Proceedings of the Musical Association.* 46th Session (1919-20): 73-97.

Tiersot, Julien. *Ronsard et la musique de son temps.* Paris: Librairie Fischbacher, [c. 1902].

Tolomei, Claudio, et al. *Versi, et regole de la nuova Poesia Toscana.* Rome, 1539.

Tomlinson, Gary. "Rinuccini, Peri, Monteverdi, and the Humanist Heritage of Opera." Ph.D. diss. University of California at Berkeley, 1979.

Topsfield, L. T. *Troubadours and Love.* Cambridge: Cambridge University Press, 1975.

Tottel, Richard, pub. *Songs and Sonnets: Tottel's Miscellany.* 1557. Reprint. Menston: Scolar Press, 1970.

Trimpi, Wesley. *Ben Jonson's Poems: A Study of the Plain Style.* Stanford: Stanford University Press, 1962.

Tyard, Pontus de. *Oeuvres: Solitaire premier.* Edited by Silvio F. Baridon. Geneva: Droz, 1950.

_____. *Solitaire second, ou prose de la musique.* Lyons, 1555.

Ure, Peter. "Two Elizabethan Poets: Samuel Daniel and Sir Walter Ralegh." In *The Age of Shakespeare.* Edited by Boris Ford, 131-46. The Pelican Guide to English Literature 2. Harmondsworth: Penguin, 1955.

Utley, Francis. "Must We Abandon the Concept of Courtly Love?" *Medievalia et Humanistica: Studies in Medieval and Renaissance Culture,* n.s. 3 (1972): 299-324.

Valency, Maurice. *In Praise of Love.* 1958. Reprint. New York: Schocken Books, 1982.

Vasari, Giorgio. *Lives of the Painters, Sculptors and Architects.* Translated by A. B. Hinds, revised and edited by William Gaunt. 4 vols. Everyman's Library 784. 1927. Reprint. London: Dent, 1963.

Villey, Pierre. *Les sources italiennes de la "Deffense et illustration de la langue françoise" de Joachim du Bellay.* Paris: Librairie Honoré Champion, 1908.

Walker, D. P. "The Aims of Baïf's *Académie de Poésie et de Musique.*" *Journal of Renaissance and Baroque Music* 1 (1946): 91-100.

_____. "Le chant orphique de Marsile Ficin." In Jacquot, ed., *Musique et poésie,* 17-33.

_____. "Ficino's *Spiritus* and Music." *Annales musicologiques* 1 (1953): 131-50.

_____. "Musical Humanism in the 16th and Early 17th Centuries." *The Music Review* 2 (1941): 1-13, 111-21, 220-27, 288-308; 3 (1942): 55-71.

_____. "Orpheus the Theologian and Renaissance Platonists." *Warburg* 16 (1953): 100-20.

_____. "Vers et Musique Mesurés à l'Antique." 4 vols. D.Phil. diss. Oxford, 1940.

_____. Review of *The French Academies of the Sixteenth Century,* by Frances Yates. *Musica Disciplina* 2 (1948): 259-61.

Warlock, Peter [Philip Heseltine]. *The English Ayre.* London: Oxford University Press, 1926.

Watson, Thomas. *The Hekatompathia or Passionate Centurie of Love (1582).* Introduction by S. K. Heninger, Jr. Gainesville, Fla.: Scholars' Facsimiles and Reprints, 1964.

Weber, Édith. *La musique mesurée à l'antique en Allemagne.* 2 vols. [Paris]: Klincksieck, 1974.

Weinberg, Bernard. *A History of Literary Criticism in the Italian Renaissance.* 2 vols. Chicago: University of Chicago Press, 1961.

Weiner, Seth. "Renaissance Prosodic Thought as a Branch of *Musica Speculativa*." Ph.D. diss. Princeton, 1981.

_____. "Spenser's Study of English Syllables and Its Completion by Thomas Campion." *Spenser Studies* 3 (1982): 3-56.

Weiss, Piero, and Richard Taruskin, eds. *Music in the Western World: A History in Documents.* New York: Schirmer, 1984.

Whythorne, Thomas. *The Autobiography of Thomas Whythorne.* Edited by James Osborn. Oxford: Clarendon Press, 1961.

Widmann, Benedikt. "Die Kompositionen der Psalmen von Statius Olthof." *VfMW* 5 (1889): 290-321.

Wienpahl, Robert. *Music at the Inns of Court.* Ann Arbor: UMI, 1979.

Wilkinson, L. P. "Propertius and Thomas Campion" *London Magazine*, n.s. 7 (April 1967): 56-65.

Willcock, G. D. "Passing Pitefull Hexameters: A Study of Quantity and Accent in English Renaissance Verse." *Modern Language Review* 29 (1934): 1-19.

Wille, Günther. *Musica Romana: Die Bedeutung der Musik im Leben der Römer.* Amsterdam: P. Schippers, 1967.

Wilson, Christopher R. "Words and Notes Coupled Lovingly Together: Thomas Campion, a Critical Study." D.Phil. diss. Oxford, 1981.

Wilson, Elkin. *Prince Henry and English Literature.* Ithaca, N.Y.: Cornell University Press, 1946.

Wilson, Thomas. *Wilson's Arte of Rhetorique 1560.* Edited by G. H. Mair. Oxford: Clarendon Press, 1909.

Winn, James Anderson. *Unsuspected Eloquence: A History of the Relations between Poetry and Music.* New Haven: Yale University Press, 1981.

Wulstan, David. *Tudor Music.* London: Dent, 1985.

Wyatt, Thomas. *Collected Poems.* Edited by Joost Daalder. London: Oxford University Press, 1975.

Yates, Frances. *The French Academies of the Sixteenth Century.* London: Warburg Institute, 1947.

Zarlino, Gioseffo. *Le istitutioni harmoniche.* 1558. Reprint. New York: Broude Brothers, 1965.

_____. *On the Modes.* Translated by Vered Cohen, intro. Claude V. Palisca. New Haven: Yale University Press, 1983.

_____. *Sopplimenti musicali.* 1588. Reprint. Ridgewood, N.J.: Gregg Press, 1966.

Index

Examples of musical settings are indicated by page references in **bold** type. Musical settings are posted by composer. A complete list of musical settings is found under "Musical Settings (examples)"

Sixteenth Century Essays & Studies
Monographs

ORDER FROM
Sixteenth Century Publishers, Inc.
NMSU LB 115 • Kirksville, MO 63501
Phone: 816-785-4665 • Fax: 816-785-4181
BitNet: SS18@NEMOMUS